Access Anything:
COLORADO

adventuring **with** disabilities

Craig P. Kennedy and Andrea C. Jehn

Fulcrum Publishing
Golden, Colorado

Text copyright © 2005 Craig P. Kennedy and Andrea C. Jehn
Photographs copyright © 2005 Craig P. Kennedy and Andrea C. Jehn, unless otherwise noted

All rights reserved. No part of this book may be reproduced, stored in a retrieval system, or transmitted in any form or by any means, electronic, mechanical, photocopying, recording, or otherwise, without written permission from the publisher.

The information in *Access Anything: Colorado* is accurate as of May 2005. Prices, hours of operation, addresses, phone numbers, Web sites, and other items change rapidly. If something in the book is incorrect, please write to the authors in care of Fulcrum Publishing, 16100 Table Mountain Parkway, Suite 300, Golden, Colorado, 80403, and please refer to the author's Web site for updates, www.accessanything.net/updates.

Neither Fulcrum Publishing nor the authors assume any liability for injury, damage to property, or violation of the law that may arise from the use of this book.

Library of Congress Cataloging-in-Publication Data

Kennedy, Craig P.
 Access anything : Colorado : adventuring with disabilities / Craig P. Kennedy and Andrea C. Jehn.
   p. cm.
 Includes index.
 ISBN 1-55591-534-5
 1. Colorado—Guidebooks. 2. People with disabilities—Travel—Colorado—Guidebooks. 3. Outdoor recreation—Colorado—Guidebooks. 4. Parks—Colorado—Guidebooks. I. Title: Colorado : adventuring with disabilities. II. Jehn, Andrea C. III. Title.
 F774.3.K457 2005
 917.88'0434—dc22
                                                              2004024352

Printed in the United States of America
0 9 8 7 6 5 4 3 2 1

Editorial: Katie L. Raymond, Faith Marcovecchio
Design: Jack Lenzo
Cover images: (counterclockwise from top right [skier in snow]): Courtesy of Dave Genchi; Challenge Aspen; Adaptive Adventures; National Sports Center for the Disabled (NSCD); NSCD; Challenge Aspen; NSCD; Adaptive Adventures; and Challenge Aspen

Fulcrum Publishing
16100 Table Mountain Parkway, Suite 300
Golden, Colorado 80403
(800) 992-2908 • (303) 277-1623
www.fulcrum-books.com

Courtesy of the
Breckenridge Outdoor Education Center

CONTENTS

Map of Colorado vi
Acknowledgments viii
Preface: The World Is Still Your Oyster ix
Introduction: Why We Live Here, Why You'd Want to Travel Here xi

CHAPTER ONE: GETTING STARTED 1
Packing and Your Own Pace 1
Adaptive Adventure Travel Introduction 5
    Emotional Help, Physical Help 5
    Adapting Activities to Your Needs 5

CHAPTER TWO: METROPOLITAN AREAS 7
Boulder 7
Colorado Springs 12
Denver 20
Ft. Collins 25

CHAPTER THREE: SMALL TOWNS 31
Scenic Suggestions 31
Southwest Colorado 32
    Crested Butte 32
    Durango 35
    Ouray 38
    Pagosa Springs 39

Ridgway 40
  Silverton 41
  Telluride 43
Northwest Colorado 46
  Steamboat Springs 46
  Winter Park 50
Central Western Colorado 54
  Aspen 54
  Black Hawk and Central City 56
  Breckenridge 59
  Glenwood Springs 61
  Idaho Springs 63
  Vail 65

CHAPTER FOUR: WINTER TRAVEL 67
  Aspen/Snowmass—*Challenge Aspen* 69
  Breckenridge—*Breckenridge Outdoor Education Center* 77
  Crested Butte—*Adaptive Sports Center* 82
  Durango—*Adaptive Sports Association* 88
  Nederland—*Eldora Special Recreation Program* 94
  Powderhorn—*Colorado Discover Ability Integrated Outdoor Adventures* 98
  Steamboat—*Adaptive Ski School* 101
  Telluride—*Telluride Adaptive Sports Program* 109
  Vail—*Vail Adaptive* 115
  Winter Park—*National Sports Center for the Disabled* 121

CHAPTER FIVE: SUMMER TRAVEL 127
  Adaptive Activity Specialists 127
    Adaptive Adventures 127
    Back Country Discovery 130
    Disabled Sports USA 130
    Just for the Fun of It 131
    Wilderness on Wheels 131
  Summer Activities 133
    Fishing 133
    Golf 136
    Horseback Riding 138
    Hunting 146

CHAPTER SIX: NATIONAL AND STATE PARKS 147
  National Parks, Monuments, Historic Sites, and Recreation Areas 151
    Bent's Old Fort National Historic Site 151
    Black Canyon of the Gunnison National Park 152
    Colorado National Monument 154
    Curecanti National Recreation Area 155
    Dinosaur National Monument 156
    Florissant Fossil Beds National Monument 159
    Great Sand Dunes National Park and Preserve 160

Mesa Verde National Park 162
　　　Rocky Mountain National Park 164
　State Parks 169
　　　Arkansas Headwaters State Park 169
　　　Barr Lake State Park 171
　　　Bonny Lake State Park 172
　　　Boyd Lake State Park 173
　　　Castlewood Canyon State Park 174
　　　Chatfield State Park 175
　　　Cherry Creek State Park 177
　　　Cheyenne Mountain State Park 178
　　　Colorado River State Park 179
　　　Colorado State Forest State Park 181
　　　Crawford State Park 183
　　　Eldorado Canyon State Park 184
　　　Eleven Mile State Park 185
　　　Golden Gate Canyon State Park 187
　　　Harvey Gap State Park 188
　　　Highline Lake State Park 189
　　　Jackson Lake State Park 190
　　　John Martin Reservoir State Park 191
　　　Lake Pueblo State Park 193
　　　Lathrop State Park 195
　　　Lory State Park 196
　　　Mancos State Park 197
　　　Mueller State Park 198
　　　Navajo State Park 199
　　　North Sterling State Park 200
　　　Paonia State Park 201
　　　Pearl Lake State Park 202
　　　Ridgway State Park 203
　　　Rifle Falls State Park 204
　　　Rifle Gap State Park 205
　　　Roxborough State Park 206
　　　San Luis State Park and Wildlife Area 207
　　　Spinney Mountain State Park 209
　　　St. Vrain State Park 210
　　　Stagecoach State Park 211
　　　Steamboat Lake State Park 212
　　　Sweitzer Lake State Park 213
　　　Sylvan Lake State Park 214
　　　Trinidad Lake State Park 215
　　　Vega State Park 216
　　　Yampa River State Park 217

Resources 218
Index 220
About the Authors 228

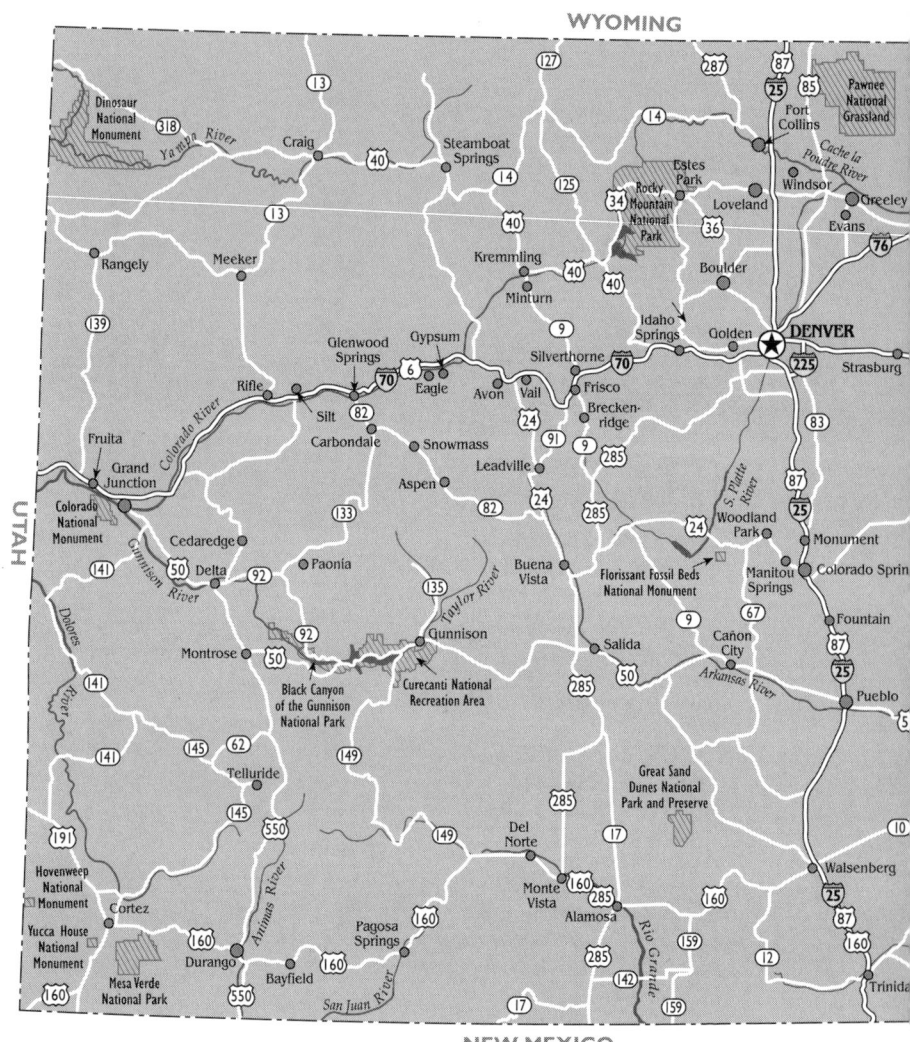

Courtesy of Marge Mueller, Gray Mouse Graphics

WYOMING
NEBRASKA
KANSAS
OKLAHOMA
NEW MEXICO
DENVER
Fort Collins
Cache la Poudre River
Pawnee National Grassland
North Sterling Reservoir
Sterling
Julesburg
Holyoke
Jackson Lake Reservoir
South Platte River
Estes Park
Rocky Mountain National Park
Loveland
Windsor
Greeley
Evans
Fort Morgan
Brush
Yuma
Wray
Kremmling
Minturn
Boulder
Idaho Springs
Golden
Byers
Strasburg
Silverthorne
Avon
Vail
Frisco
Breckenridge
Leadville
Limon
Burlington
S. Platte River
Woodland Park
Monument
Colorado Springs
Manitou Springs
Buena Vista
Florissant Fossil Beds National Monument
Fountain
Sand Creek Massacre National Historic Site
Salida
Cañon City
Arkansas River
Pueblo
Fowler
Bent's Old Fort National
Las Animas
Lamar
Rocky Ford
La Junta
John Martin Reservoir
Great Sand Dunes National Park and Preserve
Comanche National Grassland
Del Norte
Monte Vista
Alamosa
Rio Grande
Walsenberg
Purgatoire River
Springfield
Trinidad
COLORADO
N
Interstate Highways
State Highways
State Parks
National Site (Park, Preserve, Historic Site, Monument, Recreation Area, Grassland, Wildlife Refuge)
0 10 20 30 40
Miles

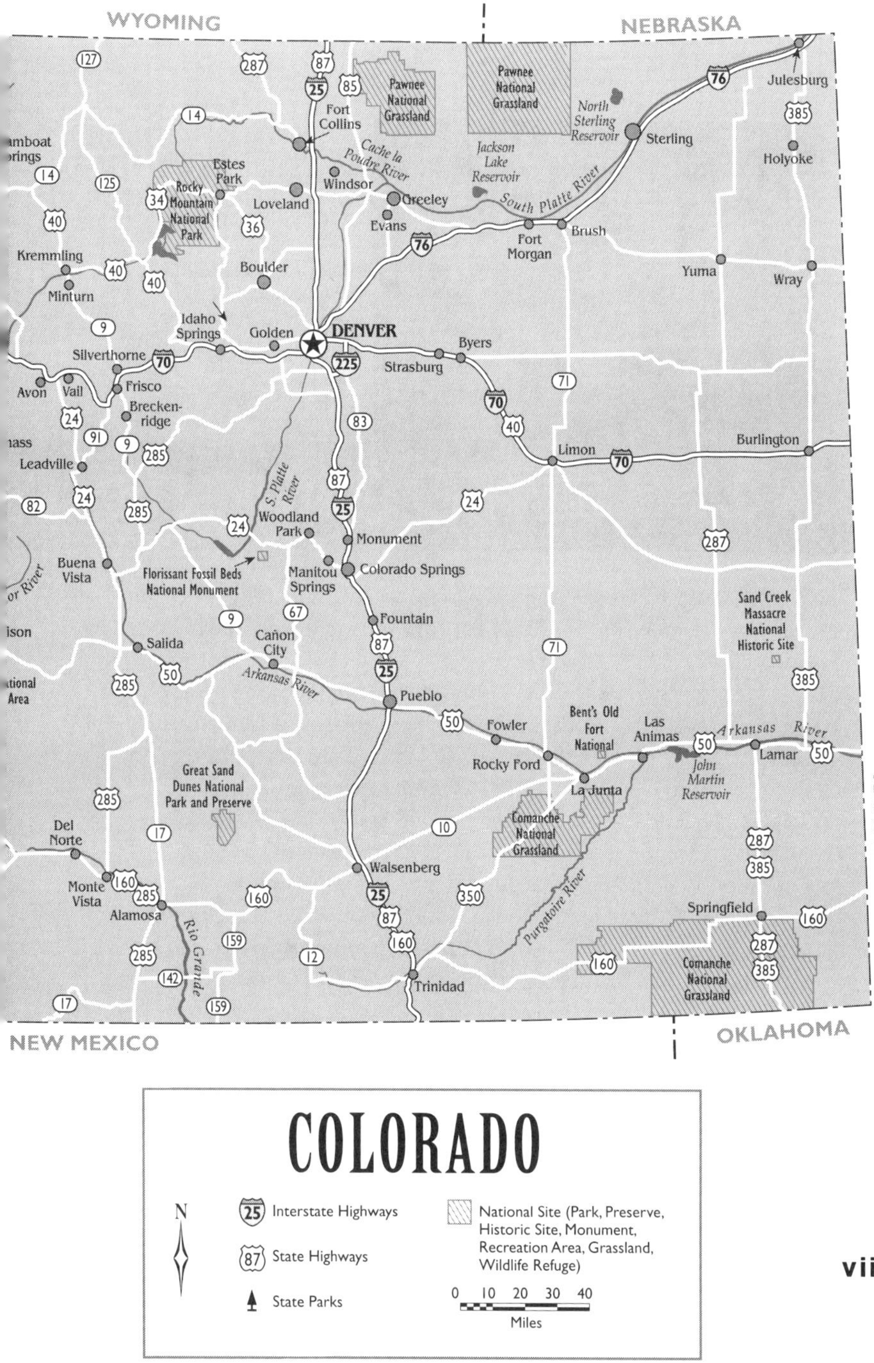

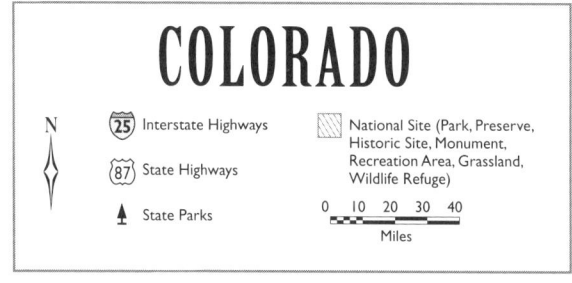

This book is dedicated to the lasting memories of our friend Tom Moore and to Christopher Reeve. Thank you for sharing your lives with us. May your light forever shine brightly for all to see.

ACKNOWLEDGMENTS

We thank our parents, Katherine and Michael Clarke, Mary Ellen and Christopher Jehn, and William Kennedy, for supporting us in everything we do.

We also extend our deepest gratitude to the following people for making all aspects of this project possible: Chelsea Faulkner, Jill Murphy Long, Mark Wellman and No Limits Tahoe, Steve Ackerman, Ruth DeMuth, Andrew and Lisa Stern, Kristi Nelson Cohen, TripStream Productions, Krauthamer and Stahl, Shaw Pittman, Adaptive Adventures, Challenge Aspen, Breckenridge Outdoor Education Center, Adaptive Sports Center, Adaptive Sports Association, Eldora Special Recreation Program, Colorado Discover Ability, Integrated Outdoor Adventures, Steamboat Adaptive Ski School, Telluride Adaptive Sports Program, Vail Adaptive, the National Sports Center for the Disabled, Fulcrum Publishing, and everyone else who touched this book with their love. Thank you very much!

Courtesy of the National Sports Center for the Disabled

PREFACE

THE WORLD IS STILL YOUR OYSTER

Travel guides have long served as keys to helping people choose where, when, and why to travel. They also provide important and essential information for making the right decisions once you have arrived. When it comes to making your trip worthwhile, affordable, and memorable, research is an absolute necessity. When a wheelchair is your mode of transportation, this research is invaluable.

While my partner and I were researching a recent trip to Alaska, it became apparent to us that the word "accessible" is consistently misinterpreted. While many businesses assured us that their facilities were accessible, they were only partially accessible according to the Americans with Disabilities Act standards. Some were denoted accessible in the travel books we had purchased. However, the universal accessible symbol is not a consistent standard but merely each individual's interpretation of what they think accessible means. This interpretation is usually through the eyes of the able-bodied, affected greatly by the individual's own awareness. Extensive travel throughout the United States by car and plane has opened our eyes to the needs of travelers similar to me.

With approximately 55 million people with disabilities living in the United States and more than 11,000 new spinal cord injuries each year, the need for information and opportunity is now greater than ever. Information provides opportunity, and opportunity provides hope. Hope is the cornerstone for much-needed positive outlooks and better quality of life for all those who are living with disabilities. Accessibility information breathes this hope into the lives of the disabled, and it is the best way to educate people about what they can do, not what they are limited to.

By providing people with the information to travel, I hope to inspire within them the sense of freedom that I feel when I am traveling. To me, freedom is getting out of my wheelchair and being able to go places and do things that nobody expects me to do. It's liberating because it makes me forget about my disability. To me, freedom is mono-skiing fast enough to feel like I'm flying. To me, freedom is waterskiing on a sunny mountain lake. To me, freedom is Colorado!

Road-tested by an avid wheelchair traveler and his partner, this book is an important tool in providing travelers with disabilities a more objective review of what to expect while traveling throughout Colorado. This adventure travel guide addresses the needs of travelers young to old, paraplegic to quadriplegic, manual to power chair. From the most mobile to the least active person, this book will help readers decide where they can go and what they can do once they get there. So, get out there and enjoy life. Happy travels!

—Craig Kennedy

Courtesy of
the National Sports Center for the Disabled

INTRODUCTION

WHY WE LIVE HERE, WHY YOU'D WANT TO TRAVEL HERE

We've found Colorado to be one of the more accessible states in the country, as well as one of the more adventurous destinations in the world. Outdoor lovers are attracted to the endless mountain landscapes, the bountiful rivers and lakes, and the four seasons of fresh air, blue skies, and perfect weather. Adaptive travel here is expanding each year, attracting all abilities to the adventurous lifestyle of this magnificent state. But that's not why we live here.

The attitude alone is enough to make any visitor a resident, along with small-town friendliness present even in the bigger cities and progressive mentalities on sustainability, urban sprawl, and outdoor living. The motto of many small towns is "The wilderness is my backyard," and what a beautiful backyard it is! With more than 104,000 square miles, Colorado is only the eighth largest state in the country but ranks as the tallest, with more than 55 peaks greater than 14,000 feet tall, a whopping 900 peaks more than 11,000 feet tall, and an average altitude of 7,000 feet. This may be a mouthful of altitude statistics, but that's what makes up the unmistakable mountain scenery that exists around every corner of every town in this diverse state. That is why we live here. The views, the unavoidable feeling of exploration and adventure, and the friendly neighbors make Colorado the best place in the world to come home to.

Nationwide, there are more than 10 million motion-challenged people with disabilities in wheelchairs and 50 million people with disabilities overall. More than 20 million visitors book their vacations to or in Colorado each year, and with disability travel expanding annually, the total number of vacationers can only increase with the expansion of adaptive adventure travel awareness and modification.*

General Travel Information:
Colorado State Tourism Office
1625 Broadway #1700
Denver, CO 80202
800-COLORADO (265-6723) or 303-892-3840
www.colorado.com

Travel Advisories and Road Conditions: 303-639-1111 or 877-315-ROAD (7623)

* This statistical information was acquired from www.colorado.com, www.denver.org/maps/stats.asp, www.boulderchamber.com, and www.bouldercolorado.com.

CHAPTER 1

GETTING STARTED

Packing and Your Own Pace

As you probably already know, packing everything you need for a comfortable trip is nearly impossible. Depending on your disability, you may need medical supplies, health-care equipment, such as shower chairs and toilet seats, and spare tubes for the wheelchair, as well as any toys you're bringing for your adventure trip (hand-cycle, mono-ski, film equipment, extra padding, etc.). So, while you're preparing for your trip, make sure you take the following preparatory steps to ensure comfort while you're on the road.

1. Make sure all your medical needs are taken care of. For example, if you need oxygen, is it available? Colorado is a high-altitude state, and with altitude topping out at above 14,000 feet, oxygen is no joke. If you can only bring a few bags and may need to restock on supplies, is there a store or medical supply nearby for you to do that? Phone calls ahead of time are invaluable when you're 120 miles from the nearest pharmacy.

2. Is your lodging fully or appropriately accessible? We've provided many options per town, but not all. Those off-the-beaten-path cabins for fishing or those cozy bed-and-breakfasts for a perfect start to skiing might *say* they're accessible, but make sure to check the smaller details that able bodies don't think of—shower size, door size, steps to a back porch, and conditions of dining facilities, for example. Again, call ahead. Doing all of this makes for hefty prep work—and, perhaps, phone bills—but it's well worth the hassle. Both where you lay your head at night as well as where you clean off your sweat from the day's adventures are the most important details to iron out. We've found that lodging managers prefer to be called with questions ahead of time rather than be thrown off guard by a shower chair that's too big for their shower.

3. Allow enough time for everything. The most important factor for disability travel is time. As you know (or, perhaps, deny), it takes wheelies longer to do just about everything—though in most independent cases, not much longer. Allowing yourself an extra hour for everything travel-related may seem liberal, but, perhaps, is not enough in some cases. For example, if you have a connection in Denver or Chicago, make sure your flights are far enough apart. For wheelies, an hour apart is barely enough to make connecting flights in most major airports, especially when boarding and deboarding last on a full airplane.

4. Make plans ahead of time for getting around while you are on your trip. If you are planning on renting a vehicle to get you to your destination(s), we have some suggestions. First, many major car companies will say they offer hand controls on their vehicles; however, only one (so far) offers a guarantee of that special request: Avis. As of 2003, Avis guarantees this. However, other requests, such as a Global Positioning System or ski racks, are not guaranteed. Guaranteeing requests for hand controls will probably become the norm, as these are necessary for most people who request them. However, it is not the norm yet, so it is best to check ahead of time.

Another transportation option is adapted van rentals. This option is one of our favorites, as having enough room for all your gear is a must. There are several agencies that will rent converted vans in the Denver area, listed below.

7550 S. Emerson St.
Centennial, CO 80122
Phone: 800-456-1371, ext. 226, or 303-797-0999
Web site: www.wheelersvanrentals.com
E-mail: co@wheelersvanrentals.com
Wheelers has been around since 2002, is locally owned, and offers vans with or without hand controls that are available for rent on a weekly or monthly basis. This agency prides itself on quality and service, offering delivery and pickup, information on local accessibility, and 24-hour emergency assistance.

315 Evergreen Ave.
Boulder, CO 80304
Phone: 800-238-6920 or 303-674-1498
Web site: www.wheelchairgetaways.com
E-mail: co@wheelchairgetaways.com
Wheelchair Getaways is a national agency that started in the late 1970s as a bus company that had requests from many schools for special needs. Their vans are now offered in most states and offer many amenities, including power doors, hand controls, and outside entry controls for full-size and minivans.

FREEWHEEL VANS
Free to move about the Rockies

303-467-9981
719-262-6640
800-728-5313
WWW.FREEWHEELVANS.COM

4901 Ward Rd.
Wheat Ridge, CO 80033
Phone: 800-728-5313 or 303-467-9981
Web site: www.freewheelvans.com
E-mail: freewheel@freewheelvans.com

Aiming to be more cost effective, Freewheel Vans starts their daily rentals at only $100 per day and drops their rates for longer stays. They offer full-size and minivans as well as hand controls and steering knobs upon request.

5. **After your prep work, make sure to make a list of all the items you need to bring.** Forgetting something is inevitable, but it's always better to put the essentials in a list.

6. **Be flexible.** Something frequent travelers know with certainty is that the more flexible you are while you're traveling, the more fun your trip will be. This starts with your flight—allow a day or two between your flight and your first planned activity in order to settle in. In the case of storms or other uncontrollable events, if you have allowed for them, your travel stress dissipates.

This philosophy continues throughout the trip as well. Something we've learned from trial and error is allowing way more time than you think you need—for those stops you hadn't read about, the sights you just can't pass by quickly, etc. Allow a cushion in travel time for scenic drives especially, factoring in scenic pullouts or getting stuck behind slow drivers.

Between preparation and flexibility, you are ensuring a hassle-free vacation and allowing yourself the best opportunity to discover the good surprises that arise while on the road.

Now, get out there and recreate!

Adaptive Adventure Travel Introduction

Once you're packed and feeling anxious, settle into a good travel magazine, such as National Geographic's *Adventure*, to get you psyched up for your trip. Pull out those brochures from the adaptive program you're visiting as well, and look over what your week or two will entail.

Emotional Help, Physical Help

One thing you'll probably always need, but don't necessarily like to ask for, is help. Carrying extra luggage and equipment is a start. However, it's not necessary to have a traveling companion so long as you're prepared to ask for help when you need it or are sufficient enough on your own without it.

If you're new to adventure travel, keep in mind that you may very well be pushed more physically or emotionally than you have been in some time. This is good for both your mind and body and will bring you fulfillment and independence, *but make sure to discuss your adventure travel and all strenuous activities with your physician first.*

Discuss any emotional or physical questions with all tour operators or adaptive programs before finalizing your trip. The world of adaptive travel is greatly expanding as we write, and activity companies are eager to adapt their product for any needs, but much of it is still trial and error, and completely explaining any special needs ahead of time is for your benefit and safety.

Adapting Activities to Your Needs

Some adaptations may require your insight. ATV tour companies may not have an automatic machine, for example, but don't let that stop your visit to the backcountry. Many agencies will have the guide put your machine into second gear and keep your speed at a safe level for both you and the machine. This is a fine example of knowing ahead of time what works and what doesn't.

Know your limitations. Sea kayaks, for example, are not as easily toppled as river kayaks, and if you have some of your stomach muscles, this is a valid option for you to see the myriad wildlife on the uncountable lakes and reservoirs in the state. But if you do not have ample muscle capabilities, your option is a tandem kayak, steadied by your companion or the tour guide, and still offering the world of riparian habitat for your viewing.

Another popular Colorado activity is biking, but say you've never taken a hand-crank cycle out before. Many adaptive agencies mentioned in this book offer clinics and instructors to teach you how to safely enjoy these sensitive cycles before heading out on your own. This is one way to ensure your safety before attempting a new activity, while also enjoying the company of other newcomers to the world of adaptive sports.

All of the adaptive agencies for winter activities listed in chapter four provide full instruction in skiing. Most of these agencies provide activities during the summer months as well, such as biking and rock climbing, which are included in chapter five.

Also, in chapter six we list a few major adaptive agencies in the state that put together tours, events, camps, and clinics for groups if you're planning on getting together with a local or nationwide network of friends with similar abilities. You can also join these groups individually if you're seeking adventure without your own network of friends.

Have fun!

Courtesy of
the Boulder Convention and Visitors Bureau

CHAPTER 2

METROPOLITAN AREAS

Boulder

Parking and Transportation

Metro Taxi: 303-666-6666
Super Shuttle: 303-444-0808
Avis (Adapted Vehicles): 303-449-1136

Directions from Denver International Airport (DIA): Exit DIA onto Peña Blvd. Continue for 9 miles until you reach I-70 west. Take I-70 west to the I-270 north exit (279) toward Ft. Collins. Take I-270 north to the U.S. Hwy. 36 west exit toward Boulder.

Activities

With a median age of only 29 years old and the Rocky Mountains as a backyard, it's no wonder Boulder was voted the number-one sports town in America by *Outside* magazine in 2003. The city of Boulder, at slightly greater than 1 mile in elevation, also boasts 300 days of sunshine per year, 200 miles of public hiking and biking trails, and 30,000 acres of open space to recreate.

There is truly no limit of options available to outdoor enthusiasts in Boulder. Mountain biking, hiking, backpacking, camping, rafting, kayaking, flyfishing, horseback riding, snowshoeing, alpine and Nordic skiing, rock and ice climbing, hot air ballooning, gliding, and windsurfing are just some of the activities that can be enjoyed in and around the city. If you don't have your own equipment, the plethora of sporting-goods stores and specialty outdoor shops has you covered.

View of the Flatirons from the Chautauqua Trailhead.

The **Colorado Chautauqua Association**, founded in 1898, comprises 26 acres of public land at the base of Boulder's famous Flatirons. Historically, this association was created by Texans as a refuge from the hot summer months, with a cultural and educational focus for families. Today the association prides itself on land preservation and is partly responsible for the continuing accessibility initiative that helps to make Boulder more accessible every day. The tradition of bringing lectures, concerts, and other performances to the Boulder area is still alive here.

The **Chautauqua Ranger Cottage** is the headquarters for all of Boulder's mountain-park activities and information and is very accessible, including a ramp to the many trailheads and accessible restrooms and water fountains. Most of the trails at this site are not wheelchair friendly, but the main trail is doable for the first .25 mile or so.

If you want to try any sport while you're in town, call the **Boulder Outdoor Center** (2707 Spruce St.; www.boc123.com). Here is a company that does it all. What's their motto? "Expertise is our difference." These guys are willing to go anywhere and do anything every chance they get. Try kayaking, canoeing, rafting, snow sports, and more.

If you are interested in rafting, we recommend contacting **Noah's Ark Rafting** (719-395-2158; www.noahsark.com). This is one of the companies used by the **Breckenridge Outdoor Education Center**. If you require significant assistance, call ahead to inquire about their trips. You will probably want to have an able-bodied partner along to assist you.

Lodging

As with any large city, Boulder has many accessible lodging options for travelers with disabilities. **Hotel Boulderado** (800-433-4344) is a historic hotel located 1 block from Pearl St., close to the University of Colorado–Boulder (CU) campus. They have nine Americans with Disabilities Act (ADA)–compliant rooms, and a choice of valet or self-parking (accessible parking spots are in the back). They also supply shower chairs, if needed. Check out **Q's**, their four-star restaurant, for great fine dining.

The **Boulder Marriott** (303-440-8877) is located in between campus and Pearl St. at 2660 Canyon Blvd. All of the rooms are doable, with five that are ADA compliant. Two of those rooms have roll-in showers with benches. Accessible parking is available underground or at the front entrance. We also recommend trying the Marriott's own **JW Steakhouse** for a juicy Colorado steak.

The **Colorado Chautauqua Association** (303-442-3282, ext. 11) is located just up the hill from the ranger station and offers almost 100 cottages operated by Chautauqua. They have two fully accessible, ADA–compliant cottages available for rent, including one with a roll-in shower. The best time to rent these is during the summer, as many of the cottages are leased during the winter.

Super 8 Boulder (800-800-8000) is directly across the street from the CU campus and about 2 miles from Pearl St. All of the rooms on the first level are accessible, including one with a roll-in shower. Shower chairs are available as well.

We also found two accessible bed-and-breakfasts in Boulder. We absolutely loved the **Lookout Inn** (800-233-5633; www.guest-house.com) in northern Boulder. It has one fully accessible unit with a roll-in shower and bath bench and is just far enough from downtown to make your stay quiet and peaceful. If that room is not available, most of the other units are doable. The dining room is also accessible.

The **Briar Rose** (303-442-3007; www.briarrosebb.com), located only 1 mile from the Pearl St. Mall, has one unit that is very doable. It is a ground-floor room with a stall shower, but you will need to bring your own bath bench. The dining room is not accessible, due to a few stairs, but the staff is more than happy to deliver breakfast to your room.

Dining

From classic American to Mediterranean to authentic Asian and Italian cuisine, Boulder's 300-plus restaurants offer visitors incredible dining choices from around the world. Boulder is also home to the award-winning **Mountain Sun and Oasis Brewery** and a wealth of great bars and music venues. Smoking has been prohibited in all bars, taverns, and restaurants since 1995, making Boulder's nightlife even more fun for everyone.

The **14th St. Bar and Grill** (303-444-5854) serves bistro-style American cuisine and is open for lunch and dinner. It is located on the pedestrian mall at Pearl St. This entire mall is accessible, and there is always some kind of live entertainment during the summer months. **Foolish Craig's** (303-247-9383) has a fun atmosphere and serves great pub-style food. It is also located on Pearl St. We went for burgers and beers here and had a blast with the friendly and lively staff.

City Street Bagels (3070 28th St.; 303-442-0049) serves fantastic bagels and breakfast and lunch sandwiches of all kinds, and is fully accessible, including its bathrooms.

Boulder's Pearl St. Mall. Courtesy of the Boulder Convention and Visitors Bureau

The Sink (1165 13th St.; 303-444-7465) is known as the most famous spot to eat "on the hill." It once employed Robert Redford as its janitor! They serve great American food in a college atmosphere. For some of Boulder's best homemade barbecue, get full at **KT's BBQ Outback** (303-442-3717), located at on 13th St. as well.

The **Khow Thai Café** (303-447-0273) offers the best Thai food in Boulder—and, perhaps, in Denver as well—so, if you like Thai cuisine, try not to miss this one on 1600 Broadway St.

Last, every town has great Mexican food and this is it for Boulder, **Serrano's Southwestern Grill** (6525 Gunpark Dr.; 303-530-7423).

Entertainment and Nightlife

Located on the CU campus, **Fiske Planetarium** and **Sommers-Bausch Observatory** (303-492-5002) is a very hip way to learn about our planet and solar system, as well as black holes and extraterrestrials. The laser show at the planetarium is set to music by Pink Floyd, Bob Marley, the Beatles, Dave Matthews, and more. You can also request your own music. Classes, observation sessions, and laser shows are offered on Friday nights and Saturdays, occasionally with special shows on Tuesdays. The planetarium has fully accessible seating and restrooms and is open year-round. Depending on your disability, the telescopes may not be accessible.

Our favorite stop for live music in the area is the **Fox Theater** (303-443-3399, www.foxtheater.com). This venue has an old-fashioned theater feel, with a roll-in entry and plenty of options for wheelchairs, though they are currently working on improving the accessible seating even more.

Contact Information
Boulder Convention and Visitors Bureau
2440 Pearl St.
Boulder, CO 80302
Phone: 303-442-2911
Web site: www.bouldercoloradousa.com
E-mail: visitor@bouldercvb.com

Colorado Springs

Parking and Transportation

We have found that the best way to get around any big city is to take advantage of mass transit. City-run buses can usually accommodate any person with a disability.

The **Colorado Springs Transit** (719-385-2489; www.springsgov.com) is the best place to start. All city buses are equipped with wheelchair lifts and reserved-seating areas and can be picked up all over the city. If you are unable to use the fixed-route buses because of your disability, **Springs Mobility** (719-392-2396; www.springsgov.com/Page.asp?NavID=1196) can arrange a ride for you. Call or visit their Web site for punch cards and daily prices.

Yellow Cab (719-634-5000) is another easy option for getting around while in the city. They have four lift-equipped minivans in circulation that can be ready to use in minutes. We also recommend using them for airport transports. The service is very friendly and the prices are reasonable.

Activities

Pikes Peak (719-385-7325) is at 14,110 feet in elevation and is one of the most famous and most recognized peaks in the United States. It is one of 54 Fourteeners in Colorado. More than a million visitors per year come to the mountain to take advantage of the incredible views from the top of the Pikes Peak Hwy., which is 19 miles long and takes about an hour to navigate through the 60-plus curves as you climb to the top. There is also an accessible restaurant, the **Summit House**, at the top for good eats and spectacular views of the Continental Divide, Sangre de Cristo Mountains, Denver, Colorado Springs, and into New Mexico.

From I-25, head west on U.S. Hwy. 24 toward Manitou Springs. Pikes Peak Hwy. is a left turn as you enter the town of Cascade.

Since 1916, auto racers have been competing for one of the most coveted racing trophies in the world and the title of Pikes Peak International Hill Climb Champion. **Pikes Peak International Hill Climb** (719-685-4400; www.ppihc.com), or "The Race to the Clouds," is the second-oldest motor-sports event in the United States, second to the Indianapolis 500. The race comprises 12.4 miles of twisting road, including 156 dangerous gravel turns and 2,000-foot drop-offs with no guardrails. Today auto and motorcycle racers typically reach speeds of more than 130 miles per hour in their sprint to the top of America's Mountain, as it is known throughout the world. The race usually takes place annually at the end of June and is televised in more than 50 countries. The Web site has all of the information necessary for racers and fans alike. This is an incredible race to see live.

First discovered around 1860 by explorers scouting the area for the perfect place for a new township, the **Garden of the Gods** (1805 N. 30th St. [at Gateway Rd.]; 719-219-0108; www.gardenofgods.com) is an amazing display of huge, red-sandstone pillars situated at the base of Pikes Peak. It is owned and operated by the city of Colorado Springs and is a national natural landmark.

The visitors center, located at Gateway Rd., is fully accessible, complete with accessible restrooms and plenty of accessible parking. Make sure to check out the 12-minute movie, titled *How Did Those Red Rocks Get There?* Using time-lapse photography, four movie screens, and a laser-light show, this film shows how the Garden of the Gods came to be. There are also free nature talks, exhibits, a café, and a gift shop to check out while you are there.

The Garden of the Gods in Colorado Springs.
Courtesy of Experience Colorado Springs—
The Colorado Springs Convention and Visitors Bureau

There are a few paved trails that are navigable in a wheelchair and several that are not. The most accessible area is the **Central Garden Trail**, which gives a tour of most of the major rock formations in the park. You can take a guided tour daily, offered at 10 A.M. and 2 P.M., or you can take a self-guided tour. The Garden of the Gods is a truly unique place that represents the raw beauty of Colorado. If you are in the area, this is a very worthwhile stop and is free of charge to all visitors.

From I-25 exit 146, head west on Garden of the Gods Rd. Then turn left and head south on 30th St. From exit 145, head west on Fillmore St., then turn right on Mesa Rd., and then left on 30th St. From exit 143, head west on Uintah St. and then right on 30th St. From exit 141, head west on U.S. Hwy. 24, turn right at 21st St., left at Colorado Blvd., and then right on 30th St.

Seven Falls (P.O. Box 118; 719-632-0765) is one of the more beautiful and easy-to-access sites in the Colorado Springs area. Seven Falls is a 181-foot multistep waterfall located in South Cheyenne Canyon, about 10 minutes from downtown. It is the only Colorado waterfall listed on National Geographic's International Waterfall List, and it is breathtaking. What really makes it unique is that during the summer the entire canyon is illuminated at night. The lights on the falls create an amazing display of colors as they are reflected off of the water and granite walls. Practiced photographers can catch incredible stills with vibrant rainbow colors.

The 1-mile drive to the base of the falls takes you through sheer cliff walls along South Cheyenne Creek. An elevator inside the mountain takes you to the top of the falls at the **Eagle's Nest Observation** platform. This is the only place for people in wheelchairs to get a perfect view of the falls. There are also two hiking trails at the top of the falls, but these can only be accessed via the 224-step stairway and, obviously, are not accessible for most people with disabilities.

You can also check out the **Indian Dance Presentations** that take place in the circle at the base of the falls. Performed by Native Americans, these take place on an hourly basis during summer hours.

To get to Seven Falls, take Cheyenne Blvd. west about 7 miles and follow the signs.

The **U.S. Olympic Training Center** (1750 E. Boulder St.; 888-659-8687) is an amazing $8 million facility. It is the main source of information about the U.S. Olympic Committee, U.S. Olympic training centers, and the Olympic movement. There are plenty of things to see here, including the **Olympic Hall of Fame** and **Olympic torch display**, and the best way to see them all is to take the free tour. Tours leave the visitors center on the hour, starting at 9 A.M., with the last leaving at 4 P.M., and include a short, informative film and a 45-minute walking tour. There are no tours on Sundays. Most of the tour

Sculptures outside the U.S. Olympic Training Center.
Courtesy of the Colorado Springs U.S. Olympic Training Center

is outside and everything is accessible, as this is also the Olympic training center for members of the U.S. Paralympic team. This facility sees about 140,000 visitors per year and is a must-see when in Colorado Springs. We had a chance to see many Olympians training for many different sports and will never forget the intensity. Check out the Web sites www.olympic-usa.org or www.usparalympics.org for more details and information about training schedules.

The training center is located on the corner of Union Blvd. and Boulder St., with the gated entrance off of Boulder St. From I-25, take exit 143 (Uintah). Go east on Uintah to Union Blvd. Take a right on Union Blvd., then go south on Union Blvd. to Boulder St. and take a right on Boulder St. The entrance to the U.S. Olympic Complex is off Boulder St.

Buried deep inside Cheyenne Mountain is **NORAD**. This base represents one of nine strategic-defense locations in the United States and Canada aimed at protecting the skies over America.

At the base of the mountain is the **Cheyenne Mountain Zoo** (4250 Cheyenne Mountain Zoo Rd.; 719-633-9925; www.cmzoo.org). A philanthropist named Spencer Penrose, who believed it was important to have a zoological park in the community, started this unique collection of animals in 1926. All exhibits at the zoo are accessible, as is the tram if you want a guided tour of the park. You can also arrange for lunches ahead of time by calling the concession stand (719-575-0536). Make sure to ask about the special rate for people with disabilities, and make sure to enjoy this one-of-a-kind zoo.

From I-25, take exit 138, the Circle Dr. exit, and drive west to the Broadmoor Hotel. Turn right at the hotel and follow the signs to the zoo.

The **Cog Railway**, or Manitou and Pikes Peak Railway (515 Ruxton Ave., Manitou Springs; 719-685-5401; www.cograilway.com), is the highest train of its kind in the world. Passengers have been taking advantage of this incredible journey for more than 100 years. The trip takes you through amazing boulder fields and past waterfalls as it heads for Hell Gate, a natural gateway to the mountains. As the train approaches the timberline (the altitude at which trees stop growing), it passes by some of the oldest living trees on the planet, bristlecone pines, some of which are more than 2,000 years old. Steep climbs through herds of bighorn sheep complete the journey to the top. The train stops for about a half an hour at the summit, giving passengers time to use the restrooms and get something to eat before the return trip.

Travelers with disabilities can board the train without assistance via the platform, but there is no restroom onboard, so be sure to use the restroom at the depot beforehand. The railway is open from mid-April through early January, depending on the weather. The route is almost 9 miles long and takes slightly more than three hours round-trip. The **Summit House** at Pikes Peak summit is accessible and has accessible restrooms. (It's a good idea to bring your own food and beverages, as the Summit House sees thousands of visitors per day during peak season and lines can be very long.) If you are not used to the altitude, remember to drink plenty of water, as the summit is located at more than 14,000 feet in elevation.

From I-25, take exit 141 (U.S. Hwy. 24) and go west (toward the mountains) on U.S. Hwy. 24 for 4 miles to the Manitou Ave. (Manitou Springs) exit. Go west on Manitou Ave. for 1.5 miles to Ruxton Ave. Turn left and go to the top of Ruxton Ave., .75 mile.

The **U.S. Air Force Academy** (719-333-2025; www.usafa.af.mil) is located off of I-25 just before entering Colorado Springs. For visitors who wish to tour the facility, it is open seven days a week between 5:30 A.M. and 6 P.M.

Lodging

The **Broadmoor Hotel** (1 Lake Ave.; 719-634-7711) is easily the most famous building in Colorado Springs today and has been an icon since 1891. It was turned into a resort in 1918 and has been considered one of the premier resorts in the world since. The resort is incredibly accessible, considering its age. They have really gone out of their way to accommodate people with disabilities.

The hotel has 15 ADA–compliant rooms. Half of these rooms have roll-in showers with fold-down benches, and shower chairs are available for rooms with tubs. The Broadmoor is also home to nine different restaurants, all of which are accessible. Our favorite was the **Tavern**.

The Broadmoor is situated in the foothills of Cheyenne Mountain, about 20 minutes from downtown Colorado Springs, and only 8 miles from the Colorado Springs Airport.

We always manage to find a great bed-and-breakfast to stay at when we are traveling, and in Colorado Springs the place to stay is the **Room at the Inn** (888-442-1896; www.roomattheinn.com). This incredible Victorian home is centrally located, within a short drive of downtown, and is very easy to get to from I-25. The owners have made one of the units ADA compliant, with a roll-in shower and removable bath bench, and they are very familiar with wheelchair users. The dining room is also accessible, and the breakfast was one of the best home-cooked meals we have ever had. In the same vicinity, and only 1 mile from downtown, is the **Holden House** (719-471-3980; www.holdenhouse.com). They have one room that could be considered doable, although you should bring a shower chair with you. A fabulous breakfast will be delivered to your room since the dining room is inaccessible. This is a perfect place to stay if you are planning to visit the **Garden of the Gods**.

We also suggest contacting any of the major motel and hotel chains, such as **Super 8**, **Marriott**, **Holiday Inn**, and **Sheraton**, for accessible lodging options in and around Colorado Springs. The major chains always have accessible accommodations. Call ahead for reservations.

Dining

With more than 750 restaurants to choose from in Colorado Springs, finding an accessible place to eat should be no problem. In our travels we have come across some wonderfully unique and delicious favorites.

Adventures in BBQ (114 S. Sierra Madre St.; 719-471-1705; www.adventuresinbarbecue.com) is a new favorite in The Springs. Owners Michael and Kelly Davis have been studying the art of BBQ since the 1970s and it shows. The restaurant, located just off of I-25, is very accessible, including the restrooms, and has one of the friendliest staffs we have ever encountered. Our biggest challenge was deciding who would get the last rib!

The **Elephant Bar Restaurant** (7585 N. Academy Blvd.; 719-532-0032; www.elephantbar.com), located less than a mile from the Air Force Academy, and even closer to the Chapel Hills Mall, is one of the coolest and most unique restaurants at which we have dined. Aside from the leopard-skin carpet, waterfall, and giant stone elephant, we especially enjoyed the Thai cuisine and the amazing homemade specialty drinks. Make sure to ask about the "Rumble in the Jungle."

For a little lighter fare in a distinctive setting, try **The Warehouse** (25 W. Cimarron St.; 719-475-8880; www.thewarehouserestaurant.com). The Warehouse is a restaurant and art gallery, as well as the home of the Palmer Lake Brewing Company, and is housed in a historic downtown building just blocks from I-25. The pub-style food is as good as it gets, but no meal is complete without a glass of the brewery's famous stout. After our meal, we had a great time checking out the local and regional artists' work showcased in the gallery.

For accessible fine dining in downtown Colorado Springs, we recommend **MacKenzie's Chop House** (128 S. Tejon St.; 719-635-3536; www.mackenzieschophouse.com). We took the elevator down to the dining room and immediately took advantage of the martini menu, which boasts more than 40 varieties. After sampling the beef and the seafood (we were equally impressed with both) we enjoyed an after-dinner drink on the patio, a perfect way to end the evening.

If you're looking to have dinner and be entertained all in one place, the **Ritz Grill** (15 S. Tejon St.; 719-635-8484; www.ritzgrill.com) is that place. We really liked the variety on their menu. We ordered homemade pizza and some good New Orleans BBQ and were stuffed within minutes. We were so full, in fact, that we just hung out and listened to one of the free bands that play four nights a week. Although we didn't have a chance to check it out, many locals we met bragged about the Ritz's Sunday brunch as well.

Entertainment and Nightlife

There is no shortage of fun to be had in The Springs in the evenings. Here are just a few of our favorite always-have-a-great-time suggestions.

The **Golden Bee** (1 Lake Ave.; 719-577-5776; www.broadmoor.com) was brought by the Broadmoor Hotel piece by piece to Colorado Springs from England nearly 40 years ago and is as genuine today as the day it left its homeland. There are three steps to get into the building, but the staff is more than willing to help you, and we always have a fantastic time. Once inside, the club and its restrooms are accessible. The best part about the Bee isn't even the authentic English pub–style food, it is the ragtime piano player that invited the entire room to sing along. We made an entire evening of it, and managed to drink a couple of half yards of English beer too!

Loonees Comedy Corner (1305 N. Academy Blvd.; 719-591-0707; www.loonees.com) is Colorado Springs's only comedy club and features national touring comedians on a regular basis. They have live shows Wednesday through Sunday and have featured stars such as Jerry Seinfeld, Sam Kinison, and Ellen DeGeneres. Accessibility is no problem at Loonees, but reservations can be, so we strongly recommend making them in advance. We also recommend eating before you go to a show, as they only serve wings, nachos, and other bar foods.

Guthries Bar and Grill (1410 Kelly Johnson Blvd.; 719-260-8486) is another consistent favorite of ours. Besides the fact that we are suckers for a good oyster bar, which Guthries has, we love that we can see live music on the weekends, play pool, watch sports on the big screens, and drink incredible margaritas all in the same place. This bar is best on weekends if you're looking for the action.

For a variety of choices in arts and entertainment, the **Pikes Peak Center** (190 S. Cascade Ave.; 719-520-7453; www.pikespeakcenter.org) offers all kinds of shows for all kinds of audiences. "From Bach to Rock, and Broadway to Ballet" is what they advertise, and this really says it all. There is plenty of accessible parking and seating available, as well as assistance for the hearing impaired. The sound in the auditorium is unbelievably crisp, and the support staff has a lot of experience, hosting some 200 shows per year. After being very impressed with the few concerts we've seen here so far, we are looking forward to checking out some of the other offerings.

Contact Information
The Greater Colorado Springs Chamber of Commerce
2 N. Cascade Ave., Ste. 110
Colorado Springs, CO 80903
Phone: 719-635-1551
Web site: www.coloradospringschamber.org
E-mail: info@cscc.org

Denver

Parking and Transportation

One thing we have noticed when in Denver is that we are never short of a good, accessible parking space. If there isn't one visibly near your location, check nearby intersections, or ask your hotel or restaurant representative for the nearest location of one.

If you don't have your own vehicle, there are many options in this large city for alternative modes of transportation. Denver is home to the **RTD**, or Regional Transportation District (303-299-2960; TTY: 303-299-2980; www.rtd-denver.com), the city's bus and light-rail system. All buses are equipped with wheelchair lifts, and special drop-offs can be reserved up to three days in advance. The light-rail is also 100-percent accessible at all 20 stations, with ramps to the train stops. This vast system covers a total of 179 routes within Denver's city limits and is half price for riders with disabilities (60 cents per ride). Maps, prices, times, and additional information can be obtained from RTD's Web site.

Denver also has many taxi agencies to call upon for door-to-door service, but we've found a few that seem more flexible for wheelchair riders. **Denver Pro Limousine** (800-959-9868; www.denverprolimo.com) and **Harts Towncar Service** (303-237-2740) are two classier driving services that we've always had great luck with for groups of two to eight passengers who want to ride in style. **Freedom Cab** (303-292-8900), **Metro Taxi** (303-333-3333), and **Yellow Cab** (303-777-7777) are Denver's three main taxi companies. Always make sure to request the largest car possible for your special needs.

Denver is home to DIA, and there are many shuttle services that will take you from the airport to anywhere in Denver, Boulder, and even some mountain towns, such as Vail, Winter Park, and Aspen. One of our favorite DIA-informative Web sites is **www.usairport parking.com**, for a wealth of information on parking, shuttle services, rates, and discount information. Two services we've tested and return to are **Super Shuttle** (800-525-3177) and **Trans Shuttle** (303-377-7786), both for their competitive rates and timeliness.

Activities

Home of the Denver Broncos professional football team, **Invesco Field at Mile High** (1701 Bryant St.; 720-258-3000; www.invescofield.com) opened in August 2001 to replace the quarter-century-old Mile High

Disabilities disappear at Mile High's new stadium—the seats include a spacious section with electrical outlets and great views.

Stadium. The facility is state-of-the-art and completely accessible. Seating for people with disabilities is scattered throughout the stadium, and ticket prices vary. Accessible parking is close to the building and a little bit cheaper than most lots. For event information and tickets, visit their Web site. The complex is easily accessed from I-25, just south of I-70.

The **Pepsi Center** (1000 Chopper Circle; 303-405-1100; www.pepsicenter.com) opened in October 1999. This facility is also very accessible, with accessible seating available on each of the five levels. This arena is home to two professional sports teams, the Colorado Avalanche and the Denver Nuggets, as well as Arena Football's Crush and the National Lacrosse League's Mammoth. The Pepsi Center also sponsors live-music concerts and other gala events. For event information and tickets, visit their Web site.

Coors Field (2001 Blake St.; 303-ROCKIES; www.coloradorockies.com) has been the home of the Colorado Rockies professional baseball team since opening in 1995. The entire ballpark is accessible, with several accessible seating sections to choose from. Accessible parking is nice and close to the park. For more information, or to purchase tickets, visit their Web site.

As the premier outdoor venue to see live music in Colorado, **Red Rocks Park and Amphitheater** (Morrison; 303-640-2637; www.redrocksonline.com) offers an otherworldly combination of music and natural beauty. The park is located only 15 miles west of Denver on I-70 at the Morrison exit. Prime season runs from May through September. There is an entire accessible parking lot available, with a shuttle service that drops you off right at the stage entrance. Accessible seating is plentiful, and it's the front row of the amphitheater. Private, accessible restrooms are close by and easily accessible. Visiting Red Rocks is an absolute dream for people with disabilities, and we have never seen a bad show there. For information on events and tickets, visit their Web site.

Located in Denver's City Park, between Colorado Blvd. and York St., the **Denver Zoo** (2300 Steele St.; 303-376-4800) is home to more than 4,000 animals and is considered one of the most popular zoos in the country. Paved concrete pathways make it very easy to navigate in a wheelchair, and there are accessible restrooms throughout the park. The Denver Zoo prides itself on exceeding accessibility standards, and it shows. If you have the time, make sure to spend half a day touring this amazing facility.

Some 200 parks within Denver's city limits make up the largest **city parks system** (www.denvergov.org/Recreation) in the country.

With more than 300 days of sunshine a year, and the Rocky Mountains right next door, it is no wonder Denver is one of the nation's fastest-growing cities.

Lodging

Your best bet for lodging in Denver or near DIA is to contact major motel and hotel chains such as **Super 8**, **Marriott**, **Holiday Inn**, and **Sheraton**. The major chains always have accessible accommodations. Call ahead for reservations.

If you are looking to get away from the typical chain-hotel scene, there are a handful of accessible bed-and-breakfasts in Denver that will make you forget that you are in the capital city. The **Gregory Inn** (800-925-6570; www.gregoryinn.com) is just around the corner from Lower Downtown, or LoDo, as it is known to locals, and Coors Field, and it is a very elegant yet affordable bed-and-breakfast. They have one fully accessible room with a tub/shower and bath bench, and a wheelchair ramp to your private porch. We absolutely loved the location, and the hosts were very friendly. Also in downtown Denver, and within walking distance of the capitol and the **16th St. Mall** shopping center, is the **Queen Ann Bed and Breakfast Inn** (800-432-4667; www.queenannebnb.com). There are three steps to get into the building, but the staff is more than willing to help, and if you ask for the Calder Suite, you are guaranteed an accessible room with bar in the tub. It doesn't take long to figure out why they have won many awards for their service and accommodations. Finally, there is the **Capitol Hill Mansion Bed and Breakfast Inn** (800-839-9329; www.capitol hillmansion.com), also located near the capitol. They have one fully accessible room with a roll-in shower, although you will need help up the few stairs. The atmosphere and food here are fantastic.

Dining

There are several hundred restaurants, pubs, bars, and taverns within the city limits and surrounding towns. We found accessible dining in every corner of the capital. Here are our favorites.

The **Denver Buffalo Company** (1109 Lincoln St.; 303-832-0880) is a great fine-dining option if you want to see downtown. This has been one of our frequent stops in Denver for years, as they are fully accessible and serve the most unbelievable buffalo filets and other wild game. We recommend making advance reservations, especially on the weekends.

More recently added to our list of favorites is the **Kona Grill** (3000 E. 1st Ave.; 720-974-1300; www.konagrill.com). While they call it American cuisine, you can get all kinds of food here, from ribs to seafood. They are located in the Cherry Creek Mall and are ADA compliant. Definitely ask about the late-night sushi specials.

Coors Field. Courtesy of Patty Maher

Our preferred brew house in Denver is the **Wynkoop Brewing Company** (1634 18th St.; 303-297-2700; www.wynkoop.com). With a fantastic menu and the best brewery food we have had, this is not your typical brew house. They are located in LoDo, within walking distance from the 16th St. Mall, and are equipped to handle people in wheelchairs. We love the Wynkoop because we can have a great dinner and then hang out and play pool, darts, and shuffleboard when we're done.

Bob's Steak and Chop House (121 Clayton Ln.; 303-398-2627) is another fine-dining option, located in the Cherry Creek district of Denver, that has been recommended to us over and over again by several of our Denver friends. They are also fully accessible and offer some of the best beef and seafood in town. If you love lobster, we recommend the Australian lobster tail.

Entertainment and Nightlife

The **Fillmore Auditorium** (1510 Clarkson St.; 303-837-0360; www.fillmoreauditorium.com) is, by far, our favorite place to see live music in Denver. They have two reserved-seating areas for people with disabilities, accessible restrooms and bars, and remarkable lights and sound. At a capacity of around 4,000 people, every show is intimate.

The locals' secret jazz stash is at **El Chapultepec** (1962 Market St.; 303-295-9126). Located in LoDo near Coors Field, this is the most happening jazz club in Denver. We have never been disappointed with the music, nor with the frequent surprise guests that grace the stage. It is a very small bar, and the restroom is not wide enough for a wheelchair, but it is a must.

Another smaller music venue that is worth the trip is the **Gothic Theater** (3263 S. Broadway St.; 303-788-0984). We love this small venue, in particular because of the great music they attract, the great dancing, and the incredible mural that covers the entire ceiling and walls. The Gothic is about 10 minutes south of Denver, in Englewood, and is worth the drive.

If you're looking for a college-age crowd, check out the locals' favorite pair of bars at **Sancho's Broken Arrow** (741 E. Colfax Ave.; 303-832-5288) and **Cervantes Masterpiece Ballroom** (2637 Welton St.; 303-297-1772). Sancho's caters to the beer-drinking, pool-playing, Grateful Dead crowd, while Cervantes caters more to the fast-paced live-music scene. Although they are several miles apart, they share an owner, and both are accessible. Depending on your disability, you may be able to take advantage of the shuttle that runs between the two on big music nights, which would save you some cab fare.

Contact Information

Denver Metro Chamber of Commerce
1445 Market St.
Denver, CO 80202
Phone: 303-534-8500
Web site: www.denverchamber.org
E-mail: dmcc@den-chamber.org

Ft. Collins

Parking and Transportation

As with the other big cities, Ft. Collins is quite easy to get around in, whether you have your own vehicle or not. The city's bus system, **Transfort** (970-221-6620; www.ci.fort-collins.co.us/transfort), covers the majority of the city. Every bus on the regular system has a wheelchair lift, and fares are half price (60 cents) for seniors and riders with disabilities. Full bus routes are available by calling directly or visiting their Web site.

There is also an additional on-call system, **Dial-a-Ride** (970-224-6066), for seniors and riders with disabilities, which runs from Monday through Saturday and also operates on Sundays during the regular school year.

Ft. Collins has one main taxi service that also runs limousines and an airport shuttle to DIA, **Shamrock Shuttle Service** (970-482-0505).

Activities

There are several options while in Ft. Collins for public camping, fishing, and hiking for people with disabilities. The **Larimer County Parks and Open Lands** department oversees these areas. All of the reservoirs and lakes here are part of the Colorado–Big Thompson Project, which diverts water from the West Slope to the East Slope to be used as drinking water. The **Bison Visitors Center** welcomes all guests visiting Carter Lake, Pinewood, and Flatiron Reservoirs, and the Ramsay-Shockey Open Space. The visitors center is accessible for people with disabilities.

If you are in town and want to do some hand-cycling, or just want to get some exercise away from the city streets, check out the multiuse trails that run throughout the city. The **Poudre Trail** follows the Poudre River for almost 8.5 miles. Currently it runs between the trailhead at N. Taft Hill Rd. and the Environmental Learning Center on E. Drake. The **Spring Creek Trail** follows Spring Creek for 6.5 miles, hitting several city parks along the way. It runs from W. Drake Rd. to the confluence of Spring Creek and the Poudre River, and then connects with the **Poudre Trail**. The **Fossil Creek Trail** is a paved path that runs through the Cathy Fromme Prairie Natural Area along Fossil Creek for about 2.5 miles. **City Park** is a good stop along the **Spring Creek Trail**, or a great spot to fish if you're in the city; there is an accessible fishing platform on the lake.

Carter Lake is located in the foothills just west of the town of Loveland. The first .5 mile of the **Sundance Trail** is wheelchair accessible from the **South Shore** trailhead. The four campgrounds here, Big Thompson, Carter Knolls, Eagle and Lowells, and South Shore, each have one fully accessible, ADA–compliant campsite, with an accessible restroom at each. We recommend reserving these sites ahead of time, as they are limited. The fishing is good at Carter Lake year-round. There are no great spots for those in wheelchairs to fish from the shore, so we recommend boat fishing. If you don't have your own boat in tow, the **Carter Lake Marina** (970-667-1062) will gladly rent one to you. They also provide a restaurant, fishing and picnic supplies, firewood, and boat mooring. To get to the marina from Ft. Collins, take I-25 south to exit 250. Then head west on CR 56 and follow the signs to the lake.

Carter Lake has many accessible options. Photo by Charlie Johnson/Larimer County Parks and Open Lands

There are no accessible trails at **Flatiron Reservoir**, but there is one fully accessible, ADA–compliant campsite. This campground is very busy during summer months, so make sure to call ahead and reserve it. The reservoir is stocked with trout several times a year, and there is a beautiful, accessible fishing pier on the west side. The fishing is good year-round. To get to the reservoir from Ft. Collins, take I-25 south to exit 257, then head west on U.S. Hwy. 34 toward Estes Park. Turn left on CR 29 and follow the signs to the reservoir.

There are no accessible trails at **Pinewood Reservoir**, but there is one fully accessible, ADA–compliant campsite. This campground is very busy during summer months, so make sure to call ahead and make a reservation. Fishing is very good here also, but there is no marina, so if you plan to fish, you will need to bring your own boat. Boating is allowed at wakeless speeds only. To get here from Ft. Collins, take I-25 south to exit 257, then head west on U.S. Hwy. 34 toward Estes Park. Turn left on CR 29 and follow the signs to the reservoir.

Ramsay-Shockey Open Space has a 1-mile wheelchair-accessible boardwalk along the Pinewood Reservoir. The boardwalk is split, with about .5 mile at each end of the **Besant Point Trail**. The middle section is doable with little or no assistance.

The City of Ft. Collins has a unique program called **Adaptive Recreation Opportunities** (214 N. Howes St.; 970-224-6027; www.fcgov.com/aro). Through this program, the city's recreation division makes huge efforts to ensure that residents with disabilities have equal opportunities to participate in any recreation program they wish to. For more information on their ongoing programs, call or visit their Web site.

Founded as an agricultural school, **Colorado State University** (CSU) (www.colostate.edu) has been around since the 1800s. Today they are a leader in agricultural, human, and natural sciences and have a student body of about 24,000 students. They offer campus tours daily. For more information, visit their Web site.

The **New Belgium Brewing Company** (500 Linden St.; 970-221-0524) is responsible for brewing Colorado's most famous and most popular beer, Fat Tire. You can take a guided tour or tour the brewery yourself Monday through Saturday; they are closed on Sundays. The building is very accessible.

Lodging

The **Super 8** (800-800-8000 or 970-493-7701) is an easy stop-off at the junction of I-25 and CO Hwy. 14 (Mulberry), about 3 miles from downtown. They have one ADA–compliant room and will provide a shower chair, if needed. The **Bud Events Center** is nearby, as is the **Budweiser Brewery**.

The **Hampton Inn** (1620 Oakridge Dr.; 970-229-5927) is located on the south side of town and sees mostly a business crowd, so it's nice and quiet if that's what you're looking for. They have eight ADA–compliant rooms, including two with roll-in showers and permanent benches. They also have one shower chair available for the other rooms. We found them to be very wheelchair friendly, and you can actually choose between two queen beds or one king, which we have found to be a rare and welcome choice. The **Comfort Inn** (970-407-0100) is at the junction of I-25 and CO Hwy. 14 (Mulberry). They have four ADA–compliant rooms, including one with a roll-in shower, but all of the rooms are doable. Bath benches are provided for the rooms with tubs.

Best Western University (970-484-1984) is one of the finest chain hotels we have seen. The entire building has been remodeled and upgraded within the past year, so it is very clean and very wheelchair friendly. They don't have any ADA–compliant rooms, but they do have four rooms that are doable, and the hotel has accommodated people in wheelchairs in the past. You will need to have your own shower chair, as they do not provide them. This is a good central location, right across the street from the CSU campus, which worked out great for our overnight trip.

Although none of the bed-and-breakfasts in Ft. Collins are really accessible or doable due to the many stairs that the Victorian-style houses have, we do have three wonderful recommendations for bed-and-breakfasts outside of the city, all of which are ranches and offer more rustic Colorado experiences, along with delicious breakfasts. All have excellent Web sites where you can learn more about ranch histories, menus, and activity information, and they have photographs posted as well.

Open year-round, **Beaver Meadows Resort Ranch** (970-881-2450; www.beavermeadows.com) offers cabins, campsites, horseback riding, fishing, camping, and plenty of other winter and summer activities on 850 beautiful acres, which are located about 50 miles northwest of Ft. Collins in a little ranch community called Red Feather. Only one cabin has a level entry, "Beaver 1," which we recommend calling in advance to reserve. If you're arriving at the last minute, the campground is totally accessible, aside from areas of bumpy ground. The campground's main complex has accessible showers as well as restrooms. The on-site restaurant offers good ol' western food and is fully accessible via their entry ramp. Beaver Meadows hosts many groups during summer months, so we recommend calling ahead to ask any questions about specific needs and to make reservations.

Also located in Red Feather is **Red Feather Ranch Bed-and-Breakfast and Horse Hotel** (970-881-3715; www.redfeatherranch.com). This is another beautiful ranch with horse stabling and riding options, as well as other outdoor activities, such as fishing and rafting. Red Feather offers a wonderful alternative to the average bed-and-breakfast. Three of their five themed rooms are on the ground level of the ranch house, as is the kitchen and dining area, where breakfast is served. One of these three rooms is more accessible and has wider doors than the rest, so definitely specify your needs when making your reservations, as we recommend requesting this specific room. The friendly owners are very accommodating, but they do prefer an advance phone call to make sure all your special needs will be met.

Last, and closest to Ft. Collins, is **Sylvan Dale Guest Ranch** (970-

667-3915; www.sylvandale.com), located about 15 miles south of Ft. Collins in Loveland, not to be confused with Loveland Ski Area, which is located an hour west of Denver. Open year-round, this working cattle ranch offers bed-and-breakfast stays, either as part of vacation packages during the summer or by nightly reservations during the rest of the year. There are several cabins of various sizes, guesthouses, and lodge units at this dude ranch. Two cabins are fully accessible, so you'll want to call in advance to reserve these.

Dining

Bisetti's Italian Restaurant (120 S. College Ave; 970-493-0086), located downtown near the college, seems to be everyone's favorite place in all of Ft. Collins for great Italian food. The prices are very reasonable for both lunch and dinner. The building and restrooms are accessible.

CooperSmith's Pub and Brewery (5 Old Town Square; 970-498-0483) is one of our favorites spots in Ft. Collins, and we will always go back. This is a fun restaurant with great pub-style food on one side and pool tables and a bar menu on the other. The building and restrooms are accessible, with the exception of a 6-inch step into the main dining area. I had no problem with this in my manual chair, but power chair users may want to sit in the bar area or outside, weather permitting.

The Crown Pub (134 S. College Ave.; 970-484-5929) is referred to as a "beer bar" by their employees, but we found it to be much more than that. The food is definitely a step above bar food. They advertise a mix of American and Irish cuisine, but the food is mostly American. They also offer about 15 beers on tap and have a small patio that's great during the summertime. The building and the restrooms are accessible.

Farmer's Table (1035 S. Taft Hill Rd.; 970-493-3249) is our personal favorite breakfast spot in The Fort. It offers your typical fast-paced college-town atmosphere, serving huge portions and with a friendly staff. We haven't missed a breakfast here on any visit to Ft. Collins. **Rainbow Limited** (212 W. Laurel St.; 970-221-2664) is the best spot in town for a fresh and healthy meal. This is mostly American cuisine, with an emphasis on vegetarian dining. The prices here are fantastic, averaging from $8 to $10 per entrée. Both the restaurant and the patio-seating areas are wheelchair friendly, and accessible restrooms are available.

Entertainment and Nightlife

CSU breathes a true college lifestyle into Ft. Collins, visibly affecting its culture with entertainment, nightlife, and the arts. There are many restaurants that offer live music regularly, so it's always helpful to pick up a local paper, such as *Free*, that come out on Fridays, for an update during your stay. Two of our favorites are **Avogadro's** (605 S. Mason St.; 970-493-5555), host to mostly live bluegrass on their large outdoor summer patio, and **Jay's Bistro** (135 W. Oak St; 970-482-1876), more of an upscale restaurant with a jazz lounge. Both are fully accessible.

One of the most famous spots in The Fort is the **Aggie Theater** (204 S. College Ave.; 970-482-8300; www.aggietheater.com), entertaining this fun city since 1907. There is a ramp down to the open dance floor and accessible bathrooms. Mostly a venue for concerts, the Aggie is home to some of Colorado's best music acts.

Another ideal spot for entertainment is **Mugs Underground Lounge** (261 S. College Ave.; 970-472-MUGS; www.mugscoffeelounge.com). Don't let the "underground" fool you; this spot has an accessible entry in the rear of the building. A local favorite, Mugs offers live music, local DJs, and drink specials nightly.

Ft. Collins is also home to a large arts community, and if you're looking for operas, plays, musicals, alternative movies, and symphonies, the **Lincoln Center** (417 W. Magnolia St.; 970-221-6735) is the stop for you. Originally the location of Ft. Collins's Lincoln Junior High School, the Lincoln Center has been sharing its talents with the city since 1977. Now the epicenter of the city's cultural arts, the center boasts two indoor performing-arts halls and is home to the Ft. Collins Symphony Orchestra.

Contact Information

Ft. Collins Chamber of Commerce
225 S. Meldrum St.
Ft. Collins, CO 80521
Phone: 970-482-3746
Web site: www.fcchamber.org
E-mail: general@fcchamber.org

CHAPTER 3

SMALL TOWNS

Scenic Suggestions

Every drive in Colorado can be called a scenic one, but we have a few select roads that we recommend for the drivers. Follow along with us throughout this chapter with "Scenic Suggestions" sidebars. Sometimes getting to your destination is almost as much of an adventure as the activities you do once you're there! Check out the national Web site on byways and scenic drives for the full list of options for visitors who love to drive: www.byways.org.

Southwest Colorado

Southwest Colorado is yet another expansive portion of this wonderfully adventurous state. With quaint but feisty little mountain towns such as Telluride, Durango, Pagosa Springs, Ouray, and Silverton fueling the adventure travel industry, it's exciting to find that the options for travelers with special needs are only expanding. A very popular activity in this area is Jeeping, something that doesn't seem to have taken off in the northern regions of Colorado as much as it has south of the I-70 corridor. Many companies offer excellent explorative trips with spectacular scenic viewing from the safety of these semi-amphibious vehicles. It seems to us that all companies offer both self-driven or tour-guide options, and all towns offer this information at their visitors centers. Some companies are even starting to offer Hummers instead of Jeeps, which can be more versatile in some areas, but are also bigger and more enclosed, which makes them less versatile in others. We see using these high-end, slow-selling vehicles as kind of a gimmick, so we recommend sticking with the Jeeps, unless you absolutely have to climb a mountain with a 90-percent-grade incline!

CR 12—The "quick" way to Crested Butte

Known as the "quick" way to Crested Butte from the north, this twisting dirt road from Leadville through Paonia is only recommended for four-wheel-drive vehicles. The highlight of the drive is the largest stand of aspen trees in the country, covering more than 10,000 acres, making it a downright breathtaking drive in the fall. There is no other way to get to Crested Butte from the north, unless you want to loop around to the east and then south, so this dirt road offers a shorter drive with more scenery.

Crested Butte

This small town of 2,000 has a unique heart of its own, and its locals are not only friendly but courteous, and very cooperative as well, willing to lend a hand whenever and wherever it's needed. As emphasized in the winter section, some of their dining options may be technically inaccessible, but their staffs are determined to prove otherwise. See pages 85–86 for dining and lodging suggestions.

Crested Butte has much to offer to the visiting adventurer,

Loading a downhill mountain bike from the
Adaptive Sports Center at Crested Butte in the summer.

including horseback riding, fly-fishing, Jeeping, mining tours, tennis, kayaking, outdoor music festivals, scenic drives, and cycling. For specific adapted sports, the **Adaptive Sports Center** has some wonderful, adventurous options, but if you're looking to go out on your own, we have a few recommendations of activity companies that are more than willing to adapt to your special needs.

We recommend **Big Horn Balloon Company** (970-596-1008; www.balloon-adventures.com) in Montrose for hot air ballooning. Other than needing some help to get in and out of the basket, this is the easiest way to get a bird's-eye view of this amazing area.

For guided fishing, rafting, or kayaking trips, we suggest **Alpine Outside Recreational Adventures** (800-833-8052; www.3rivers outfitting.com) in Crested Butte.

Adaptive Sports Center Crested Butte (ASC) (970-349-2296; www.adaptivesports.org) offers a wide range of summer programs in addition to their winter adaptive skiing (see the winter activities section on page 84). With safety in mind—but your mind left somewhere up at the top of the ski hill—riding down Crested Butte Mountain on one of the five "gravity-downhill" bikes with ASC will be freedom as you've never felt before during the summertime. There's no hand-cranking with these bikes, just the feel of gravity pulling you downhill for a nice, long half-hour ride. Two ski lifts take riders and hikers up to the top of the mountain, and the ASC has taken this reasonably new opportunity to offer their famous gravity-downhill rides on their own mountain. (ASC offers these clinics at many other ski-area mountains around the state during the summer, but has only recently had the opportunity to offer them on their own soil.) If in the area, this activity is a must.

ASC also offers rafting trips and a fully accessible ropes course for team building and adventurous souls. Call the ASC for more up-to-date information on camps and opportunities that will spice up your adventure.

Contact Information

Crested Butte Chamber of Commerce
P.O. Box 1288
Crested Butte, CO 81224
Phone: 800-545-4505 or 970-349-6438
Web site: www.cbchamber.com
E-mail: info@cbchamber.com

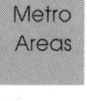

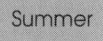

Durango

Home to the **Adaptive Sports Association** (ASA) (970-385-2163 or 970-259-0374; www. asadurango.org), Durango has plenty of summer options to offer guests with disabilities. ASA has been around since 1983, when they began offering adaptive skiing. (For further information, see pages 89–90 in the winter activities chapter.) For the last five years, ASA has given visitors with disabilities a piece of Durango adventure—the town is known for its water sports, such as rafting, kayaking, canoeing, and fishing. ASA also offers day trips to **Old Hundred Mine** and the **Anasazi Heritage Center**, and overnight trips to **Molas Lake** and rafting the **Gunnison River**.

Durango is perhaps most famous for its Class 5 Animas River, which has been tempting the fates of white-water kayakers and rafters for decades. In the early spring, this river is no place for the beginner.

Ouray to Silverton to Durango— The Million Dollar Hwy.

Known as The Million Dollar Hwy. (because of the money it has cost the state to maintain year-round during the last 50 years), this road from Ouray to Durango offers one of the most magnificent views in the entire country. The 240-mile stretch climbs to 11,000 feet in elevation. Red Mountain Pass is the first of three as you depart Ouray, and it is aptly named as the surrounding 13,000- to 14,000-foot peaks are nearly flaming red. Winding above the multithousand-foot-deep canyons below, the avalanche-prone highway only gets hairier, summiting Molas Divide Pass and Coalbank Pass as well. From above Silverton, riders get glimpses of the Animas River below and, occasionally, can spot the historic train, which we highly recommend taking. Look back as you depart Ouray, climbing high through the narrow break in the mountains: this is one of the most famous, photographed spots in the area, for obvious reasons. The views from up here are not for the weak-stomached, nor the sea-level drivers, and, although there are no guardrails, rest assured, it is safe.

However, if you're planning on coming after the water flow eases into the slow season (usually after mid-July), this river has some of the most superlative views in the state. The southwest portion of the state is well-known for its abundance of Fourteeners (mountains taller than 14,000 feet). With 54 of these tall peaks scattered throughout the state, the Durango area boasts the highest concentration of these foreboding crests, the jagged views that photographers dream of.

The area is an adventurers paradise, offering everything the outdoorsman can think of, including a nearby national park (see Mesa Verde, page 162), golf, horseback riding, rafting, Jeeping, fishing, biking, hiking, and, of course, hot-spring soaking. **Mild to Wild** (800-567-6745; www.mild2wildrafting.com) offers rafting and Jeep tours for individuals and groups of all ages. Their listing is extensive, with 27 trip options lasting from two hours to four days. They are more than happy to work with any and all abilities and were the most accommodating for families and larger groups that ASA couldn't handle.

Grand Mesa Scenic Byway

This 63-mile drive takes you through the Plateau Creek Canyon to the top of Grand Mesa, which is what was known to the Utes as Thunder Mountain, just southeast of Grand Junction. Also called the Alpine Oasis, this area is lush with aspen and evergreen forests and hundreds of lakes of all sizes.

Follow the Lands End Rd., along the ridge of the world's largest flattop mountains, and stop to take in the views of the La Sal Mountains to the west, in Utah, and the San Juans to the south, near Durango. There is an accessible visitors center with accessible restrooms at the top of the road, along with countless lakes. The Crag Crest National Recreation Trail is not wheelchair friendly, however. Driveable during all seasons, we most recommend taking this scenic tour during the fall, but don't miss it during any month if you're in the neighborhood.

This drive along CO Hwy. 65 has five scenic overlooks, five campgrounds, a dozen lakes, and two visitors centers along its route. If you're starting in Powderhorn or Mesa, head south along CO Hwy. 65 until you get to the Pioneer Town and Welcome Center. This would also be the alternate starting point. A photographer's mecca, this area is for the artists!

Durango is also proudly home to many accessible trails, including the 7-mile paved bike trail along the Animas River, the **Rio de los**

Animas Perdidas River Trail, offering use for all types of wheels, as well as great views of the valley. The two other accessible trails that the ASA uses for its summer guests are the **Animas Overlook Trail** and the **Big Al Trail**. The **Animas Overlook Trail** is located at 25th St., past the **Colorado Trail** trailhead, and is .25 mile of a wide, paved loop trail with interpretive signs and Animas Valley views. The **Big Al Trail** is named after a local Forest Service firefighter injured by a falling tree. The trail is .25 mile of hard-packed gravel that crosses a creek, takes you through a thick aspen grove, and has beautiful views of the LaPlata Mountains from an overlook deck at the end of the trail. The trail is just north of Mancos. It has a picnic area and fully accessible restrooms.

See the winter activities section on Durango for lodging and dining suggestions in this area (pages 91–92).

Contact Information
Durango Area Tourism Office
P.O. Box 2321
Durango, CO 81302
Phone: 800-463-8726
Web site: www.durango.org
E-mail: visitorcenter@durango.org

Ouray

Located just south of Ridgway is Ouray, historically more civilized, due to its population of families versus miners since its early inception. It is surrounded by astounding scenery. This area has become a mecca for hot-spring enthusiasts. Coined "The Switzerland of America," Ouray beckons with waterfalls, hot springs, and more than 500 miles of trails to offer adventure to hikers, bikers, and Jeep enthusiasts. Surrounded by red-rock walls and waterfalls, Ouray is one of the most beautiful areas in the state.

Located just off U.S. Hwy. 550 is **Box Canyon Falls**. Complete with its own visitors center, this should be your first stop to get more information on the area.

The **Ouray Hot Springs Pool** sits in **Hot Springs Park** and offers a playground, a .25-mile running track, tennis courts, a softball diamond, picnic areas with barbecue grills, and a gazebo for afternoon get-togethers or lunch after a long soak. The pool has been open since 1927 and has been updated wonderfully for accessibility. The pool and bathhouse are fully accessible, including a ramp for wheelchair entry into the pool itself. There is ample accessible parking, and the nearby trail system is also accessible. This is a wonderful place to bring a group or just have an afternoon soak in an amazingly scenic valley.

Contact Information
Ouray Chamber Association
1230 N. Main St.
P.O. Box 145
Ouray, CO 81427
Phone: 800-228-1876 or 970-325-4746
Web site: www.ouraycolorado.com

Pagosa Springs

Another not-to-be-missed portion of the southwest corner of the state is Pagosa Springs, located only one hour east of Durango. Smaller in size, Pagosa is something that most people glance over too quickly. *Pagosa* is the Ute Indian word for "healing waters," and the town is well-known for its naturally hot, therapeutic mineral springs and surrounding waterfalls. This area of Colorado is a water-lover's haven.

The most popular spot in the area is the **Hot Springs Resort** (800-225-0934, www.pagosahotsprings.com), located in the center of town on Hot Springs Blvd. This terraced resort offers 17 individual pools, two of which are located at the top of the resort and have accessible roll-in entry, offering great views of the pools and San Juan River below. The pools range in temperature from 84° to 114° F, and the water is free of chemicals as it cascades from the top pools to the river. The resort offers massage and spa services, a juice bar and café, a sports shop, and a boutique, as well as spacious locker rooms with large roll-in showers for those with special needs. Towels are available for rent, as are rooms next door at the Spring Inn, which offers one accessible room with a roll-in shower and can be booked through the main Hot Springs Resort info. above.

Stop in at the Tourist Center, located next door to the resort, for pamphlets on driving tours of the seven popular waterfalls or self-guided driving tours in the area.

Hot Springs Resort in Pagosa Springs.

Contact Information
Pagosa Springs Chamber of Commerce
402 San Juan St.
P.O. Box 787
Pagosa Springs, CO 81147
Phone: 800-252-2204 or 970-264-2360
Web site: pagosaspringschamber.com

Ridgway

Dubbed "The Gateway to the San Juan Mountains," the town of Ridgway not only offers anything and everything for the outdoorsman, but also boasts one of Colorado's finest and most accessible state parks with the same name. The town's bike path links you to the park by foot or wheels for easy accessibility, and the park offers nearly every water sport imaginable, including scuba diving. (See page 203 for **Ridgway State Park**.)

Orvis Hot Springs (970-626-5324) is a clothing-optional hot-springs resort with seven large soaking areas, four outdoor and three indoor pools. All pools have at least two steps to their entry, except the largest, the Indoor Pool House, and although this one has to be accessed from behind the building, it is definitely doable. There are two shallower pools, the Smokers and the Island Pools, that are the easiest for accessible entries. We only recommend this resort if you have assistance, as even the lodge rooms have seven to eight steps up to them as well. The resort and the views from town are amazing, so if you do have help, we advise making this a stop.

Contact Information

Ridgway Chamber of Commerce
150 Racecource Rd.
Ridgway, CO 81432
Phone: 800-220-4953 or 970-626-5181
Web site: www.ridgwaycolorado.com
E-mail: racc@gwe.net

Silverton

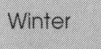

This small, historic town takes you back in time, with only 500 year-round locals, dirt streets, and some really interesting, old-fashioned shops and buildings. Silverton watches two to four trains of hundreds of visitors roll in each day all summer long and offers guests a quaint piece of historic Colorado. Home to a mix of artists, miners, adventurers, and hermits, Silverton is what Colorado once was. The **narrow gauge train ride** tour from Durango gives you about 90 to 120 minutes of time in Silverton, which is enough to wander its two main streets and have a bite to eat, but not nearly enough to take in the full splendor this tiny town has to offer. We highly recommend this amazing train ride, but also suggest you spend a day or two here to take the mine tour (see below), a Jeep tour, see the historic hotels, and experience the small-town friendliness that will keep you coming back.

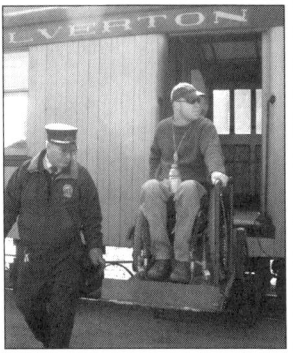

During the summer months, with its wealth of backcountry trails and deep wilderness location, this town is a hotbed for Jeeping and mountain biking. Silverton is also known for its five major nearby waterfalls, three of which are visible by car once the snow melts in early spring: **Highland Mary Mills**, **Eureka**, and **Niagra**. **Crystal Lake Falls** and **Deadwood Falls** are located farther in the backcountry, but Crystal Lake is on a four-wheel-drive road. Maps for these can be picked up at **Fetch's Mining and Mercantile Shop**. Owner Scott Fetchenhier designed the maps with all the Silverton highlights.

The accessible railcar of the Durango-Silverton Narrow Gauge Railroad.

From mid-May to mid-October, Silverton also offers a daily **Gold Mine Tour** (800-872-3009), which we think is Colorado's best mine tour for its accessibility and authenticity. The train cars are small, but they do offer one car that they can bring only one wheelchair in with a ramp. Underground, in the mine itself, the surfaces are compact gravel but mostly smooth, and the mine does offer accessible bathrooms. Guests are allowed free gold panning. Reservations are not needed, but we recommend calling ahead to book the one wheelchair seat, if needed.

A major highlight of this region is the **Durango Silverton Narrow Gauge Railroad** (888-872-4607 or 970-259-3372; www.durangotrain.com). Originally designed to transfer mined materials, mostly silver and gold, out of this rich area, these tracks and train wind through the narrow canyons along the Animas River. It only took railroad workers 11 months, from 1881–82, to finish this 45-mile track through one of the most inhospitable canyons in the state. Because of the beautiful scenery, however, the Rio Grande Railway began offering rides to passengers immediately and has now provided more than 120 years of continuous service to this valley.

There is only one railcar that is fully accessible, via a mechanical lift, but it's first in line behind the engine. The best part of this accessible car is the enormous bathroom. The engineers always offer to make more room for guests in wheelchairs, and they will gladly remove as many cushioned benches as needed to make the car as comfortable and accessible as possible. Never exceeding 20 miles per hour, the train still runs on steam and makes two stops for water during the three-and-one-half-hour ride to Silverton. This is a delight to watch. The engineer pulls the huge water line over to the engine and fills her up. She coughs out some more steam from two smokestacks, black (from the burning coal) and white (from the boiling water), and off you go.

The train crawls alongside the Animas River, sometimes gaining breathtaking elevation above it, but never climbing anywhere near the 14,000-foot peaks that surround this beautiful valley.

The train ride is the only fully accessible way to return from Silverton, and return trips take about eight hours total. The train always starts in Durango in the morning, with a long lunch stop in Silverton, and returns at supper time. The railroad provides its own buses in Silverton as a return option for those with less time. However, the buses do not have lifts, and although they save you two hours of riding, the views from the train on the return trip are just as magnificent as they are going in. We managed to get assistance for Craig up into the bus, but strapping young gentlemen are not always available to help, and we suggest you take the train back home unless pressed for time.

Winter trips are shortened, as parts of the river valley become impassable from the heavy snowfall, but if you're in the valley to ski, this is an added bonus for a relaxing afternoon among some amazing scenery.

Contact Information

Silverton Chamber of Commerce
P.O. Box 565
Silverton, CO 81433
Phone: 800-752-4494
Web site: www.silvertoncolorado.com
E-mail: chamber@silvertoncolorado.net

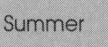

Telluride

The attraction most worth exalted recognition in Telluride is their ever-expanding tram, or **gondola system**, from the historic town of Telluride to Mountain Village, traversing to the top of the ski area itself. This impressive and free gondola has fully accessible cars, as well as separate pet cars, and picks up at the base of the mountain in the town of Telluride at Oak St. Plaza. From here, it takes you to the trail access routes at the top of Telluride Ski Area, then down the other side to Mountain Village, and, lastly, out to the Village Parking Station. This may very well have been our favorite item to report on in all of Colorado, and should be something of a model to all ski areas and their potential for adaptive modifications. The gondola runs from 7 to 12 A.M. daily and is closed for a month during their "mud season" (April 7 to May 22).

Telluride is also known for its famous **Bridal Veil Falls**, Colorado's longest free-falling waterfall. It is viewable at a distance at the far east end of town, and the switchbacking, four-wheel-drive road up to the falls will get you there and beyond. There is a second waterfall, **Ingram Falls**, above on the same dirt road, but this section is recommended for experts in four-wheel driving only. Do not attempt to do either of these roads in a low-clearance or two-wheel-drive vehicle.

Telluride's gondola has wide doors and ramps for full accessibility.

Telluride offers guided fly-fishing, horseback riding, rafting, glider rides, trails, and all-terrain vehicle tours for the adventurers. Current information on companies that provide these services can be accessed at the tourism center on Main St.

Telluride is also home to the **Telluride Adaptive Sports Program** (TASP) (970-728-7537; www.tellurideadaptivesports.org), which offers summer adaptive horseback riding in addition to their famous winter ski program. (See additional information on TASP on pages

The Anasazi Area West of Mesa Verde

This is not the typical Colorado scene as we've described throughout the rest of the book, but if you're near Mesa Verde National Park, driving this route is a must-do. This is the land of the Anasazi, which is a Navajo word for "Ancient Ones." No one knows what the Anasazi called themselves, as they were a pictographic culture and did not have a written language. They were highly sophisticated for their time, building livable spaces such as those seen in Mesa Verde and nearby, and they have stamped this region with their unmistakable heritage.

The Anasazi Heritage Center is home to more than 2 million artifacts of southwestern Colorado and should definitely be a stop on this drive, along with nearby Dominguez and Escalante Ruins.

The center is just west of Dolores, only 17 miles west of the entrance to Mesa Verde, and lies on the McPhee Reservoir, which offers rustic camping and semi-accessible sites. The natural landscape of this area is rock formations: plateaus, canyons, and mesas scattered with sage and other shrubs. There are a few smaller mountains, such as Ute Peak and Marble Mountain, between Mesa Verde and Hovenweep National Monument, located west of U.S. Route 666. But it's not for the natural landscape that we recommend this drive; it's for the unforgettable human landscape that remains somewhat a mystery. It's the cliff dwellings, the pictographs, and the nomadic leftovers that make this area fascinating. Between these two monuments lie several Anasazi ruins and unmarked pictograph sites. All of these can be found on a map you can pick up at the Anasazi Heritage Center. Make sure to have the staff point out directions to the Lowry Ruins, Crow Canyon, and the Yucca House, for starters.

109–10 in the winter activities chapter). One of the state's many proud North American Riding for the Handicapped Association (NARHA) chapters, TASP offers riding as their only summer activity thus far. (See page 138 for further information on NARHA.)

Open year-round, **Telluride Outside** (P.O. Box 685 or 121 W. Colorado Ave.; 800-831-6230; www.tellurideoutside.com) offers fly-fishing, Jeeping, rafting, biking tours, and guide services for all ages, and although they do not specialize in adaptive adventure, they have the spirit of adaptation that we've seen in most Coloradans. If they can make it work, they will!

The Telluride area offers more than a dozen trails for the biker, hiker, or four-wheeler, ranging from easy to expert. The three easiest trails we found were **San Miguel River Trail**, **The Spur Path**, and **Mountain Village Trail**. San Miguel is a small, 170-foot-elevation-gain trail stretching more than 2.5 miles one way. It starts at the southwest bridge into Town Park and continues along the river through town. Excellent for river viewing, dog walking, and town access, this trail was one of our favorites. The Spur Path is a little longer, at 3 miles one way, but has the same elevation gain as San Miguel and is a paved path that parallels the highway, starting at the west end of town. Mountain Village Trail is a well-maintained trail and the widest of the three. It is 1.5 miles one way and begins at the information center in Mountain Village.

For local lodging and dining suggestions, see the winter activities chapter on pages 112–13.

Contact Information

Telluride and Mountain Village Convention and Visitors Bureau
630 W. Colorado Ave.
P.O. Box 1009
Telluride, CO 81435
Phone: 888-605-2578
Web site: www.visittelluride.com

Northwest Colorado

Northwest Colorado has as much to offer during the summertime as southwest Colorado does. Off-roading with Jeeps is much more popular down south, but the alternative to that in the north is off-roading with ATVs. Most activity agencies can give you more information on their own adaptability options, and we've found that most are willing to offer options for all clients with variable abilities.

Steamboat Springs

The first summer highlight of this beautiful valley is the **Yampa River Core Trail**, a multiuse, paved trail system running the length of town and beyond for a total of 7.2 miles. The hope is to eventually connect this trail to the neighboring town of Hayden, 25 miles west of Steamboat, along the length of the Yampa River and U.S. Hwy. 40. The trail offers several picnic areas, boat launches, and a new boardwalk section, opened in 2004, that offers accessible fishing along the banks of the river on the eastern end of the trail. There are two parking areas, one at Walton Creek Rd. and one at Pine Grove Rd., both of which offer accessibility. The core trail is quite popular during the summer months for kayakers, canoers, anglers, photographers, and tubers, so plan accordingly. There are ball fields in the midsection of this trail that host several tournaments throughout the summer months. Restrooms are also located here. There is more parking here, as well as a beautiful botanical park, which has a loose-gravel trail loop and blooms from spring to late summer. This section of the trail can be accessed at the intersection of Trafalgar Rd. and Lincoln Ave. Head toward the river on Trafalgar and take a left on Pamela Ln.

While checking out the Yampa River Core Trail, you don't want to miss out on the brand-new, accessible **Boardwalk at Rotary Park**. This 8-foot-wide walkway is an offshoot of the south end of the core trail and is a great way to check out the Yampa River up close. It is a short loop, at nearly .25 mile in length, and is complete with handrails, benches, and three piers adjacent to the river. A small wetland area, it is an ideal spot for a relaxing stroll or watching for wildlife and waterfowl. When the water is high during the spring, it serves as a great accessible fishing pier. There is accessible parking available in the Rotary Park parking lot at the bottom of the Mt. Werner Rd. exit ramp, and access to the boardwalk is located about 200 yards from the parking lot to the east.

Cameron Pass to Rabbit Ears Pass—
The Crags and the Ears!

This back road from Ft. Collins to Steamboat ever-so-slowly climbs a 12,000-foot pass by the name of Cameron. The entire three-hour drive is gorgeous, starting out in the jagged Cache La Poudre Canyon along the Poudre River. This winding river drive offers picnic pull-outs, hiking trails, and kayak-viewing during the summer months, all frequently used by travelers and Ft. Collins locals alike. Winter hits this road hard at the top, so unless you are in a four-wheel-drive vehicle and have snow-driving experience, make sure ahead of time that you'll have clear weather for the drive. It's also somewhat deserted during winter months at the top, with little or no cell-phone service, so come prepared. The forest area at the apex of the pass has a number of camping options for the summer outdoor enthusiast, along with magnificent views of the famous Crags, a jagged, foreboding-looking mountain to the left if you're heading west. (See chapter six for more information on camping in this area.) Coming down from the apex through the small, sleepy town of Walden, you're blessed with 360-degree views of the surrounding, distant jagged peaks of the Never Summer Range; Routt National Forest, including the Rabbit Ears rock formation; and the Zirkel Mountain Range, one of our favorites!

Another wonderfully accessible site is **Fish Creek Falls Recreation Area**. There is a per-car fee, payable at the fee booth at the first parking lot, but the views are well worth the nominal charge. This historic canyon offers a winding, paved trail system from the top parking lot to an overlook of **Fish Creek Falls**, a narrow, 280-foot falls at the confluence of Fish Creek and North Fork Fish Creek. This long trail has only a moderate incline at the apex viewing spot and has interpretive signs along the entire .5-mile trail. The trail forks in the middle (marked by a blacktop-paved trail, versus the sidewalk trail), with one section winding down to the picnic area and bathrooms and one winding down to the falls. There are also accessible restrooms with vault toilets located at the top parking lot, as well as a water fountain and fill station. The packed-dirt trail down to the falls has a long and steep incline and is not recommended for wheelchairs, although it is doable with a strong pusher or two. There is a map in the parking lot and, usually, a ranger manning the pay station who can answer specific questions.

Most boating operations in the area are more than willing to help adapt their gear to your needs. The Elk and Yampa Rivers are the closest, but only have enough water flow for rafting during the spring months. The **Colorado** and **Arkansas Rivers** are the next closest rafting opportunities, but be prepared for at least a 45-minute drive to these during the summer months. For rafting companies in the area, we recommend **Bucking Rainbow** (888-810-8747 or 970-879-8747; www.buckingrainbow.com). This outfitter is located within Steamboat and offers transportation to their put-in sites. They run the Elk, Eagle, and Colorado Rivers, and also offer guided fly-fishing. **Buggy Whips and Blue Sky West** (970-871-4260; www.blueskywest.com) is an all-seasons outfitter that runs rafting, tubing, and fly-fishing during the summer months, as well as winter skiing during the winter months (see page 103 for their backcountry ski trips). They are the only other outfitter with an office within Steamboat, and they offer transportation to their put-ins as well. **Colorado River Runs** (800-938-7238 or 970-638-9742; www.raftcolorado.com) offers more for the novice rafter and families on both the Colorado and Eagle Rivers. Their office is located just outside of State Bridge, about 50 miles south of Steamboat, on CO Hwy. 131, and requires guests to provide their own transportation to the office and take-out site, but will provide transportation to the put-in, which is several miles upstream.

Steamboat to I-70 to Vail— CO Hwy. 131 along the Colorado River

Rafting is one of the best ways to see a river's historic course as it first broke its way through the tall mountains around it. But the stretch of road down Hwy. 131 is as winding as the river it parallels, and if you've come into Steamboat via U.S. Hwy. 40 over Rabbit Ears Pass, we recommend taking this alternate route back to I-70. You'll pass through old mining towns, a rafter's paradise, red-rock canyons, and fields of sagebrush. It may not be as jaw-dropping as some of the other high-altitude drives we've suggested, but this one is better for the weak-stomached and serves as good access to the western portion of I-70.

Steamboat Ski Area (800-922-2722) offers summer fun at its base with a bungee jump, a zip line, gondola rides to the top, and biking trails down the ski area. Most of these activities are not fully accessible, but longtime Steamboat Adaptive Program coordinator Johanna Hall (jhall@steamboat.com) can be contacted through the main number for any updates while Steamboat spends the next few years improving its base area accessibility. Steamboat Ski Area proudly started this development in 2005, with a fully accessible gondola car for its pre–ADA gondola, equipped with wider doors and folding interior benches for all manual and power wheelchairs.

Contact Information
Steamboat Springs Chamber Resort Association
1255 S. Lincoln Ave.
P.O. Box 774408
Steamboat Springs, CO 80477
Phone: 970-879-0880
Web site: www.steamboatsummer.com

Winter Park

The sound of laughter and screaming freedom fill the air at the base of Winter Park Resort in the summertime. From the trampoline bungee jump to the alpine slide, kids of all ages have something to do with the town's many **resort activities** (800-979-0332; www.skiwinter park.com).

This kind of summer fun is a growing attraction, more and more common at the base of ski areas each year, and there is no better agency to make it accessible than the **National Sports Center for the Disabled** (NSCD) (970-726-1540; www.nscd.org). Summer camps are available to children for these activities as well as for rock climbing and horseback riding. For individuals, however, guides will accompany you, if requested.

The NSCD has also established a very impressive, fully accessible campground. There is no charge for using this facility; however, you must leave your car at the trailhead and be creative to get your gear to the sites. There is a boardwalk for the first .125 mile of the trail, which is a little more than 1 mile total, and then there is a fairly level, wood-chipped trail that gradually climbs through .75 mile of trees to the picnic sites. The campground is beyond that, another .125 mile or so. The NSCD offers group events at this site and help getting your group's gear in by van, if reserved ahead of time. Individuals like us, however, had to choose between making several trips in or carrying a very heavy load uphill all at once. After trying both, we recommend bringing many people that have able bodies to take two trips for more gear.

Horseback riding is a sport for all abilities. See pages 138–145 for more information. Courtesy of the National Sports Center for the Disabled

We haven't yet seen a town more accessible than Winter Park. The NSCD has worked with nearly every business in both the resort town and neighboring Fraser to ensure that visitors with disabilities are welcome everywhere. This is an amazing feat for a town of such historic age and building structures and is definitely a draw. See our winter activities chapter on pages 124–26 for lodging and dining suggestions. (However, Winter Park is so accessible, it's safe to assume that nearly all of your dining and lodging choices will be doable.)

The many other common Colorado outdoor activities are plentiful in the Winter Park area too. First worth mentioning is the paved, 5-mile multiuse **Fraser River Trail**, which extends from Winter Park to Fraser and offers picnic tables and a paralleling gravel trail next to the Fraser River.

Mad Adventures (970-726-5290, 800-451-4844; www.madadventures.com) is the major rafting company in Winter Park, offering full-day or half-day trips for all ages and abilities. Rafting trips in the area are also operated by agencies outside of Winter Park, such as **Colorado River Runs**, out of Bond (see Steamboat on page 48).

Trail Ridge Rd.

If you're in Rocky Mountain National Park, you're already on this road, but if you care to miss most of the camping and just take the scenic drive, there isn't another one like this in the country. Nestled at the highest elevation for a road nationally, reaching 12,183 feet at its crest, this drive boasts some of the most spectacular views in the state. Surrounded by the endless, daunting peaks of Rocky Mountain National Park, this road is inaccessible and closed during winter months, due to heavy snow. It's not the quickest way from the mountains to the Front Range, but it sure is the nicest. Allow yourself the entire day for this one, for the many picture-perfect viewpoints and wildlife.

One of our favorites is the flight-seeing option, a magnificent way to see the mountains without needing a mule to get you to the top of them. **Blue Sky Balloon and Airplane Adventures** (800-696-1384; www.blueskyballooning.com) out of Granby offers both balloon and plane rides at affordable prices.

One activity we recommend worthy of an evening of fun in

Winter Park is the **High Country Stampede and BBQ** at the John Work Arena in Fraser on Saturday evenings during July and August. This is Wild West and rodeo fun for families and groups as well as the individual looking to fill their Saturday night the old-fashioned way.

Hot Sulphur Springs Resort (800-510-6235; www.hotsulphursprings.com) is an obscure resort along U.S. Hwy. 40 between Winter Park and Steamboat Springs, one of the nation's oldest and largest hot-springs resorts and spas, in full operation for 140 years and renovated most recently in 1996. With a full campground on the Colorado River, many motel rooms, one private "honeymoon" 1840s cabin, 22 hot-springs pools, a swimming pool, and on-site massage, this is an extensive resort with plenty to offer.

The campground is a recognized state wildlife area with fire rings, fishing, 20 campsites, and an 18-hole Frisbee golf course. The course is through the brush, so during the spring (when the brush is still young), we would call it

Hot Sulfur Springs Resort's fully accessible Elk Pool.

partly accessible and, with minimal assistance in the rough, definitely a possibility for people in wheelchairs.

The motel has two accessible rooms, with ramp entries and large interiors, located near the pools. The rooms are adjoining and, therefore, nice for large parties. The "honeymoon" cabin is up several flights of stairs from the main parking lot, and 10 or so stairs from its own private parking lot, so it does not, unfortunately, pass the accessibility test.

The two-story building that houses the check-in desk and massage rooms has two designated accessible parking spots next to the rear entrance and a ramp to the second level of the building. From here, the hosts will direct you to the "locked" gate for access to the pools; the general public enters the pools from the front desk, down five stairs. The gate really isn't locked and does have a sign designating it an entrance for visitors with disabilities. From here you can access the swimming and the only truly accessible hot spring, the **Elk Pool**.

This accessible hot-spring pool is very large and covered for all-season use. It has about a 2-foot drop down into the pool, but there are ledges all around the pool for easy transferring. The rest of the facility is multilevel, but there are only a few steps to each level, and, therefore, it is doable with assistance.

Overall, it's a beautiful facility, butted against a rock wall with mural paintings and modern décor. We recommend it during all seasons, whether on your way to Steamboat or Winter Park or out of Rocky Mountain National Park.

Contact Information

Winter Park Chamber of Commerce
78841 U.S. Hwy. 40
P.O. Box 3236
Winter Park, CO 80482
Phone: 970-726-4118
Web site: www.winterpark-info.com
E-mail: visitorcenter@winterpark-info.com

Central Western Colorado

Aspen

The Aspen area and surrounding Pitkin County is an outdoorsman's paradise during the summertime, offering horseback riding, wildlife trails, Jeeping, rafting on the Roaring Fork and Frying Pan Rivers, outdoor music festivals, and, of course, scenery, with the famous Maroon Bells towering above at more than 14,000 feet.

As with most of the ski areas and small towns in Colorado, Aspen's history lies in mining, and updating their buildings for accessibility is a slow and ongoing process. See our winter activities section on Aspen for dining and lodging information (pages 73–75).

Activities are plentiful here. Following are a few of our recommendations for agencies that are happy to adapt to your special needs.

For Jeeping, rafting, cycling, fishing, and even relaxing sunset dinners, we recommend **Blazing Adventures** (800-282-7238; www.blazingadventures.com). This company has seen more than three decades of change in Aspen, and their staff is not only accommodating but also very enthusiastic and full of suggestions, no matter what your ability.

Challenge Aspen Summer Programs (CA) (970-923-0578; www.challengeaspen.com) offers an abundance of camps and clinics during the summer months, in addition to their excellent adaptive skiing during the winter (see page 72). The large amount of activities they offer is commendable, including, but certainly not limited to,

Rock climbing is for everyone!
Courtesy of Challenge Aspen

fly-fishing, rafting, horseback riding, hiking, biking, tennis, golfing, and kayaking. If there is something that you want to try but they don't offer it yet, they are always willing to take suggestions, as their motto is "Making Possibilities for People with Disabilities."

Our favorite parts of CA are their international trips, feats, and acclaim. They've been party to opening new programs across the globe and have traveled to Chile, Iceland, France, Italy, and Germany, to name a few, to spread awareness and motivation to encourage adventure for all abilities. CA is truly an asset to this community.

Contact Information
Aspen Chamber Resort Association
425 Rio Grande Pl.
Aspen, CO 81611
Phone: 970-925-1940
Web site: www.aspenchamber.org
E-mail: info@aspenchamber.org

Aspen to the Maroon Bells

Among the most famous and photographed of the Colorado mountain ranges are the Maroon Bells in the Snowmass Mountains just west of Aspen and accessed by Maroon Creek Rd. off of CO Hwy. 82. The road dead-ends at Maroon Lake, with camping along the way, and is a continuous stretch of Fourteeners, from Snowmass Mountain to the north to Castle Peak to the south. One of our shorter drive suggestions, this one is too easy to skip but well worth the extra few hours of mostly gawking, not driving.

Oh My Gawd Rd.

This drive from Idaho Springs to Central City takes you up the Virginia Canyon along a historic mining trail on CR 279 for 9 miles. Named for the drop-off cliffs on either side, this road is the long and scenic way to Central City and Black Hawk. There are four historic mines along this road, Cornerstone Mine, Druid Mine, Scandia Mine, and Glory Hole Mine, just to name a few of more than 20 in this local area. Something special to do if you're staying in the area, Oh My Gawd Rd. is one of the shorter scenic drives in the state.

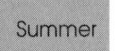

Black Hawk and Central City

There is not a chamber of commerce in the town of Black Hawk. The Web site www.blackhawkcolorado.com contains most of the information you will need on the town and the casinos. The closest information center is located in Idaho Springs, which is about 15 miles south. They have a couple of brochures about the town and also carry *The Gambler*, a comprehensive guide to all of Colorado's casinos. You can contact them by calling 303-567-4382 or visiting their Web site at www.idahospringschamber.com.

Similar to many small Colorado towns, Black Hawk and Central City (just 1 mile farther up the road) find their roots in the gold rushes that brought thousands of settlers to Colorado in the mid-1800s. Thanks to the coming of the railroad and the constant source of water provided by Clear Creek, most of the gold ore mined in the ravine came through Black Hawk for milling and the town prospered. Prosperity did not last long, however. Frequent floods and heavy pollution chased most people away, until the 1930s, when the price of gold got a big boost. This, again, was short-lived, and then Black Hawk became nearly a ghost town for almost 60 years. Facing sure extinction, the town's leaders got together and lobbied for the legalization of gambling in 1990. By 1991, historical buildings were opening in both Black Hawk and Central City as casinos and investors were flooding money in for development. Today visitors coming to gamble and to see some of the oldest cities in Colorado sustain both towns.

Small-stakes gambling has been legal in Black Hawk and Central City since 1991. Most of the casinos in town are filled with slot machines and video poker, but some do offer table games such as blackjack and poker. With a maximum bet of $5 at a time, this is a great place to gamble without losing your nest egg.

To make things easy, we recommend staying in one of the hotels that are attached to a casino. The larger, newer buildings are the most accessible. There are also a few bed-and-breakfasts in town if you prefer quaint accommodations, but these are not wheelchair friendly.

The **Isle of Capri** (401 Main St.; 800-843-4756) is one of the newest, and probably the most luxurious, of the casinos and hotels in Black Hawk. With more than 1,100 slot machines, poker and blackjack tables, and every type of video gambling game you can imagine, this casino is a must-see. The hotel has six ADA–compliant rooms, some with roll-in showers and some with tubs. There are also three restaurants on-site. This is the most upscale of the accommodations in the area. They also offer three restaurants to choose from. **Farraday's** is their fine-dining restaurant which serves steaks and other American cuisine. **Calypso** is their huge buffet-style restaurant, which is complete with a fresh seafood bar, pasta bar, and pizza station. They also have an à la carte grill called **Trade Winds**. They serve made-to-order burgers and sandwiches and lighter fare. The buffet is the best value in town. It's a good thing I had a wheelchair to roll myself out!

The **Golden Gates Casino** (261 Main St.; 303-582-1650) is the locals' favorite. They have available almost 300 slot- and video-gambling machines, blackjack, and poker and offer free sandwiches while you are gambling. There are no dining facilities here, but a covered walkway connects it to the Mardi Gras Casino across the street.

The **Mardi Gras Casino** (208 Main St.; 303-502-5600) is a little bigger than the Golden Gates and has a year-round New Orleans–style theme, with both a deli and a New Orleans–style fine-dining restaurant. They have about 700 slots and video machines and live poker and blackjack. They also have wonderful Cajun and Creole food, so we had to eat at the **Café Orleans**. They serve all kinds of New Orleans fare, including gumbo and great po' boys.

The **Lodge Casino and Hotel** (303-582-1771) is another good all-inclusive spot, offering gambling, lodging, and dining. The hotel has four ADA–compliant rooms, one with a roll-in shower. Shower chairs are available for rooms with tubs. For fine dining, check out the five-star **White Buffalo Grill**. The buffalo filet is one of the best we have ever had. **Season's Buffet** is an all-you-can-eat buffet featuring seafood and pastas. **Jake's Deli** offers large and delicious sandwiches.

Mountain High Inn (303-582-5415), formerly known as the Gold Dust Lodge, is a much less expensive option than the other hotels in Black Hawk and is only about 1.5 miles down the road. They don't have any rooms that are ADA compliant, but they recently installed ramps and have several rooms and a couple of suites that are certainly doable. You will need to bring your own shower chair, however. They also run a free shuttle to the casinos, but you will need to be strong or have a helper as it does not have a lift. We do not recommend this option for people in power chairs.

Fitzgerald's Casino (303-582-3203) has a unique Irish fine-dining restaurant called the **Shamrock Café**. For a real taste of hearty Irish cuisine at not-too-expensive prices, it's worth stopping here.

Almost all of the 40 casinos in town have some kind of food to offer, whether it's free sandwiches, pizza, buffet, or fine dining. Several establishments have more than one option, making your stay in Black

Hawk much easier.

Central City is just 1 mile from Black Hawk and is considered within walking distance, but the hill is quite steep in spots. There are also shuttles with wheelchair lifts that run between the towns to make travel easier.

Coach U.S.A. and Ace Express (303-421-2780) is a service that offers regular bus trips from Denver to Black Hawk, with pickups in Arvada and in Golden. They have a wheelchair lift on the side of the bus with reserved accessible seating onboard. Call for schedule times and prices.

Contact Information

There is no chamber of commerce in Black Hawk. Please see the Idaho Springs Chamber of Commerce information on page 64.
Web site: www.blackhawkcolorado.com

Breckenridge

Breckenridge is another adventure mecca of the state, offering biking, four-wheeling, fishing, rafting, horseback riding, and train rides, to list just a few activities that can be found here.

Home to the **Breckenridge Outdoor Education Center** (BOEC) (970-453-6422; www.boec.org), there are even more adaptive options in Breckenridge during the summer months than during the winter (see pages 77–81 for winter activity information). Perhaps the finest summer activity that BOEC has to offer is their fully accessible ropes course, used for groups and individuals who want a team-building experience or an adventurous afternoon. The center offers summer wilderness and adventure camps, canoe and kayak camps, an annual "Blue River Run and Roll" event, and financial aid for those in need.

If you're a history buff, the **Summit Historical Society** (970-453-9022) is the place to start and offers a very inexpensive glimpse of the early mining days of Breckenridge.

The ski area also offers some summer fun at the **Peak 8 Fun Park** (970-453-5000), with a .5-mile alpine slide and horseback riding being the most accessible options.

Four-wheeling is an amazing way to get into the backcountry in any mountain area, and semi-automatic ATVs and Jeeps are available in Breckenridge. At the highest elevation ski area in the state, this area offers some magnificent views from their mountain trail systems. It is the only ATV outfitter in this area. For more information, contact **Tiger Run Tours** (970-453-2231) and let them know of your special needs. With the BOEC bringing in adaptive clients, Tiger Run Tours are more than willing to adapt their programs to this clientele.

For rafting, Breckenridge has many nearby outfitters that are happy to assist adaptively. The BOEC runs groups if you have a larger number of people who would like to go, but if you're an individual

Kayaking camp with the Breckenridge Outdoor Education Center. Courtesy of the Breckenridge Outdoor Education Center looking for a day on the river, we recommend **Performance Tours Rafting** (800-328-7238; www.performancetours.com).

For the truly adventurous, there is the **Paved Bike Trail System** (www.summitnet.com), which runs through Breckenridge, Frisco, Dillon, Copper Mountain, Vail, Avon, Silverthorne, and Keystone. There are starting points with parking, trailheads, rest stops, and signage at all of these towns on what is known as an unquestionably vast network of paved trails. This uniquely progressive and incredible trail system for all abilities, ages, and uses offers everything from easy cruising sections along Lake Dillon to challenging hill climbs atop Vail Pass. The local chamber offices in these areas have maps and more information if you are seeking descriptions of terrain. All sections are paved, and local bike shops are available for rentals, but, as of yet, no local bike shop offers hand-cycles, so bikers with disabilities must provide their own or inquire about rentals at the adaptive centers in Breckenridge and Vail.

If you're looking for a break from the adventure, **Riverwalk Center** (970-547-3100) is Breckenridge's primary summer outdoor venue with live music all summer long. The center seats 800 to 2,000 guests, depending on allowed lawn seating, and is a great, flat location for all types of abilities to relax to some good music.

For lodging and dining information in Breck, see our winter activities section on this area on pages 80–81.

Contact Information

Breckenridge Resort Chamber
311 S. Ridge St.
P.O. Box 1909
Breckenridge, CO 80424
Phone: 970-453-2913
Web site: www.gobreck.com

Central Reservations
Phone: 888-251-2417 or 970-453-2918
E-mail: cenres@gobreck.com

Activity Center
Phone: 877-864-0868 or 970-453-5579
E-mail: acenter@gobreck.com

Information Center
Phone: 970-453-6018

Glenwood Springs

Glenwood Springs was one of the areas that was home to the Ute Indians. They came for its sacred and medicinal hot pools, as well as to rest, fish, and heal their wounded. Discovered by explorer Captain Richard Sopris in 1860 and claimed by Captain Isaac Cooper soon thereafter, the town was not established until the early 1880s and was formally named in 1885 after the town of Glenwood, Iowa.

In 1886, the three Devereux brothers purchased the springs pools and surrounding land for a whopping $125,000, with plans to build the largest hot-springs pool in the world. After diverting the Colorado River south around the springs pools, construction began on the first pool, the Natatorium, with local materials such as sandstone. It was 615 feet long, 75 feet wide, and as deep on one end as 5.5 feet. It was completed in 1888 and, indeed, became and remains the largest natural hot-springs pool in the world. Two years afterward, the main bathhouse and lodge were completed, with tubs, Roman vapor baths, and dressing and lounging bathrooms. To finish the vacationers' lure, the Devereux also added one of the largest hotels in the state, which cost more than $850,000 at the time and is still in use, the Hotel Colorado.

The Glenwood Hot Springs Lodge and Pool is fully accessible and ADA compliant.

For the next 30 years, Glenwood Springs hosted U.S. visitors by railroad, including U.S. senators, presidents, and movie stars, as well as European royalty, until its decline during the Depression and World War II. During World War II, the Hotel Colorado became a therapy center for disabled veterans and was closed to the public until it reopened in 1950. Sold in 1956 and renovated in 1960, the springs underwent a major facelift: shops, restaurants, an athletic club, childrens' pools, and a miniature golf arena were added. In 1986, the resort built a new hotel, the Hot Springs Lodge, and was renovated again in 1993.

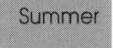

The overall accessibility of the **Glenwood Hot Springs Lodge and Pool** (P.O. Box 308, Glenwood Springs; 800-537-SWIM or 970-945-6571; www.hotspringspool.com) is amazing. From the moment you enter the wide entry gates, anyone and everyone feels welcome in this large recreation and relaxation center. Because of its size, it's atypical of a relaxing hot-springs retreat and is more for families and groups wishing to relax together than for the couple seeking a romantic getaway. The ADA–compliant bathrooms have accessible showers and stalls and large changing and lounging areas. The pool even has a lift for those who need assistance transferring into it, and the staff is very helpful to those with special needs. Lifeguards are on duty, and you can rent lounge chairs, towels, and other items you need for relaxing by the pool during summer months. The hot-springs pools are open year-round. For pricing, refer to their Web site or call the lodge.

There are two lodge rooms that are fully accessible, but they do not have roll-in showers, and they must be reserved in advance.

Contact Information
Chamber Resort Association
1102 Grand Ave.
Glenwood Springs, CO 81601
Phone: 970-945-6589
Web sites: www.glenwoodchamber.com or
www.glenwoodsprings.net
E-mail: info@glenwoodchamber.com

Idaho Springs

Located only 30 miles west of Denver in the first western stretch of the Rocky Mountains along I-70, Idaho Springs is a small, historic town that has had a big tourism pull since the first discovery of gold in Colorado in 1859. Preserved for its historic past, Idaho Springs offers mine and mill tours, gold panning, a microbrewery, **Bridal Veil Falls** and **Historic Charlie Taylor Water Wheel**, and the famous, relaxing mineral hot springs, as well as the usual abundance of Colorado outdoor activities such as rafting and horseback riding.

One of the best attractions of the Idaho Springs area is the very scenic loop train ride over stomach-dropping, 96-foot-tall **Devil's Gate Viaduct trestle**. **The Georgetown Loop Railroad**'s (800-691-4386; www.coloradohistory.org/hist_sites/Georgetown/G_general.htm) historic, narrow-gauge train crosses over the Devil's Gate Viaduct, a 300-foot-long and 100-foot-high rise that shows the remarkably progressive engineering of its time. When the industry no longer called for this area to be operating, the railroad was closed and not reopened until 1975, when the Colorado Historical Society decided to begin offering trips to the public.

The railroad is currently under a sensitive contract with the Colorado Historical Society and has changed operation vendors as of 2005, so make sure to check with local or Web updates on the operation of this amazing historic sight. It is one of our favorite activities in this area and is definitely worth the stop and your support.

There are two local gold mine tours. The first one runs inside what is still a working mine, and the second operates as a full historic and educational museum. Both are open daily from mid-April to mid-October. **The Phoenix Gold Mine** (303-567-0422; www.phoenixgoldmine.com) is fully accessible and even offers free admission for persons with disabilities. The **Historic Argo Gold Mine Hill and Museum Adventure Tours** (303-567-2421; www.historicargotours.com) has stairs down into it that will impede some disabilities, but the museum itself is fully accessible.

There are two rafting companies in the Idaho Springs area that run trips for all abilities. As with all rafting agencies, we advise you to specify your exact needs and abilities in a conversation ahead of time to allow for your guide's full assistance and your own safety.

Both **Clear Creek** (800-353-9901; www.clearcreekrafting.com) and **Raft Masters** (800-568-7238; www.raftmasters.com) offer tours on the Arkansas River through Royal Gorge, Bighorn Sheep Canyon, or Brown's Canyon. Both companies offer free helmets and wet suits, group discounts, and a history of the area for full entertainment and safety. They do recommend making reservations in advance since they are one of the larger operators in the state and book up early with concierge referrals and return visitors.

Contact Information

Idaho Springs Chamber of Commerce
P.O. Box 97
Idaho Springs, CO 80452
Phone: 303-567-4382
Web site: www.idahospringschamber.com

Vail

Conveniently located off of I-70, the scenic area known as Vail Valley was picked out by the U.S. Army Corps of Engineers for one thing and one thing only: skiing. Its bowls enticed the corps to build a made-to-order ski area in the 1960s, and, as with most ski destinations, the town became somewhat of a ghost town during summer months, until the last few decades when Colorado tourism increased tremendously.

Today the summer visitor can't get enough during the warm months, and there's nothing quite like the dry and breezy mountain air and that close, hot sunshine that warms the river rats and tans the shoppers. Vail Valley isn't short on activities for the outdoor enthusiast, including white-water rafting, Jeep and the newly introduced Hummer trips, fishing, camping, and ballooning, to name a few.

Following is a list of activity companies in the area, and, as usual, we recommend an advance phone call before your trip to hold the space and discuss your specific needs.

Action Adventure Rafting and Timberline Tours (970-476-1414; www.timberlinetours.com) was established in 1971 and takes visitors on rafting and Jeep and Hummer trips and offers rock climbing and team-building programs. They specialize in customized tours and operate out of nearby Mintern.

Balloon America (970-468-2473; www.balloonrideusa.com) is the closest hot air balloon option to Vail. Typically plush for the area, Balloon America offers leather seating and seatbelts for the thrill-seeking adventurer who's after an early-morning view of this beautiful valley. They also offer specified trip photos via e-mail within 24 hours of your trip. This company is truly top-notch Vail material.

Nova Guides (888-949-6682; www.novaguides.com) is proud to be Vail's only year-round recreation agency. During summer months, they offer rafting, fishing, Jeeping, biking, four-wheeling, and even paintball. Willing to take anyone out for a good time, this group of adventure-seeking guides will adapt to your needs whenever possible.

Piney River Ranch and Conference Center (866-447-4639; www.pineyriverranch.com) is tucked away at the base of the Gore Mountain Range. This guest ranch offers a wide range of activities; hay rides and canoeing are the most adaptive adventures they offer. Their ranch offers all-inclusive packages, gourmet dinners, and Wild West entertainment for families and groups alike.

Vail Resorts On-Mountain Activities (877-204-7881 or 970-476-5601; www.vail.snow.com) offers the only fully accessible gondola in the state. With all cars of the Eagle Bahn gondola accessible and the views magnificent, this is a wonderful way to spend a sunny afternoon having a high-altitude lunch and getting a bird's-eye view of the largest ski area in the state.

Vail to I-70 to Glenwood Springs— Glenwood Canyon

This 20-mile stretch just before Glenwood Springs is, by far, the most amazing section of I-70. Cut through Glenwood Canyon along the Colorado River, the road is surrounded on both sides by rock walls rich in color and varied in formation. There are a few pullouts along this short stretch, and there is a paved bike path below the highway for closer views of the river. This is a main route for bikers and joggers in the area, so it is frequently busy. Stop at the end in Glenwood for a soak in their large, historic hot-spring-pool recreation center.

Adventure Ridge is the only fully on-mountain adventure center in the state and is complete with biking, hiking, golf, trampoline, lawn sports, a BMX course, a discovery center, nature tours, and laser tag. This center is open from mid-June to early September and all activities have fees, including the gondola, which is not discounted during the summer months as it is during winter.

See the winter activities chapter on Vail for lodging and dining suggestions in the area (pages 117–19).

Contact Information

Vail Valley Chamber Tourism Bureau
100 E. Meadow Dr., Ste. 34
Vail, CO 81657
Phone: 970-476-1000
Web site: www.visitvailvalley.com
E-mail: info@visitvailvalley.com

Courtesy of
the National Sports Center for the Disabled

CHAPTER 4

WINTER TRAVEL

With great pride, ski-town locals will defend and argue their respective snow stats to death. But when it comes to travelers with disabilities, accessibility is as important to us as snow depth is during midwinter to many others. In this section, we've researched the ski resorts with adaptive programs and their respective ski towns to help you choose which one or ones are right for you and your family.

Skiing or riding is a wonderfully easy way to explore the outdoors and focus on your abilities, not your disabilities. Ski equipment is varied for all types of injuries and mobility. For instance, a bi-ski (a balanced and steady sit-ski rig with two skis) with an instructor in tow to gait your speed would be appropriate for quadriplegics. All of the programs detailed in this chapter offer the full range of lessons and equipment for para- and quadriplegic riders, amputees, and those with developmental disabilities, as well as for the visually and hearing impaired.

Of the 25 ski resorts in Colorado, eight offer adaptability programs with a plethora of equipment and a wonderfully experienced and dedicated staff. With adaptive programs expanding every year, now is the perfect time to get out and enjoy the Colorado winter sun and snow.

Aspen/Snowmass—*Challenge Aspen*
Breckenridge—*Breckenridge Outdoor Education Center*
Crested Butte—*Adaptive Sports Center*
Durango—*Adaptive Sports Association*
Nederland—*Eldora Special Recreation Program*
Powderhorn—*Colorado Discover Ability Integrated Outdoor Adventures*
Steamboat Springs—*Adaptive Ski School*
Telluride—*Telluride Adaptive Sports Program*
Vail—*Vail Adaptive*
Winter Park—*National Sports Center for the Disabled*

These eight resorts offer a variety of skiing and riding choices, dedicated instructors and leaders, and more snow than imaginable. Winter Park, Vail, and Steamboat rank as three of the five towns with the largest snow averages in all of Colorado. Whether a novice at your first lesson or an old pro on your Revolution, snow conditions do matter when it comes to landing soft and learning fast. *Don't be discouraged by limitations, hit one or all eight of these resorts with passion!*

If you are staying at one of the larger hotels or hotel chains, keep in mind that there will be a concierge desk for any last-minute activities you might want to tack onto your adventure. You can always call them in advance for additional suggestions, as they are usually well versed in the town's options for activities and dining.

Winter Travel Tip

Driving in winter conditions isn't hard, it just takes practice, but if you're doubtful, you have another option. First, and easiest, all ski resorts offer shuttle service from their closest airports, as well as from Denver International Airport (DIA). When calling to make airline reservations, request this service. Sometimes it's cheaper to fly to the ski areas that are closest to the airport, and sometimes it's cheaper to fly into DIA and take the shuttle from there. Check both options.

Second, there are quite a few agencies that rent accessible vans and vehicles. If you are comfortable with winter driving, you will need to know the mountain pass information of the areas in which you will be driving, such as the rules, whether conditions are safe, and important phone numbers. The Colorado Department of Transportation can be reached at 303-639-1111, 877-315-7623, or www.cotrip.org.

Aspen/Snowmass—Challenge Aspen

History

Much of northwestern Colorado's mountain ranges were once roaming lands for the Ute Indians. Aspen was one of several areas the many Ute tribes used for resources, and with respect to the area's abundance of silver they named the range "Shining Mountains."

Gold and silver miners arrived in the Roaring Fork Valley during the summer of 1879, just before a Ute uprising forced many of them back across the Continental Divide. The few that remained began governing themselves, naming the newly forming city Ute City, growing in numbers to nearly 300, and renaming the town Aspen in 1880. During the next 10 years, Aspen became one of the largest silver-mining towns in the West, and by 1893 was home to 12,000 people, six newspapers, two railroads, four schools, three banks, electric lights, a modern hospital, two theaters, an opera house, and a small brothel district. But this was the year the Sherman Silver Act was passed, demonetizing silver, which sent Aspen into an economic decline.

Mono-ski camp for all abilities in Aspen.
Courtesy of Challenge Aspen

During the following three decades the decline was catastrophic, and something was needed to bring Aspen out of these hard times. As with several other Colorado ski areas, a member of the U.S. Army's 10th Mountain Division helped develop the existing town of Aspen into a beloved ski area. Based near Vail at Camp Hale, just outside of Leadville, the army forces were training for World War II and Europe's unforgiving mountain ranges. It was army man Friedl Pfeifer who began planning Aspen's ski slopes, and in 1945, plans were finally completed. Chicago industrialist Walter Paepcke joined forces with Pfeifer, forming the Aspen Skiing Corporation in 1946. In 1950, Aspen hosted the International Ski Federation World Championships, transforming the resort's status to worldwide acclaim.

Today the Roaring Fork Valley is bubbling over with options. With four mountains of terrain to ski, rivers to raft, live music, good food, and plenty of friendly faces, Aspen/Snowmass is as perfect for the independent traveler as it is for the family vacation.

An Aspen tip: Ask a local ski patroller about shrines on the ski area—you just might see Elvis!

Challenge Aspen

The Aspen Ski Area managed a small adaptive program through the 1980s and early 1990s that was directed mainly by an organization for the seeing impaired, **Blind Outdoor Leisure Development** (BOLD). In 1995, Houston Cowan and paraplegic Amanda Boxtel turned the ski area's adaptive program into a nonprofit organization open year-round named **Challenge Aspen** (CA), a sister organization of BOLD. With the help of individual contributions, fund-raisers, and local and state grants, what started out as a small ski camp grew into an internationally known adaptive-adventure corporation. CA is based in Aspen/Snowmass, but their treks take them far and wide, such as rafting trips down the Grand Canyon portion of the Colorado River or paragliding over nearby mountain ranges. The cofounders have shared their inspiration and technique with adaptive clubs at ski areas in Iceland and Chile. There are no boundaries for outdoor adventure at CA.

Mountain Stats

Snowmass
Typical ski season: Approximately November 28 to April 13
Base elevation: 8,104 feet
Summit elevation: 12,510 feet
Vertical rise: 4,406 feet
Terrain: 3,010 acres
Trails: 84
Pipes and parks: 1 half-pipe and 2 terrain parks
Lifts: 20 total; 18 primary: 7 high-speed quad chairs, 5 double chairs, 2 triple chairs, 2 platter pulls, and 2 magic carpets; 2 secondary: 1 double (Naked Lady) and 1 platter pull (Cirque)

Aspen Mountain ("Ajax")
Typical ski season: Approximately November 23 to April 20
Base elevation: 7,945 feet
Summit elevation: 11,212 feet
Vertical rise: 3,267 feet

Terrain: 673 acres
Trails: 76
Pipes and parks: Special Spring Jam terrain park on Little Nell in April
Lifts: 8 total; 6 primary: 1 gondola (the Silver Queen Gondola goes from the base to the summit in 14 minutes), 1 high-speed quad chair, 1 high-speed double chair, 1 quad chair, and 2 double chairs; 2 secondary: 1 quad (Little Nell) and 1 double (Bell Mountain)

Aspen Highlands
Typical ski season: December 14 to April 6
Base elevation: 8,040 feet
Summit elevation: 11,675 feet
Vertical rise: 3,635 feet
Terrain: 790 acres
Trails: 131
Pipes and parks: N/A
Lifts: 4 total: 3 high-speed quad chairs and 1 triple chair

Buttermilk
Typical ski season: December 14 to April 6
Base elevation: 7,870 feet
Summit elevation: 9,900 feet
Vertical rise: 2,030 feet
Terrain: 420 acres
Trails: 41
Pipes and parks: 1 half-pipe; 2-mile-long Crazy T'rain Park. A permanent ESPN Winter X Games slope-style course is to be integrated into the terrain of the park. There is a new sound system in the superpipe.
Lifts: 7 total: 1 high-speed quad chair, 5 double chairs, and 1 handle tow

Parking and Transportation

The mountain shuttle is an excellent mode of transportation for all levels of ability. It is free and all buses have lifts and tie-downs for full accessibility.

If you or those traveling with you do not have an accessible parking permit or have forgotten one, CA has up to 25 that they can loan out per day. To park closest to their facilities, park in Lot 6 (three spots) or 7 (two spots). Daly Ln. also has three slope-side spots that are nice if you don't need to meet someone at Challenge's offices.

Activities

When you contact CA, don't forget to ask about the additional activities they offer. Their best asset is the ice-skating facility. State-of-the-art and brand-new, Aspen Ice Garden operates all year and is a national training camp.

CA has a working relationship with many tour operators in town, and if you let them make the bookings for outdoor fun such as dogsledding, ice-skating, snowmobiling, and cross-country skiing, you're likely to get as much as half off the price.

Ski School, Equipment, and Lift Tickets

The winter program isn't limited to skiing. CA offers snowmobiling, ice-skating, snowshoeing, and Nordic skiing as well. The instructors and volunteers for the adaptive program make for a one-on-one personal experience, handling up to 35 participants per day.

There is no shortage of equipment or invention at CA. They like to keep their stock up-to-date with current technology, including brand-new innovations such as a two-man snowboard and adapted snowboards with a PVC-pipe handlebar for easy learning. Their mono-ski stock is mainly Revolutions, which can be rented without a lesson, considering ability and experience. They do have a buddy system if all you're looking for is a guide.

Advanced adaptive ski camps include racing opportunities and awards. Courtesy of Challenge Aspen

Perhaps best of all, CA has more-than-reasonable rates. Lift tickets are half off the normal high-end Aspen rates and include a companion ticket at no additional cost. They have also offered scholarships since the program's inception, which only about half of the participants take advantage of, something the program directors are trying to increase with better publicity.

Adaptive Camps

Challenge Aspen hosts several adaptive camps per season, including many ski camps for the blind, an annual mono-ski camp with U.S. Disabled Ski Team instructing, and a winter sports clinic for National Disabled Veterans.

On-the-Mountain Information

Although CA is based at Snowmass Mountain, their privileges span three neighboring ski areas: Aspen, Aspen Highlands, and Buttermilk. Aspen Highlands is the newest addition to this family, and, therefore, all of the buildings in the area are wonderfully accessible. Aspen is the oldest in the area and, subsequently, the least accessible. However, their newest on-mountain building, **The Sundeck Restaurant**, is totally accessible and a great place for lunch, as is Buttermilk's new building at the base, **Bumps**. Snowmass's on-mountain dining is mostly accessible. **Gwyn's High Alpine** is a one-story building with accessible bathrooms and wheelchairs just inside the entry. The **Ullrhof** and the **Café Suzanne** buildings have restrooms and wheelchairs on the lower level, but this level has small doors and limited space. We recommend using this only in case of emergency. The **2 Creeks** building on the far side of Snowmass is also accessible, quiet, and has great bathrooms.

There are nine mountain restaurants in Snowmass: **Burlingame Cabin**, **Café Suzanne**, **Cirque Bar and Grill**, **Gwyn's High Alpine**, **Lynn Britt Cabin**, **Sam's Knob**, **Two Creeks Mexican Café**, **Ullrhof**, and **Up 4 Pizza**.

In Aspen, there are three mountain dining options: **Benedicts**, **Bonnie's**, and **The Sundeck**.

In Aspen Highlands you'll find five: **Cloud Nine Alpine Bistro**, **Iguanas Bar and Grill**, **Merry-Go-Round**, **Thunderbowl Market Café**, and **Willow Creek**.

At Buttermilk there are just two: **Bumps** (located at the base) and **Cliffhouse** (located at the top).

The lifts are mainly detachable quads and are all relatively low to the ground for easy loading. Their lift operators are all very helpful and well trained to help when needed.

Lodging

The CA staff is a wealth of information for everything you may need to know about the area, including lodging options. Calling them for pricing and availability is welcomed because they have agreements with most of the properties regarding additional discounts. To start with, however, we've put together a list of properties we know have standard ADA–compliant rooms available.

If you're spending your vacation with CA, the closest place to stay is in Snowmass. The **Silver Tree Hotel** (970-923-3520) has the most ADA–compliant rooms in the area. With four amazing slope-side rooms at this deluxe property, this hotel is the one to choose if you feel like pampering yourself. The rooms do not have roll-in showers, but the hotel is a beautiful ski-in property and is mostly accessible. Next we recommend the **Mountain Chalet** (970-923-3900), which has two ADA–compliant rooms, but is also without roll-in showers. This moderately priced property is one of our favorites for its European chalet feel and friendly staff. Last worth recommending in the Snowmass area is the **Wildwood Lodge** (970-923-3550), which also has two ADA–compliant rooms, and, unlike the others, it does offer roll-in showers. This is also a moderately priced property and close to the ski area.

If you are skiing Aspen Mountain or Aspen Highlands and prefer to stay in the town of Aspen, **Aspen Meadows** (970-925-4240) offers ADA–compliant

Bi-skiing with a buddy in Aspen. Courtesy of Challenge Aspen

rooms as well as ADA–compliant suites complete with roll-in showers and a fully accessible restaurant on-site. **The Limelight Lodge** (970-925-3025) has one ADA–compliant room with a roll-in shower and is very luxurious yet offers affordable pricing. The **Sky Hotel** (970-925-6760) is a more moderately priced hotel that offers ADA–compliant rooms as well as suites if you're traveling with several family members or friends, and all units have roll-in showers. The **St. Regis Hotel** (970-920-3300) has ADA–compliant rooms as well, but none have roll-in showers. There is a restaurant and entertainment venue on-site at this deluxe hotel.

Dining

Much of the dining in Snowmass involves a few stairs or small restroom doors, however the Mall, which is the main district for shopping and dining, houses the CA offices and has multiple 24-hour accessible public restrooms that are near many favorite dining spots. The employees at each dining facility are also well versed at directing patrons with disabilities in the right direction for restrooms.

The fully accessible dining options that are our favorites are the **Brothers Grille**, for good American eats, and **Good Fellows**, for the best pizza in town. The **Paradise Bakery** is a local favorite, known for good wraps and deli-style lunches and for cheap, light-fare meals, and **The Stew Pot** is popular for their wonderful variety of soups.

Après-Ski

Aspen is a bustle of urban activity, with four ski areas contributing to the sprawl. Many venues still remain inaccessible, due to the purpose of historic preservation. The most popular places for nighttime entertainment are listed below, with some information regarding their accessibility. We've included places that are both accessible and those that are not, for people who are traveling with helpers.

The après-ski scene is big here in Aspen, and if you're on the Snowmass terrain, you want to stop into the **Cirque** for a bit of sun on the deck and some live-music entertainment. At Highlands, the local favorite is **Iguanas**, also for their deck and the music. **Zane's** is a convenient and cheap bar next to CA if you need a quick watering. **Mountain Dragon** is recommended for their appetizers. The restaurant is 99-percent accessible, with the fault of a bathroom door swinging inward. All of these restaurants are accessible, and although some of the restrooms are not, the same public restrooms as above can apply.

The **Aspen Music Tent** hosts summer concerts and festivals and has fully accessible seating and bathrooms. With seating for nearly 1,000, this is a great place to enjoy the fresh air and live music while you're in the area. For live rock and roll, the **Double Diamond** (970-920-6905) bar, located in the town of Aspen, is a multilevel venue that may require some assistance for you to access, but always has a great lineup if you're looking for late-night entertainment and music. **NXT** (970-980-0066) is another live-music spot that has a rare wheelchair lift on the staircase and accessible bathrooms. Formerly named Club Chelsea, this is a popular spot with a club atmosphere to listen to live music and have a few drinks. Last on the rock and roll list, and one of our personal favorites for its accessibility, is **Whiskey Rocks** (970-920-3300), a fully accessible nightclub located on the ground level of the **St. Regis Hotel** with accessible bathrooms.

For Memorial Day and Labor Day concerts, we recommend **Jazz Aspen** (970-920-4996) as it is always accessible at its rotating location and always provides accessible portable toilets. The **Wheeler Opera House** (970-920-5770) is a historic music venue with an elevator and accessible restrooms located on the second (lobby) level; it offers a mix of music. This building alone is worth the visit. Last but not least, the **Thunder River Theater Company** (970-963-0399) is a fully accessible, professional theater venue offering excellent live-theater entertainment for the entire family.

Contact Information

Challenge Aspen
P.O. Box M
Aspen, Colorado 81612
Phone: 970-923-0578
Web site: www.challengeaspen.com
E-mail: possibilities@challengeaspen.com

Central Reservations
Phone: 800-923-8920
Web site: www.snowmass.com

Aspen Ice Garden
Phone: 970-920-5141

Breckenridge—
Breckenridge Outdoor Education Center

History

The Town of Breckenridge dates back to the Pikes Peak Gold Rush and was officially settled in 1859. Twenty years later, huge deposits of silver, lead, and gold quartz were discovered in the hills and the town boomed. Prospectors, merchants, and settlers poured into this rich valley. By the late 1800s Breckenridge was the place to be in Summit County. Today the town still has the feel of a classic mining town, with its early 1900s–style architecture. Consequently, many of the buildings are not accessible. At 9,600 feet, Brecken-"fridge" has the reputation of being chilly, so don't forget your sweaters.

Breckenridge Outdoor Education Center

Founded in 1976 and staffed entirely of volunteers, the **Breckenridge Outdoor Education Center** (BOEC) brags that their adaptive program is the best in the West. Although they don't push through as many guests as Winter Park's National Sports Center for the Disabled program does each season, BOEC still maintains at least one instructor for every guest for the personalized one-on-one feeling. Their staff of nearly 200 paid and volunteer employees has assisted an average of 2,000 guests per winter season for the last six years. They aren't looking to raise those numbers, unwilling to sacrifice income for their personal touch, and, therefore, the BOEC boasts a high return rate for visitors. Their large program houses three departments—Wilderness, Team Building, and Adaptive Programs. The Wilderness and Team Building Programs run during summer months only. The Adaptive Ski program is one of the most respected in the country and runs in cooperation with the Breckenridge ski area. The following BOEC information is ski-program related only.

The Breckenridge Outdoor Education Center has offered adaptive skiing since 1976. Courtesy of the Breckenridge Outdoor Education Center

Mountain Stats

Typical ski season: Thanksgiving Day to the third Sunday in April
Base elevation: 9,600 feet
Summit elevation: 12,998 feet
Vertical rise: 3,398 feet
Terrain: 2,208 acres
Trails: 146
Pipes and parks: Freeway and Trygves terrain parks on Peak 8; Country Boy, Eldorado, and Gold King terrain parks on Peak 9
Lifts: 16 total: 2 6-packs, 6 quads, 1 triple, 6 doubles, and 1 T-bar

Parking and Transportation

The BOEC office is located below the "Maggie" building at the base of Peak 9 in the Village at Breckenridge. The closest parking lot to the facility is the F Lot, and it does have a daily fee. The next-best option is to drive up to Beaver Run to the first parking lot on the left on Village Rd. at the base of the Quicksilver chairlift. There are only five spots here, but they are virtually on the slopes, so if your visit doesn't require a lesson with the BOEC, these spots are free.

None of the public buses in Breck are accessible; however, staff are willing to work with anyone, so in a pinch give them a call. They're associated with Central Reservations. Call their toll-free number (888-251-2417) and ask for the transportation department.

Activities

Tiger Run Tours and **Good Times Tours** both offer many options for activities such as dogsledding and snowmobiling and come highly recommended by the staff at the BOEC.

In addition to these options, Breckenridge also has a few small theaters. **The Speakeasy** (970-453-7243), located just a few steps off Main St. on S. Harris St. at the Colorado Mountain College, shows first-run movies. They are wheelchair accessible and provide hearing-aid assistance, if needed. For live-theater entertainment, **the Backstage Theater** (970-453-0199) has been offering award-winning performances for almost 30 years and shows everything from modern playwrights to Shakespeare. Accessible seating is available on the floor.

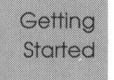

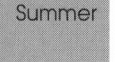

Ski School, Equipment, and Lift Tickets

Budgeted by hearty endowments and grants, the BOEC is not only able to reach many children and adults with their programs, but is also able to offer scholarships and discounts to those in need. A wonderful, far-reaching financial-aid system is applied to an average of 90 percent of the program's attendees each year. As a result, only a small percentage of the BOEC guests pay full price.

Their equipment room is a huge asset to the program and is bulging as a result of a healthy budget. Each year the stock is updated to include three to five new ski rigs, as well as many repair parts for the older ones.

No other program in Colorado has access to as many sit-ski rigs as the BOEC, therefore the instructors not only give lessons on the Breckenridge terrain, but also will take their instructions to **Arapahoe Basin**, **Copper Mountain**, and **Keystone** upon request. Their only requirement is one day of skiing in Breckenridge to fit equipment and for gait instruction.

Lesson prices include equipment, lift ticket, and instruction at very reasonable rates. There is also the option to rent a guide for the mountain if you are, for example, an advanced mono-skier and only need equipment and/or a guide. The equipment cannot be taken off-site without a staff member, however.

If you are only purchasing lifts and will be in Breckenridge for a few days, we suggest purchasing the cheap five-day adaptive pass (same as in Vail). Even if you're only there for three days, it's worth it.

Adaptive Camps

BOEC's camp options are vast and their reputation is excellent. They offer a varied array of family, child, adult, adventure, and motivational camps during both winter and summer. See their Web site for the season's schedule (www.boec.org).

On-the-Mountain Information

All of the on-mountain dining facilities of Breckenridge are basically accessible. **Bergenhaus**, **10-mile**, **Peak 9**, and **Vista Haus** are the main four buildings on the mountain and all have wheelchairs for public use. Peak 9 and Vista Haus are food court–style restaurants with multiple choices for dining. **10-mile** is the only dining facility that is multileveled. The wheelchairs are on the lower level near the restrooms. Once inside, guests can use the elevator to access the upper level.

Their recent ownership transfer to Vail Resorts has gifted Breckenridge with many new quad lifts, including one giant double six–seater, meaning 12 people load at once and the lines move fast, getting you back up the hill even quicker. Their lift operators are well trained by the BOEC, the lift-to-ground distance is low for easy loading, and there are a total of eight fast lifts (between 6.5 and 11 minutes) that seat four people or more, so don't fear loading onto any of this new, fast technology. The only place we don't recommend is the back-bowl area of the new (set up during the 2002–03 season) terrain, called **Peak 7**. This area is mostly double black diamond with a T-bar lift. We recommend it for advanced and highly independent mono-skiers only, with a guide or assisting companion.

Lodging

Breckenridge is spread out mostly over two of four bases (Peaks 9 and 8), so, unlike most small mountain towns, the lodging range is wide and construction is still continuing. The new, huge homes and resorts that are climbing up the expanded lower mountain area and the base resorts are all luxurious.

If you are spending your time here with the BOEC, the closest option is the **Village at Breckenridge**. It is one of only two ski-in, ski-out (to the Quicksilver chairlift) accessible properties and has numerous units there, including a hotel, studios, and condos. The second-best option is **Beaver Run Resort**, having only three rooms out of 500 that are *not* accessible. With unit sizes ranging from a standard hotel room to four-bedroom suites, there is something here for everyone. This is the other ski-in, ski-out property at the base of Peak 9. The **Park Avenue Lofts** were built in 2001 and are the only real ADA–compliant units here. There are one- and two-bedroom lofts, some with a private hot tub. This is next to the F Lot parking area and across the street from the Village at Breckenridge. There are also a few hotels only 10 miles away in Frisco that have ADA–compliant rooms, such as the **Holiday Inn**, the **Ramada**, and the **Alpine Inn**.

Dining

Due to the age of most buildings in Breckenridge, their accessibility has slipped through the "grandfathered" cracks. Main St. has the typical western feel of tall, angled buildings with raised doorways that have from two to five steps up to enter, considered doable by most wheelies with traveling companions. The **Breckenridge Brewery**, however, is a must-see-and-drink. There are steps up to the dining room, however, making the only accessible seating in the smoking bar or outside. The dozen or so fans in the bar keep the smoke to a minimum. The **South Ridge Seafood Bar and Grill** is a great fine-dining option, serving fresh seafood in the middle of the Rocky Mountains. The **Blue River Bistro** on Main St. has an affordable fine-dining menu and great American fare. For more casual dining, check out **Main St. Station Plaza**. The two best spots in the plaza are **Maori's**, specializing in Asian food, Thai noodle dishes, and sushi, and the **Quandry Grill**, which is renowned for their healthy servings of "real food," a mix of American and Southwestern cuisine. If you run out of options, you can always drive to neighboring Keystone and try the **Keystone Ranch**, the **Ski Tip Lodge**, or the **Alpenglow Stube**. All three are worthy of the short drive (only 13 miles north on U.S. Hwy. 6).

Après-Ski

Although it's a small area, Breckenridge isn't without a night scene. **Sherpa and Yeti's** (970-547-9299) has stairs down to an underground live-music venue, and the music is worth the bump back up afterwards. It seats 350, so its shows are intimate.

Contact Information

Breckenridge Outdoor Education Center:
P.O. Box 697
Breckenridge, CO 80424
Phone: 970-453-6422
Web site: www.boec.org
E-mail: boec@boec.org

Central Reservations
Phone: 800-789-7669 or 970-453-5000
Web site: www.townoffrisco.com

Breckenridge has two chamber locations with local information, maps, and guides. Both buildings are on Main St. but only one is accessible. That address is 137 S. Main St. The other one, at 309 N. Main St., is a very small, old building with four to five steps up to its small office doors.

Crested Butte—Adaptive Sports Center

History

The town of Crested Butte, located in what is referred to as The Gunnison Country, was one of the earliest regions explored in Colorado. Prior to the arrival of fur traders, or "mountain men," just after the turn of the 19th century, Gunnison Country was home to the Ute Indians. Explorers such as John Gunnison and John Fremont were among the first to make a name for themselves in the area as they surveyed the land and scouted routes for trade and railroad expansion. The 1860s brought gold prospectors to this valley by the trainload. Just as in Summit County to the north, millions of dollars would be mined from deep veins of gold ore. A decade later, the discovery of silver would bring some 40,000 people, two railroads, and permanence to Crested Butte and Gunnison. By the turn of the century, these two towns were known as important supply towns sustained by coal, cattle, and a brand-new college at Gunnison, which still exists today. The small-town family feel of Crested Butte, as well as a great adaptive ski program, make this stop a must when visiting Colorado.

Adaptive Sports Center

Crested Butte's adaptive program, known today as the **Adaptive Sports Center**, or ASC, was founded in 1987 as the Physically Challenged Skiing Program of Crested Butte. It was started by a motivated group of locals after former president and first lady Carter expressed personal interest in being involved. This nonprofit organization is supported annually through various fund-raisers, including a silent auction and a golf tournament. They also receive generous monies from grants and in-kind donations and have a lot of local support. The current director, Christopher Hensley, started with the program in 1991 as an instructor and a technician, quickly becoming devoted to his work. In 1997, Hensley and his codirector, Mary Manion, revamped the program with year-round status and renamed it the Adaptive Sports Center of Crested Butte.

Mountain Stats

Typical ski season: December 14 to April 6
Base elevation: 9,375 feet (lowest lift: 9,100 feet)
Summit elevation: 12,162 feet
Vertical rise: 3,062 feet
Terrain: 1,073 acres

Trails: 85

Pipes and parks: 500-foot superpipe, halfpipe, and two terrain parks on Canaan and at the top of Painterboy lift

Lifts: 14 total: 3 high-speed detachable quads, 3 triple chairs, 3 double chairs, 3 surface lifts, and 2 magic carpets

Parking and Transportation

The Mountain Express Shuttle, a *free* bus service, offers rides between downtown Crested Butte and Mt. Crested Butte every 15 minutes during the season. All of their shuttles are wheelchair accessible.

The ASC is located in the lower level of the Treasury Building at the base of the mountain and is open from 8:30 A.M. to 4 P.M. The best parking is at the Sheraton. They have four spots right next to the slopes. If you still can't find a spot, ask any local for help.

Activities

In addition to their skiing program, the ASC can help you book other winter activities as well. Dogsledding is one, and is great for families. For the more adventurous, snowmobiling and snowcat-skiing are also options. You can set these activities up on your own, but the ASC is happy to do it for you. They have the knowledge and experience necessary to set up all of your activities while in Crested Butte.

Ski School, Equipment, and Lift Tickets

The ASC offers several winter programs, including mono-skiing, bi-skiing, Nordic skiing, three-track and four-track skiing, and adaptive lessons for the visually and

Deep, light powder is always preferable.
Courtesy of Adaptive Adventures

hearing impaired. They can accommodate most disabilities and give up to 20 adaptive lessons in a day. Equipment ranges from 10 years old to brand-new and is updated every 18 to 24 months, or as needed. It can be rented without a lesson with approval.

Lessons are recommended for beginners and are offered in half- or full-day packages. The reasonable price of the lesson includes a private instructor, lift ticket, and equipment. Early reservations are highly recommended as Crested Butte sees almost 75 percent of their guests return annually or biannually. A buddy program is available for skiers who don't need a lesson but do need a guide.

The ASC has a solid base of instructors and volunteers to support a great program. Their instructors are all certified by the Professional Ski Instructors of America and have been with the program an average of seven to nine years. More than 100 volunteers are at their disposal. The center limits its yearly lesson count to about 1,200 in order to keep the program small and personalized. All guests receive an evaluation that is kept on record to track personal progress. This program has a unique feel that sets it apart from most busy Colorado resorts. The focus is on individuals having fun and gaining a passion for adventure and all winter activities. While Crested Butte Resort is definitely off the beaten path, the extra effort is well worth it.

Adaptive Camps

The ASC runs one mono-ski clinic each year for more advanced skiers, which ends with a day in the backcountry. They also run two overnight hut trips with the help of **The Arthur B. Schultz Foundation**. In addition to their time at Crested Butte, many of their instructors run adaptive clinics all over the country and in South America and Europe.

On-the-Mountain Information

The base area surrounding the **Treasury Building** is very flat and accessible, as is the **Hall of Fame Bar**. This is probably the best place to stop and eat while skiing. On-mountain dining is only partly accessible, and your best bet for food on the hill is **Paradise Warming House**, at the base of Paradise lift. This is a split-level building accessible from the front or the back without an elevator. The restrooms are on the lower level, and the restaurant is on the upper level. There is only one wheelchair for both levels and it can be found on the lower level by the entrance or the restrooms.

All of Mt. Crested Butte's lifts and runs are accessible, depending on your skill level. Beginner, intermediate, and advanced terrain are all lift accessible. Much of the expert terrain is only accessible by Poma lift or T-bar, which require quick-release straps and a little more skill to load and unload. Lift operators are well trained and always happy to offer assistance when needed.

Lodging

With the small size of the resort and the town, accessible lodging is limited but available. The resort's Web site has a lodging search form attached to the Crested Butte tab that will give you a couple of options. Their Central Reservations department is well trained to assist in ADA–related phone calls, but listed below are your best options for comfortable and accessible lodging. Contact Central Reservations to confirm location of accessible parking.

One of the two most convenient options in Crested Butte is the **Sheraton Crested Butte** (970-349-8000), located right at the base of Mt. Crested Butte. This chain hotel has 13 accessible rooms, two with roll-in showers, and an accessible restaurant. Our second recommendation at the base of Mt. Crested butte is **Club Med Crested Butte** (800-Club-Med), which has plenty of accessible rooms and offers the typical posh Club Med experience.

Not too far from the mountain, and easily reached by the free and accessible city bus, downtown Crested Butte has three options worth our recommendation. First is the **Old Town Inn** (888-349-6184), with one accessible room. There are plenty of dining options near here, and it's only a half block from the free local bus stop. Also downtown, the **Crested Butte International Hostel** (888-389-0558) is a very impressive large hostel with one quaint, accessible room, excellent rates, and is also a half block from the bus stop. We recommend calling well in advance to reserve this room as it is one-of-a-kind and usually books early. The **Inn at Crested Butte** (970-349-1225) is also located in downtown Crested Butte and has one accessible room. This old-style inn is 1.5 blocks from the bus stop and has a very home-away-from-home feel to it.

Dining

Crested Butte has several great dining options. All of the choices listed below are not only fully accessible but nonsmoking as well, which we consider a plus. At Mt. Crested Butte, we recommend the **Firehouse Grill** for family-style Italian. They also serve great pizza and wings. Downtown, **Lil's Land and Sea** is a must. They offer a wide variety of cuisine from fish-and-chips to steak to crab legs and have a fantastic sushi happy hour every day from 5:30 to 6:30 P.M. Also try their unique prickly pear margaritas, made from the pink juice of the prickly pear cactus. **Bacchanale** is another downtown favorite. They serve Northern Italian, fine-dining style. Make sure you try any of the veal dishes or the cannelloni.

Colorado restaurants serve the best buffalo in the country, and the **Buffalo Grill** serves the best buffalo in Crested Butte. They are a fine-dining option and offer an extensive selection of beef and seafood in addition to buffalo. For good, inexpensive Mexican and Tex-Mex and, according to our taste buds, the best margaritas, **Teocalli Tamale** is the best choice. Our other favorite spot for inexpensive dining is **The Secret Stash**. Their menu covers every kind of pizza (build-your-own) and topping you can imagine. They also serve great salads and offer a late-night menu. The **Gas Café** is also downtown and was recommended as the best burger joint in town by every local we asked. The also have terrific breakfast sandwiches.

These selections are just a few of the many dining options in the Butte, so check out the town chamber office when you arrive or call for a dining guide beforehand for specific dining needs (such as vegetarian).

Après-Ski

Après-ski fun at Crested Butte starts at either **Rafters** or **The Avalanche**. Both are located at the base of Mt. Crested Butte and feature outdoor seating and live music on the weekend. **Rafters** is accessible via an unmarked elevator, so call ahead to ask for its specific location or ask any local for help. **The Avalanche** is really the place to après-ski, but there are quite a few stairs to get to the front door. If you can find a couple of strong helpers, it is definitely worth the effort. You can also hop on the free bus and head downtown (only 3 miles away) for after-ski drinks. The best spot is the **Crested Butte Brewery/Idle Spur**. The brewery offers award-winning handcrafted beers and live music and dancing on the weekends.

For late night, it's Rafters again if you want a clublike scene with music and dancing. Supposedly, Rafters has the best singles scene in town as well. With pool tables, shuffleboard, and a small arcade, **The Talk of the Town** is a local favorite, but is definitely not nonsmoking. **Kochevar's** is another local spot, best known as the favorite watering hole for Butch Cassidy and the Sundance Kid. If you're looking for something a little more relaxing, try the **Princess Wine Bar**. They offer a great selection of wines by the glass and ports, as well as a large variety of single malt scotches and cognacs. You can also have a late-night appetizer or dessert. With the exception of Rafters, most of the nightlife happens in downtown Crested Butte.

Contact Information

Adaptive Sports Center
P.O. Box 1639
Crested Butte, CO 81224
Phone: 866-349-2296
Web sites: www.crestedbutteresort.com, www.crestedbutte.com, or www.adaptivesports.org
E-mail: info@adaptivesports.org

Central Reservations
Phone: 800-607-0050

Durango—Adaptive Sports Association

History

Durango is great city to peruse art galleries or spend an afternoon shopping. Originally named after the surrounding Animas Valley, Animas City was formed in 1960. In 1875, the native Ute tribe ceded a large portion of land to the settlers, farms began developing, and by 1877, the town even had a post office. Animas City was moved 2 miles north to the current location of Durango when the modern railroad was laid just south of the area in 1880. By 1881, Durango was filled with hustle and bustle, and for the next decade coal was mined throughout the nearby canyons, increasing attractiveness to the area.

The markets began to decline by 1910, and the mining activity decreased considerably. For the next few decades the area relied on agriculture, ranching, and logging, and it wasn't until the 1950s, when the travel market was off and running, that Durango became a tourist attraction. In 1965 the Duncan and O'Neill families developed Purgatory Ski Resort just north of Durango. Purgatory remained a family operation until 2000, when a low market forced them to sell an 80-percent share to Mountain Springs Development, who subsequently renamed it Durango Mountain Resort.

Adaptive Sports Association

The **Adaptive Sports Association** (ASA) was founded in 1983 by ski instructor Dave Spencer, who had lost his leg to a long battle with cancer that ultimately took his life in 1986. Originally named Durango/Purgatory Handicapped Sports Association, the center's facilities were named in his honor and the program's title was renamed shortly thereafter. The current program director, Scott "Grizzly" Kelley, volunteered with the program for six years before joining the staff in 2000, and he is in charge of summer activities.

Mountain Stats

Typical ski season: Approximately November 28 to April 6
Base elevation: 8,793 feet
Summit elevation: 10,822 feet
Vertical rise: 2,029 feet
Terrain: 1,200 skiable acres
Trails: 75
Pipes and parks: Freestyle arena, 400-foot halfpipe and terrain park,

Pitchfork Terrain Garden

Lifts: 11 total: 1 high-speed 6-seater, 1 high-speed quad, 4 triples, 3 doubles, 1 surface lift, and 1 magic carpet

Parking and Transportation

The ASA office is located at the Columbine base area near the beginner lifts. There are accessible parking spaces available in the adjacent lot.

Mountain Transport runs buses on a regular schedule throughout the season, taking guests between the town of Durango and the resort area. Five bucks buys you a round-trip ticket.

Activities

Even if you do ski, there are plenty of other things to do while in Durango, from snowcat-skiing to sleigh rides to dogsledding to the historic **Durango and Silverton Narrow Gauge Railroad** (888-TRAIN 07). The Durango to Silverton trip is among the most famous in the country. This railroad has been hauling passengers since the 1880s and just recently started offering trips year-round. The old baggage car, now called the Home Ranch Car, was adapted for passengers with disabilities in the mid-1980s, offering a lift and accessible restrooms. **Buck's Livery** (970-247-9000) is the place to call if you're looking for an amazing sleigh ride with incredible views. If you are really adventurous, make sure you call **San Juan Ski Company** (800-208-1780) for unbeatable backcountry skiing. With advanced notice, they will take anybody riding. The **Durango Dog Ranch** (970-259-0694) is a favorite pick of the ASA. Dogsledding is an activity for all ages, and this outfitter gives you the choice of riding or guiding the sled. All companies require advance reservations to accommodate special needs.

Ski School, Equipment, and Lift Tickets

The ASA hosts nearly 1,000 lessons per season, with a one-on-one personal touch thanks to a staff of 40 PSIA-certified instructors and more than 200 dedicated volunteers. Skiing, snowboarding, and sit-skiing options are available with state-of-the-art equipment that is updated on a regular basis. While most of their equipment can be rented without a lesson, sit-skiers not wanting a lesson must have a buddy with them. The program can typically handle up to about 20 lessons in a day. If you are traveling with your own equipment, arrangements can be made to have ASA store it on-site for you, but call ahead as space is limited.

Lift tickets are very reasonable for students, friends, and family alike, and, as mentioned above, the buddy program is available if you just want a local tour guide for the day. If money is an issue, ask about the ASA scholarship program, which offers assistance to qualified students on a sliding scale. They assured us that they would never turn a student away because of monetary reasons, which helps to account for their 75-percent return rate for local and out-of-town adaptive guests.

Adaptive Camps

The ASA coaches several local Special Olympic teams during the winter, leading up to the annual regional Special Olympics races held every year during February. In March, the **Dave Spencer Ski Classic** takes over Durango Mountain Resort as people flood into the resort from all over the country for this commemorative fund-raiser. Ask to participate if you are interested. Everyone leaves with an award.

On-the-Mountain Information

There are several options for eating while on the mountain. There are four restaurants on mountain: **Bucks Cabin**, **Café de los Pinos**, **Dante's**, and **Powderhouse**. Of the four, Dante's and Powderhouse are the accessible options. Powderhouse is located almost halfway down the Engineer lift line and is a split-level building. If you need to use the bathroom, you'll want to stop at the upper level, and food service is on the lower level. Dante's is located just off of the Grizzly lift and has bathrooms on the lower level and a restaurant on the top level. Both buildings have doable bathrooms, but neither have an elevator, so you will need to get back in your sit-ski to access the other floor of the structure.

Views from Purgatory on a mono-ski.
Courtesy of the Adaptive Sports Association

The **Columbine Station** is the most accessible place at the base to eat; it is located at the Columbine base, very close to ASA's office. The rest of the base area is very accessible, with ADA–compliant bathrooms and regularly maintained or heated ramps.

All trails and lifts are accessible, but watch out for the three "old school" double chairlifts as they are a little trickier to load, especially for sit-skiers. The lift operators and adaptive instructors are well versed in assisting ASA's guests, so don't be afraid to ask for help.

Lodging

Because all of the condominiums at Durango Mountain Resort are privately owned, there's not much available to travelers with disabilities. The best accessible lodging is located in the city of Durango. As with any city, all of the typical chain hotels are available. You can usually count on these hotels to have at least one ADA–compliant room on the property. The **Hampton Inn** (970-247-2600) is totally accessible, offering four ADA–accessible rooms, one with a roll-in shower. These rooms all have only one king-size bed, but have adjoining rooms available with two queen-size beds. The rest of their rooms are doable if you don't need a roll-in shower or bars in the restroom. The ASA highly recommends them, thanks to a great track record with their guests. The **Double Tree** (970-259-6580), considered a luxury hotel, is another great option. They have two ADA–compliant rooms available, with roll-in showers and bars in the restrooms. They also have a restaurant, hot tub, and pool, all of which are accessible. The **Super 8** (800-800-8000) ties for the most ADA–compliant rooms with four. You have a choice of one king- or two double-size beds, and all of the rooms have bars in the bathrooms. **Residence Inn by Marriott** (970-259-6200) has three ADA–compliant rooms, including a two-room suite with a roll-in shower. All have bars in the bathrooms. **Best Western** has a location in Durango (800-547-9090) and one at the resort (800-637-7727). The **Comfort Inn** (970-259-5373), **Days Inn** (970-259-1430), and **Econolodge** (970-247-4242) each have one or two accessible rooms as well. Call for details.

Dining

The town of Durango is much larger than most ski towns and, subsequently, offers plenty of accessible options for dining out. Most people staying in the resort make the 30-mile trip from the ski resort back to town for this selection. These are not the only accessible restaurants in Durango. As always, if you're not sure about access, call ahead and ask. We found everyone to be very friendly and accommodating.

If you're not in the mood for the half-hour trip into Durango, there are a few options close to the resort area. **The Sow's Ear**, located about 1 mile south of the resort, is famous for its huge, hand-cut steaks.

Just north of the resort entrance, you'll find the **Hamilton Chop House**. They are 100-percent accessible, offering amazing wild game and an extensive selection of wine in an upscale atmosphere. The **Cascade Grill** is also close to the resort, and although getting into the restaurant is little tricky, the bathrooms are accessible and the prime beef and seafood are worth the effort.

Away from the resort, a definite favorite among Durango locals and tourists is **Ken and Sue's Place**. We can see why, with their extensive menu offering everything from burgers to pasta or even Asian cuisine. They have two locations on Main Ave. (the second is **Ken and Sue's Place East**), both of which are accessible. For something different, stop in to the **Cypress Café**. They serve great Mediterranean food at affordable prices. For fine dining, try **Randy's**, on the corner of College and Main. They specialize in prime rib, steaks, and seafood. They are wheelchair friendly, but we recommend calling ahead to make sure the side door is open and the ramp is in place. If you are looking for more-casual dining, we really enjoyed **Christina's Grille and Bar** on north Main. Known for their homemade soups and fresh, made-from-scratch cuisine, they are reasonably priced and fully accessible.

Après-Ski

The first stop on the après-ski circuit has to be **Purgy's Pub**, at the base of the mountain. The beers are cold and sometimes they have live music. The locals hang out a couple of miles south of the resort at the **Olde Schoolhouse Café**. They specialize in huge calzones and free pool.

It seemed to us that most people go into downtown Durango to really get their après-ski on. If you've lasted this long, don't leave Durango without stopping at the **El Rancho**. "The Ranch" has been the bottom floor of the Central Hotel for as long as locals can remember and was rumored to have been the home of famous boxer Jack Dempsey's first knockout. With Ft. Lewis College right around the corner, the mix of college students, locals, and tourists means a guaranteed good time. There are lots of bars in Durango, so don't forget to cruise Main St. for all kinds of après-ski options.

In the city of Durango there are endless ways to entertain yourself. **Sky Ute Lodge and Casino** is home to blackjack, bingo, poker, and slot machines if you want to whet your gambling appetite. Ask about the shuttle at the activity desk at the resort. There are also several entertaining and educational museums, such as the **Railroad Museum**, the **Animas Museum** (970-259-2402), and the **Children's**

Museum of Durango (970-259-9234), to keep everyone interested. Families can also find theater shows such as **Melodrama**, an 1800s-period genre of theater, at the **Diamond Circle Theater** (970-247-3500). Rated by *Time* magazine as one of the top three melodramas in the country, this is entertainment not to be missed if you're in Durango.

Contact Information

Adaptive Sports Association
P.O. Box 1884
Durango, CO 81302
Phone: 970-385-2163 (winter); 970-259-0374 (summer)
Web site: www.asadurango.org
E-mail: asa@frontier.net

Central Reservations
Phone: 800-982-6103
Web site: www.durangomountainresort.com

Nederland— Eldora Special Recreation Program

History

The town of Nederland was incorporated in the mid-1800s as a silver-mining town. By the end of the century, the mines ran dry and Nederland nearly became a ghost town with just a few families staying behind. The town was revived in the early 1900s, with the discovery of tungsten, which was valuable for making steel, but this ore ran out around 1950, and, eventually, Nederland became an easy getaway from the Front Range heat and city life. As Boulder continued to grow, so did the need for a nearby place to recreate during the winter. Today this small, picturesque town is conveniently located just a few miles from Eldora Ski Resort, which opened its doors for skiing in 1962 and slowly developed into a multiuse resort. Alpine (downhill) and Nordic (cross-country) skiing and snowshoeing are all available. The mountain gets more than 300 inches of snow each season.

Eldora Special Recreation Program

The **Eldora Special Recreation Program** (ESRP) has been introducing people with disabilities to winter activities and recreation since 1975. The program was started as a nonprofit organization with a mission to "provide integrated recreational opportunities for people with disabilities that will foster independence through the acquisition of lifetime skills." Located only 21 miles west of Boulder, Eldora Mountain is the perfect destination for children and adults with special needs living in or visiting the Boulder area.

Mountain Stats

Typical ski season: December through early April
Base elevation: 9,200
Summit elevation: 10,800
Vertical rise: 1,600 feet
Terrain: 680 acres
Trails: 50-plus
Pipes and parks: Terrain park and quarter pipe
Lifts: 12 lifts total: 2 quads, 2 triple, 4 doubles, 1 Poma lift, 2 rope tows, and a conveyor lift

Parking and Transportation

Regional Transportation District (RTD) is a mass-transit bus system that is operated in Denver, Boulder, and the surrounding area. They offer rides from Boulder to Eldora and back for just a few dollars and are completely accessible, with lifts and accessible seating. This is a great, inexpensive option, especially if you don't like driving in winter conditions. For a complete schedule, visit Eldora's Web site, www.eldora.com, or RTD's Web site, www.rtd-denver.com.

There's nothing quite like the views from Colorado's many ski areas. Courtesy of Adaptive Adventures

To get to Nederland from Boulder, head west on CO Hwy. 119 through the town of Nederland for 21 miles. The ESRP headquarters is in the modular trailer right at the base of the slopes. Accessible parking and restrooms are available.

Activities

Cross-country skiing, skate skiing, and snowshoeing are available only steps away from the ski lifts at the base of Eldora Mountain. The Eldora Nordic Center provides more than 25 miles of trails in a very peaceful winter setting. Lessons for guests with disabilities are available through the ESRP and should be set up in advance. You are welcome to bring your own cross-country equipment and use the trail system with or without a lesson.

Ski School, Equipment, and Lift Tickets

As a nonprofit organization, this program is not part of Eldora's main ski school and operates out of a modular trailer at the base of the mountain. ESRP can accommodate almost any mental or physical disability, including spinal-cord injuries, cerebral palsy, spina bifida, and amputations. If you are unsure whether they can handle a certain special need, feel free to call them directly and ask. The ESRP staff of more than 100 volunteers is well trained and always eager to meet new challenges and help individuals achieve their personal goals.

The program has accumulated a large variety of equipment throughout the years, and, thanks to generous local supporters and in-kind donations, they are able to keep their equipment updated every year or two. They provide mono- and bi-skis, three-track, four-track, snowboarding, and cross-country equipment. Although most students use the equipment provided, you are welcome to bring your own.

ESRP operates every Friday, Saturday, and Sunday from January through the end of March, handling about 1,000 lessons per season. Private lessons are also available on other days with advance reservations. With a 90-percent student return rate each year, very reasonable prices, and limited scholarships available for those in need of financial assistance, this program is highly respected in the world of adaptive recreation.

Adaptive Camps

In addition to the regular lessons and special weekly school groups that take advantage of this program, students can also train here for the Colorado Special Olympics in alpine, Nordic, and snowshoe racing at regional and state levels.

On-the-Mountain Information

There are four places to eat at the resort, but two are considered fully accessible. **The Lodge** is fully accessible and serves a selection of hot foods, including homemade soups, chili, hamburgers, and pizza. Accessible restrooms are also available here. **Indian Peaks Lodge** is the newest building and, therefore, the most accessible. It overlooks Challenge Mountain and serves homemade soups, sandwiches, and other snacks. There is an elevator inside to access the upper level as well.

With only 680 acres of skiable terrain, Eldora is the smallest of the mountains with an adaptive program. The entire mountain is accessible to people with disabilities if you are an expert skier; otherwise, you will want to stick to the blue and green runs or request a guide.

Lodging

Best Western Nederland (800-279-9463) has two ADA–compliant rooms with bars and benches in the showers, but all of the first-floor rooms here are doable if you don't need the ADA–compliant amenities. There is also a continental breakfast served daily.

There are plenty of accommodations available in Boulder, which is just a 30-minute drive from Eldora. See the Boulder section of chapter two for our recommendations or visit the chamber's Web site at www.bouldercoloradousa.com.

Dining

There are no restaurants to dine at past closing time at Eldora Mountain, and only a few in Nederland. Once again, we strongly recommend making all of your post-skiing plans in the city of Boulder.

Après-Ski

There is some après-ski action at Eldora, but only on the weekends. The bar is located on the upstairs level of The Lodge, however, and there is no ramp or elevator to access it. We recommend heading down to Nederland or back to Boulder to check out the bar scene.

Other entertainment and nightlife options are also best explored in Nederland and especially Boulder.

Contact Information

Eldora Special Recreation Program
P.O. Box 19016
Boulder, CO 80308-2016
Phone: 303-442-0606
Web site: www.esrp.com

Powderhorn—Colorado Discover Ability Integrated Outdoor Adventures

History
Powderhorn Resort is located in western Colorado, about 35 miles east of Grand Junction. The first skiers to hit the slopes were a crew of ambitious, adventure-seeking locals who built a rope-tow lift on the western slope of Grand Mesa in 1937. The resort has changed hands quite a few times throughout the years, but it remains a quiet, family-oriented place to ski and have fun.

Colorado Discover Ability Integrated Outdoor Adventures
Colorado Discover Ability Integrated Outdoor Adventures (CDA) is a nonprofit organization that provides winter- and summer-adventure opportunities to people with disabilities and at-risk youth. They offer exciting white-water rafting and kayak trips during the summer and have been teaching adaptive ski and snowboard lessons for more than 20 years. CDA started as Powderhorn Resort's adaptive program in 1980.

Mountain Stats
Typical ski season: December 1 to March 31
Base elevation: 8,200 feet
Summit elevation: 9,850 feet
Vertical rise: 1,650 feet
Terrain: 510 acres
Trails: 29
Pipes and parks: Freestyle terrain park under main Take Four lift and beginners terrain park on the beginner hill. No pipe.
Lifts: 4 lifts total: 1 quad, 2 doubles, and 1 surface lift

Parking and Transportation
There are accessible parking spaces available in the main parking lot. Adaptive guests meet at **The Day Lodge** at the base of the slopes.

Amtrak provides daily accessible rail service to Grand Junction from Denver and Salt Lake City. **American Spirit Shuttle** (888-226-5031) can transport people in manual chairs with a little assistance and have in the past. They handle a lot of Powderhorn's guests.

Ski School, Equipment, and Lift Tickets
The entire adaptive ski and snowboarding program at Powderhorn

Resort is operated by CDA. All of their instructors are PSIA trained and/or certified and can accommodate physical, developmental, and cognitive disabilities, as well as the visually impaired.

They have a complete inventory of adaptive equipment, including mono- and bi-skis, three-track and four-track skis, and snowshoes. Equipment is purchased and upgraded yearly or as needed as they like to keep their stock up-to-date.

Private and group lessons are available from December 1 through the end of March and are offered at a very reasonable rate. Scholarships are available to area schoolkids in need of assistance.

Adaptive Camps

CDA is an annual host for a local Special Olympics Colorado team and, with help from School District 51, provides training and preparation for regional and state competitions at no cost to team members.

On-the-Mountain Information

The Day Lodge is the main ski lodge at the base area. The lodge is accessible using an elevator to reach the upper level. **The Sunset Grill** serves mainly grill-style food, such as burgers, hot dogs, and soups, while some people prefer the get-your-hands-messy barbecue served on the deck.

All 29 trails on the mountain are accessible to adaptive skiers and snowboarders, depending on your ability level. Your best bet for restrooms is also the **Day Lodge**, as the on-mountain restrooms are not accessible.

The **Take Four Quad lift** is the newest and fastest of the three chairlifts, but you'll also want to ride the doubles to access the entire mountain.

Lodging

There are plenty of places to stay when visiting Powderhorn. There are resort-owned accommodations at the base of the mountain and condos within shuttle distance. The nearby towns of Grand Junction, Cedaredge, and Rifle provide even more options. **The Inn at Wildewood** (970-268-5170) is a full-service ski-in, ski-out inn owned and operated by Powderhorn Resort. They have one ADA–compliant room, which is a deluxe suite with a roll-in shower and fold-down bath bench. The restaurant on the upper level is not accessible, due to a long stairway. **Goldenwoods/Valley View Condos** (970-268-5040) offer one- and two-bedroom condominiums with views of both the slopes and the valley. There are no ADA–compliant rooms available, but there are four units that are doable. Guests taking advantage of the adaptive program at Powderhorn often use these rooms. We liked both options here and would stay at either.

Dining

The only true restaurant at the slopes is the **Wildewood Restaurant**. Unfortunately, there are two sets of stairs to navigate so it is not wheelchair friendly. If you can find a couple of strong volunteers to carry you up, it is worth the trip. The menu is mainly Italian, with gourmet pizzas, calzones, pastas, and pannini sandwiches.

Due to limited options at the resort, many visitors and families head to Grand Junction or Rifle for evening meals.

Steamboat's most popular adaptive ski is the bi-ski by Bi-Unique.

Après-Ski

The Day Lodge's **Sunset Grill** is the only accessible après-ski bar at the mountain, serving icy-cold beer and cocktails. We also recommend bringing your own beverages and having the after-ski festivities at your condo.

For nightlife and entertainment, you'll definitely want to head to Grand Junction.

Contact Information

Colorado Discover Ability
P.O. Box 1924
Grand Junction, CO 81502
Phone: 970-257-1222
Web site: www.coloradodiscoverability.com
E-mail: info@coloradodiscoverability.com

Powderhorn Adaptive Ski School Office
Phone: 970-268-5700, ext. 2037
Web site: www.powderhorn.com
E-mail: ski@powderhorn.com
Contact Fruita offices during the off-season: 970-858-0200

Steamboat Springs— Adaptive Ski School

History

Steamboat's small-town feel and off-the-beaten-path location make it great for both families and adventurers alike. The town's uniqueness lies in its history. A western town turned ski town, Steamboat's history dates back to the late 1800s, when settlers and trappers found the most concentrated group of hot springs in Colorado and decided to settle.

Skiing wasn't long behind them though, and, as early as 1914, Carl Howelsen, a German Olympian, turned one of the steepest pitches in the valley into a ski-jump run that now hosts the World Cup qualifications every year. It is the oldest and most complete natural ski-jump complex in North America and has been the training ground for more than 47 Olympians, 15 members of the Colorado Ski Hall of Fame, and 6 members of the National Ski Hall of Fame.

The town's Winter Carnival dates back a tad further, to 1913, and is the oldest continuing winter carnival west of the Mississippi.

Adaptive Ski School

The adaptive program isn't large, but the ski school itself is one of the largest and most productive in the country, as Steamboat's local Winter Sports Club has coached more than 40 youths into competing Olympians. Steamboat's **Ski School** employs more than 350 staff members, and the adaptive program is run in conjunction with the main ski school. One of the oldest adaptive programs in the state, Steamboat's program was founded in 1976. It has a large percentage of return guests but still operates as one of the smaller adaptive programs in the state.

There's no question why guests are loyal to this town, where the small-town friendliness is as revered as both the skiing and the western heritage combined. Once you make friends with this valley's inhabitants, you'll always find yourself at home here.

Mountain Stats

Typical ski season: From Thanksgiving to the second Sunday in April
Base elevation: 6,900 feet
Summit elevation: 10,568 feet
Vertical rise: 3,668 feet
Terrain: 2,939 acres

Trails: 142

Pipes and parks: Longest superpipe in North America: Mavericks; SoBe terrain park on Bashor expands each year for all levels of free riding

Lifts: 20 total: 1 8-passenger gondola; 4 quads, 7 triples, 6 doubles, and 2 surface lifts

Parking and Transportation

Steamboat's main Gondola area is a multilevel complex of shops and offices that can be clarified with a map from the adaptive program. There are plenty of parking spaces on each level, but most are on the bottom Gondola parking lot. To understand this complicated area better, there is a great "Accessibility Map of Gondola Square" on Steamboat's home Web page, www.steamboat.com.

This main Gondola parking lot, a left off of Après-Ski Way, is the lowest level of this facility and has the most spaces available. From here you can head straight toward the elevator in the Gondola Building and up to the second level—ticket offices, the main gondola entrance, ski school, restaurants, and shops are here. When you call to set up lessons or purchase advance lift tickets, ask for the map of the area and the adaptive brochure to have on hand as a good visual aid when you arrive.

Most lodging companies have their own shuttle services, but none yet have a lift for motorized wheelchairs. However, the public transportation is more than sufficient to get you and your traveling companions around.

The **Steamboat Springs Transit** (SST) bus system is free, and all buses have lifts. The buses run three to four times per hour. You can also call SST directly 24 hours in advance and they will schedule their smaller bus to pick you and your family or friends up and take you where you need to go; they just need the advance warning in order to schedule the driver.

Steamboat only has one taxi company, **Alpine Taxi**. They drive minivans and full-size vans and can accommodate most manual wheelchairs. Individuals with motorized chairs have to call several hours in advance and request one of their two vans with a lift. The fares are minimal and are per mile and passenger.

Activities

The usual mountain activities are given a special western feel in Steamboat. From sleigh rides to teepees, snowmobiling to private cabins, and cowboys skiing in their chaps, you still get the feel of the Old

West here. Most activity companies are adaptable to suit the needs of the guest, and **Steamboat Central Reservations** can book many of these tours, as well as help to notify the activity manager of any special needs you require. Hotel concierges are another helpful resource if you'd like to wait until you arrive to make your bookings, but we feel it's always good to book your activities in advance to ensure care of your special needs.

For excellently guided snowmobile tours, we recommend either **Steamboat Snowmobile Tours** (877-879-6500) or **Steamboat Lake Outfitters** (970-879-4404) for two-hour, four-hour, and dinner tours. Both companies are very experienced and have been around for at least 15 years. But for the best views of the surrounding mountain ranges—and the shortest ride from Steamboat—we recommend Steamboat Snowmobile Tours, and for the tours around Steamboat Lake and historic Hahn's Peak volcano, we recommend Steamboat Lake Outfitters.

Adaptive skiers get "face shots" in Steamboat's Champagne Powder™. Courtesy of Steamboat Adaptive Ski School

For horse-pulled wagon rides, horseback rides, and excellent cowboy entertainment, we recommend both **Big Rack Horseback Adventures** (970-824-4525) and **Elk River Guest Ranch** (800-750-6220). Both offer the Old West feel and are located in the woods, not far from downtown Steamboat.

We are also very proud to recommend **Steamboat Powder Cats at Blue Sky West** (800-288-0543), a tour agency that has been operating out of Steamboat for many years taking guests into the backcountry for fresh-tracks snowcat-skiing on nearby Buffalo Pass. This agency offers something very unique to skiers and riders—a guarantee of fresh tracks and endless powder throughout the winter months. They have very recently begun to bring groups from Breckenridge's BOEC and Winter Park's NSCD for adaptive backcountry powder skiing as well, and are still perfecting this alteration to a wonderful full day of hard skiing. These newly cooperating agencies provide the guides and the mono-skis if you'll provide the muscle but, so far, for large groups only. We commend both agencies for beginning to offer this amazing sense of adventure to the adaptive community.

This kind of skiing is definitely for experienced skiers and takes serious patience and willpower, as powder skiing is really like no

other. For individuals and smaller groups, **Powder Cats** provides fatter "powder" skis and snowboards for able guests and will let you bring your own equipment (and mono-skis) if it suits their standards. Inquire directly for more information on their trips, pricing, and annual adaptive ski days.

Ski School, Equipment, and Lift Tickets

Steamboat has one of only two programs in the state (along with Vail) that is funded by its own ski school. Many of Steamboat's ski instructors remain year after year and offer familiar faces to returning guests, giving the program a high return rate for loyal skiers.

The program is the smallest in the state, serving only 150 guests per season, 60 percent of which are return visitors. Eighty percent of those use the program's equipment. They do not normally provide storage; however, several mono-skier locals have found their way around the limited storage by parking their rigs under nearby staircases, and the ski school is willing to accommodate special circumstances if you do not have a vehicle or condo where you can place your rig.

They offer limited equipment here, only a handful of ski rigs total, which are updated regularly, and they cannot be rented without a lesson. If you do not need a lesson and have your own gear, they do offer a buddy or guide for a reasonable multi-hour rate.

The program offers extremely discounted package rates for a lesson, lift ticket, and equipment, for all types of disabilities. They also offer discounted lift tickets for companion skiers at more than half off the regular skier rates.

Adaptive Camps

Due to its small size, Steamboat's adaptive program does not offer any adaptive camps.

On-the-Mountain Information

Steamboat has wheelchairs at all on-mountain dining facilities, and the ramps and accessible entrances are maintained regularly for snow removal. All of the on-mountain buildings were built pre–ADA, but are all generally accessible. Their gondola is not large enough for adaptive skiing equipment, therefore we take three lifts to get to mid-mountain for skiing: South Face to Christi III to Thunderhead puts you just next to the gondola's top entrance. If you just want to dine, Steamboat purchased one ADA–compliant car for their gondola as of

2005, but if there are more than one of you in wheelchairs, you can always transfer into the other cars and have them put your chair in the car behind.

On-mountain dining includes **Bear River Bar and Grill**, **Four Points**, **Rendezvous**, and **Thunderhead**; all are accessible. **Bear River** is at the base of the ski area and is 100-percent accessible through the Sheraton Hotel or from the slopes. The rest of the facilities are on-mountain, and, of them, **Four Points** is the only single-level building; its ramp and wheelchair are at the northeast corner of the building (to the Storm Face side). **Rendezvous** is three levels and has an elevator to access them all. The wheelchair is at the top level (from South Peak lift), where the restrooms are, but you might have to have someone bring it to you as there's a long, wooden bridge at this entrance. The only inaccessible part of the building is the outside deck (known as "the beach"), which is separated from both the mid- and bottom levels by a series of stairs. **Thunderhead** is the least accessible of these buildings, as there is no public elevator, only a service one. The wheelchair entrance is at the top of the Thunderhead lift and nearest to the restrooms. On this level is **Hazie's Restaurant** and **Stoker Bar**. The wheelchair is just inside this entrance.

Backcountry skiing on Steamboat's Buffalo Pass. Courtesy of Dave Genchi

Lodging

Steamboat's reservation agency system (800-922-2722) is vast and their agents are equipped to handle calls from individuals with questions regarding accessibility. Their booking system represents nearly 90 percent of the lodging options in Steamboat and the surrounding area. Steamboat has the most-expansive options for lodging of all the ski areas, including condominium options as well as hotel accommodations. Their staff has full information on all these. In addition to lodging, they book many activities, on-mountain dining, and transportation.

Our favorite recommendations for lodging at the base of the ski area are the **Sheraton Steamboat Resort Hotel** (800-848-8877) and the **Steamboat Grand Hotel** (877-269-2628), both of which offer plenty of ADA–compliant rooms, accessible restaurants on-site, and access to the base of the ski area. The Sheraton is right on the slopes, with a full-service ski shop that offers free ski storage to Sheraton guests and is definitely the premier spot to stay. The Grand is right across the street and right next to the main bus station. Downtown, which is about 2 miles from the base of the ski area and offers less-expensive lodging options and access to the ski area via the free city bus, also has several options that we recommend. The **Alpiner Lodge** (970-879-1528) has king-size beds in their ADA–compliant rooms and is in the heart of the downtown shopping-and-dining district, and the **Rabbit Ears Motel** (800-828-7702) offers king-size beds in their ADA–compliant rooms and a full continental breakfast, with some rooms facing the Yampa River.

One new accessible addition to Steamboat is the **Hahn's Peak Inn** (970-870-6507), which is open year-round but is mainly a summer highlight as there's not much going on in Hahn's Peak Village/Clark (located 30 minutes north of Steamboat) during the winter months. In close proximity to **Steamboat Lake State Park** (see page 212) and **Hahn's Peak Lake**, located in the historic town of Hahn's Peak, this new inn is a wonderful alternative to camping. The inn is mostly accessible. The entrance offers a ramp alternate to the few wide stairs, and there is one fully accessible suite with a queen bed as well as a trundle and a twin. The suite has a fully accessible bathroom in it, no roll-in shower, but it does have a shower chair. Breakfast is normally served on the second-floor dining area, but the deck is on the main floor and food can be served here or in your room if you do not want to ask for assistance up to the second floor. Contact the Hahn's Peak

Inn directly for reservations and questions, or visit their Web site at www.hahnspeakinn.com.

Dining

Because many of the buildings in Steamboat are as old as the ski area, finding perfectly accessible entrances and bathrooms in dining facilities would be nearly impossible. However, because of several local patrons, many owners have done the best they can to make their facilities generally accessible.

Our following recommendations are for the 100-percent accessible lunch and dinner options. For fine dining our first choice, for the elk-tenderloin steaks and varying menu, is **Café Diva**, located at the base of the ski area in Ski Time Square. The downtown area also has several excellent choices for fine dining. **Giovanni's** and **Riggio's** are known for the best Italian dining in town, both located at 10th St. and Lincoln Ave. (enter **Riggio's** at the side entrance), and the **Cottonwood Grill**, located on Yampa St., is recommended for Pacific Rim cuisine.

For the best beer within 100 miles and great food, **Mahogany Ridge**, located downtown on 5th St. and Lincoln Ave., formerly known as the Steamboat Brewery, is home to Steamboat's only microbrewed beverages and some excellent, moderately priced cuisine. Also downtown is **Azteca Tacqueria** and **Gobi Mongolian Grill**, which are two restaurants in the same building that we recommend hands-down for the best cheap burritos in town and fantastic make-your-own stir-fry dishes.

All of the breakfast places in town are excellent and accessible; however, their restrooms are small. **Freshies** is the newest addition to this list and has the largest seating area as well as the largest fully accessible restrooms. The food is fantastic, and during the summer the deck can't be beat. The **Creekside Café**, located on 11th St. in downtown, is the most unique breakfast spot, serving famous eggs Benedict.

Après-Ski

The favorite local spot to après-ski is **Slopeside Bar and Grill**. There are two steps up to the nonsmoking dining section, making it mostly accessible. The entry, bar area, restrooms, garage below, and the outside seating (for sunny spring or summer days) are all accessible; however, this place gets packed from 2 to 5 P.M. with skiers and riders. Plan accordingly. Occasionally, they host live music on Sundays on warm spring days and during the summer. Call 970-879-2916 for band listings.

For entertainment, Steamboat attracts much live music year-round; it is famous for throwing free live concerts hosted by the ski area throughout the winter (www.steamboat.com). These are usually in the main gondola area and accessible. Although most of the live-music venues aren't very accessible, all staff members are well trained by a couple of local wheelies to help in any way they can. **LevelZ** is the only clublike atmosphere in Ski Time Square, with DJs and varied live music, but it is a three-story venue with no elevator. The bouncers are well rehearsed at carrying wheelies up to hear the music. **The Tugboat**, also in Ski Time Square, hosts live-rock music regularly and has a large, accessible bathroom between the bar and the stage. There is one tall step up to the front deck and another up to the front door. Downtown, **Mahogany Ridge** is one of our favorites for free music shows as well as their great beer.

Contact Information

Steamboat Adaptive Ski School:
2305 Mt. Werner Cir.
Steamboat Springs, CO 80487
Phone: 800-299-5017
E-mail: skischool@steamboat.com

Central Reservations
Phone: 800-922-2722
Web site: www.steamboat.com

Both the Steamboat Springs Chamber of Commerce and the Forest Service offices are a wealth of information on the Steamboat area. Both are located on your way into Steamboat, on the left-hand side of S. Lincoln Ave.

Telluride—
Telluride Adaptive Sports Program

History

As is the case with many Colorado towns, Telluride was first settled by the nomadic Ute Indians. For centuries it was known as the "Valley of Hanging Waterfalls." The Spanish passed through this area in the late 1700s and are responsible for naming the majestic San Juan Mountains. The post-Ute era began around 1875, when prospector John Fallon discovered gold and established the first mining claim in this unique box canyon. Originally settled as Columbia, the town was forced to change its name to Telluride so it would not be confused with a mining camp in California with the same name. In 1890, the railroad came to town and filled the valley with more than 5,000 people from all over the world. With the onset of World War I, the mining boom ended, and by the 1950s, Telluride was practically a ghost town, with fewer than 600 residents. Thanks to longtime local Bill Mahoney Sr., the town of Telluride was revived in the 1970s with the opening of the ski area. Thirty years later, the town still thrives with year-round culture and unmatched beauty.

Telluride Adaptive Sports Program

The **Telluride Adaptive Sports Program**, or TASP, was started by Bill Glasscock in 1992 as a very small department of the Telluride Ski School. The current director, Colleen Trout, found her way to Telluride in 1993 after spending seven years creating the Challenge Alaska program at Alyeska Resort in Girdwood, Alaska, and, more recently, working for the BOEC. After running TASP for two years, she turned the program into an independent, nonprofit organization in order to address training, staffing, equipment, and fund-raising needs. Thanks to Colleen, a wonderful staff, and their direct involvement with Disabled Sports

Adaptive equipment available at Telluride Adaptive Sports Program.

USA and The Telluride Ski & Golf Company, TASP's size and reputation continue to grow.

Mountain Stats

Typical season: Approximately November 26 to April 4
Base elevation: Coonskin: 8,725 feet; Big Billie's: 9,160 feet; Station Mountain Village: 9,540 feet
Summit elevation: Lift 6: 11,975 feet; Gold Hill Summit: 12,260 feet
Terrain: 1,700 acres
Trails: 84
Pipes and parks: Terrain park and pipe
Lifts: 16 total: 1 gondola (2 lifts), 7 high-speed quads, 2 triples, 2 doubles, 1 magic carpet, and 2 surface lifts

Parking and Transportation

The TASP office is located in the mountain village and is accessible by gondola from the town of Telluride or the parking lot at the far end of the village.

You shouldn't need a car once you're in Telluride. If you do drive to the resort, you will probably leave your car parked there for your entire stay. All locations in downtown are within walking distance to the gondola and other lifts. There is also an accessible town-transit system. While you can drive to the Mountain Village from town and vice versa, the free gondola is the best way to travel back and forth, as it runs until at least midnight. You can also call **Dial-A-Ride** (970-728-8888) from 7 to 12:30 A.M. and the accessible transit will take you where you want to go.

Activities

If skiing isn't enough to quench your adventurous appetite, there are several activity companies in and around Telluride that can help. Remember that while these companies can provide services for people with disabilities, they may not have facilities, such as bathrooms, to accommodate all of your needs. A quick phone call should be enough to address your questions or concerns.

If you want to take advantage of the best views from anywhere in the valley to take pictures of some of the most photographed and picturesque mountains in the world, call **San Juan Balloons** (970-626-5495). The balloons are only accessible thanks to the strong and friendly employees, but once you're floating 1,000 feet in the air, you won't be thinking about your wheelchair. **Telluride Snowmobile**

Adventures (970-728-4475) is another option for those with good upper body strength. They will show you a whole other world of snow fun. You can also call **Winter Moon Sled Dog Adventures** (970-729-0058). **The Ouray Hot Springs Pool** (970-325-7073) is very accessible, including accessible bathrooms and roll-in showers, and they are in the process of building a ramp right into their pool. In the meantime, just ask for help if you need it. They also offer massage through a private business called **Healing Touch**. Call in advance (970-325-0415) to make reservations.

Ski School, Equipment, and Lift Tickets

While TASP can and will recommend other activities in the winter, their focus is definitely on skiing. Their staff of between 10 and 15 PSIA–certified instructors and volunteers can handle about 10 lessons per day. The executive director of the program is in charge of all staff training. They are very interactive and will always take time to speak with a guest's doctor or therapist upon request. Each adaptive guest receives a personal evaluation to address goals and equipment needs, which is also kept on file in order to track yearly progress and ability. About half of TASP's visitors are return guests each season, and they also attract several area school programs.

Currently, TASP has four bi-skis, five mono-skis, and one dual-ski in stock, and they are able to buy new and update old equipment each season. They also offer lessons for three-track and four-track skiing and assist the visually impaired. You can rent their gear without a lesson, and a buddy system is always an option if you just need a guide. They will provide storage for personal equipment, if necessary.

Lift tickets are included in the price of your lesson and are offered at half price to adaptive guests not taking a lesson. Thanks to a great relationship with Telluride Sports, family members and companions can take advantage of half-price ski rentals. The Ski Buddy program will cost you about the same as a lift ticket. Overall, the prices are very reasonable.

Adaptive Camps

The Expand Your Horizons ski camp is an annual event geared toward intermediate and advanced riders and is open to all disabilities. You must, however, be able to ski blue runs comfortably and be independent off of the mountain. Call in advance for dates as they do change each season. Recently they've started offering two Nordic, or cross-country, ski camps slated to run in January.

On-the-Mountain Information

If you are eating on the mountain, your best bet is **Gorrono**, located at mid-mountain. You can access the bathrooms, which are relatively wheelchair friendly, via the lowest level of the building, where the wheelchairs are. You will need to ask for help to access the lift that takes you to the restaurant, as there is a coffee cart blocking the entrance. **Guiseppes**, at the top of lift nine, is really not accessible, although you could have someone order food for you and eat outside in your ski(s). **Big Billies**, at the base of lift one, has accessible dining and restrooms available and a wheelchair on-site as well. If more than one chair is needed, they will make arrangements to bring your personal chair via the gondola. You can also drive to Big Billies if you are in a power chair. If you are skiing to the **Mountain Village** for lunch, the TASP office keeps a couple of chairs on hand, and all of the restaurants are accessible via the plaza elevator.

All of the lifts on Telluride, most notably the gondola, meet accessibility standards, and the lift operators will take good care of you if you need assistance. They offer plenty of terrain for beginner, intermediate, and advanced skiers alike. The steep and challenging terrain is perfect for the advanced or independent mono-skier.

Telluride Adaptive Sports Program is one of the state's newer adaptive ski schools and offers programs suitable for all levels. Courtesy of Telluride Adaptive Sports Program

Lodging

As with many ski towns, Telluride does not have a lot of ADA–compliant accommodations, but they do have quite a few that are doable. For condominium and house rentals, you should call either **Alpine Lodging** (970-728-3388) or **Mountain Management at Telluride** (970-728-6060). Although options are limited, they do have a few rentals that are accessible and/or doable. We found the **Bear Creek Lodge** the most wheelchair friendly. Most of the hotels and motels in town have at least one accessible room. The **Hotel Telluride** (970-369-

1188) is located at the west end of town and has four rooms that are accessible. All have one king-size bed and three have roll-in showers. The **Camel's Garden** (970-728-9300) is the closest to the gondola and offers two ADA–compliant rooms, but all of their accommodations are mostly accessible. The **New Sheridan Hotel** (970-728-4351), **Ice House Hotel** (970-728-6300), and **Hotel Columbia** (970-728-0660) are all recommended by AAA guidebooks and are all located in the town of Telluride. Each has one room that meets ADA standards with bars in the bathrooms and one king-size bed. In the Mountain Village, the **Inn at Lost Creek** (970-728-5678) has two ADA–compliant rooms (but no bars) and several others that are doable, including suites with one king-size bed and a pullout couch. The staff is incredibly friendly. **The Wyndham Lodge** (970-369-5000) has six rooms that are up to code. All have one king-size bed and bars in the bathrooms. Unfortunately, there is no accessible bed-and-breakfast lodging offered in Telluride at the moment.

Dining

Even with the historic stature of most of the buildings in Telluride, a surprising number of restaurants are accessible, or at least doable. For fine dining, three places really caught our eye downtown. **Honga's** is just a block off of the main street. They have a great ramp and serve fantastic Asian cuisine at $12 to $20 per plate. You shouldn't have any problem finding **221 S. Oak**. This contemporary bistro is totally accessible and offers some of the best food in Telluride, including fresh fish, pork, and wild game. Last but not least is the **New Sheridan Chop House**. Located in and accessible through the New Sheridan Hotel, the Chop House serves up the best steaks and prime rib around. There are also plenty of choices for more casual dining. **La Cochina** seems to be the locals' choice for great Mexican food. They are best known for their fish tacos, great prices, and main-street patio seating. **The Brown Bag**, located in the plaza at the center of town, is a fully accessible sandwich shop for eat-in or take-out. **Fat Alley BBQ** is also in this plaza, and although not fully accessible, it is doable with just a 1- to 2-inch lip and just enough room to get through the door. **Sophio's** is one of just a few breakfast spots in town. The food is worth waiting for, as there is usually a line, but plan to use the bathroom somewhere else because it's not accessible.

Après-Ski

For accessible action at the end of your ski day, try the **Wildflour** (in town) for lots of beers on tap and great appetizers. If you're headed to the Mountain Village, there are two wheelchair-friendly stops to make. **The Great Room** at Wyndham Peaks Resort is possibly the best place in Telluride to see a sunset and relax with a beer or cocktail. **The Skiers Union** is always hopping at the end of the day, crowded with skiers and boarders just as an après-ski bar should be.

As with any ski town, Telluride is not short on bars and nightlife. A local favorite is the **Last Dollar Saloon**, also known as "The Buck." It is one of the original buildings in Telluride, dating back more than 100 years, and is the most accessible bar in town. The Buck sees action all day long. Smugglers brewery has a ramp, with access through a side door, and great homemade beer. You can have fun at **Smugglers** for après-ski or nightlife. The **New Sheridan Hotel** also has a steady nighttime scene and a beautiful, old-fashioned bar. There are two steps to negotiate in and out of the bar area, with accessible bathrooms in the lobby. As with the après-ski scene, a lot of the popular places are inaccessible, with lots of stairs. If you don't mind asking for assistance, check out the **Fly Me to the Moon Saloon** or **Roma Bar** for late-night fun with live music.

Bridal Vail Falls is one of two spectacular waterfalls viewable from Telluride. It is one of the most famous in the world. And one of the things that keeps Telluride unique is that you won't find any chain restaurants, hotels, or businesses. This helps to keep small-town businesses in business.

Contact Information

Telluride Adaptive Sports Program
P.O. Box 2254
Telluride, CO 81435
Phone: 970-728-7537
Web site: www.tellurideadaptivesports.org
E-mail: tasp@tellurideadaptivesports.org

Vail—Vail Adaptive

History

The word "Vail" inevitably brings to mind a picture of the rich and famous playing lavishly in the Rocky Mountains. Originally thought of as an impoverished and unimportant area in terms of Colorado history, the Gore Creek Valley, where Vail lies, was unknown to skiing until the resort opened in 1962. The famous Back Bowls of Vail were first discovered in 1957 by 10th Mountain Division Army veteran Pete Seibert and local prospector Earl Eaton. Originally owned by the Ute Indians, these 4,000 acres of glades are a result of massive fires in the 1950s. Today they represent a landmark to skiers and celebrities from all over the world, and Vail is known as America's number-one ski resort. With a reputation like this and more than 2 million visits from skiers per year, it's only expected that their adaptive program uphold these standards as well.

An alternative to three-track skiing for amputees: snowboard attachments and ropes, which offer a feel similar to that of surfing. Courtesy of Toni Axelrod, Vail Resorts

Vail Adaptive

Vail Adaptive (VA) ski school was established in 1984 by Kara Heide in coordination with an existing program for the Eagle Valley school system. The current program supervisor, Ruth DeMuth, joined the staff in 1987 and maintains the program with impressive standards and dedication. She trains and leads the 30-person adaptive staff, which is larger than any other adaptive program in the United States.

Mountain Stats

Typical ski season: From Thanksgiving to the third Sunday in April
Base elevation: 8,120 feet
Summit elevation: 11,570 feet

Vertical rise: 3,450 feet
Terrain: 5,289 acres
Trails: 193
Pipes and parks: Golden Peak terrain park with 400-foot superpipe and mini quarterpipe
Lifts: 33 total: 1 gondola, 14 high-speed quads, 9 fixed-grip chairs, and 9 surface lifts

Parking and Transportation

The VA office is located across the parking lot from the Kids Ski School, at the Golden Peak area of the mountain. There are two accessible spots (which fill up early during busy season, of course) in the small Golden Peak parking lot, and there are several in the Passport Parking Garage, which is just before the Golden Peak area. Neither area charges for accessible parking.

All of Vail's public transportation vehicles have lifts and are 100-percent accessible. Call 970-479-2178 for bus schedules.

Activities

In addition to their top-rated adaptive program, Vail is also home to **Adventure Ridge**. Located only a seven-minute ride away, at the top of the Eagle Bahn gondola at Eagle's Nest, this is the place to go for nonskiing activities. They offer head-first thrill sledding, tubing, ski-biking, snowmobiling for kids and adults, and laser tag. They also offer adaptive sled-skating for quadri- and paraplegics. Adventure Ridge does not provide qualified supervisors or instructors for these activities, so plan to bring your own helper if you require special assistance.

Ski School, Equipment, and Lift Tickets

The program is funded as a branch of the Vail Ski School and, although highly priced, has been voted best in the country. Their instructors are all PSIA trained at various levels and go through an extensive multi-week training course each year. The program supervisor and/or the instructors are all willing to speak with your doctor or health-care practitioner regarding special needs. After each lesson, the instructors are required to fill out a form for their guest regarding the details of the lesson. These are kept on file and are referred to when charting guests' progress each year.

Their equipment holds to high qualifications, is updated often, and cannot be rented without a lesson, due to liability. They do, however, have a dozen rigs of various build and technique to loan with a lesson, and their lessons are very reasonable considering that they include equipment, lift ticket, and a private instructor.

If you bring your own rig and want a tour, they do offer a buddy system at a reasonable rate, and they will provide you with storage for your gear at no cost. The ski area has a deeply discounted five-day pass for adaptive skiers (nearly 80 percent off) and offers a reduced-price daily ticket for your companion as well (nearly 60 percent off). If you intend to visit Vail more than once a season, they also offer an extremely discounted price on an adaptive season pass. These prices are definitely affordable in the exorbitant land of Vail. Contact the ski area for up-to-date prices.

Adaptive Camps

Vail is lucky to have an Olympic medallist as a local resident. Sara Will, eight-time gold medallist in the Paralympics and one of the best adaptive skiers in the world, teaches weeklong adaptive clinics twice a season. Make sure to sign up early as spaces go very quickly. Go to www.sitski.com or imonoski@vail.net for more information.

On-the-Mountain Information

With a program like this, it's no wonder that 90 percent of the adaptive guests return every year, some even for a decade or more. The entire mountain is accessible, from the gondola, which boasts the only fully accessible cars in the country, to the on-mountain dining. Each on-mountain dining facility has at least one wheelchair, ramps, accessible bathrooms, and lipless entryways. The base of the ski area is a little different; some of the buildings are definitely pre–ADA, however, all have been modified to suit all special needs.

Lodging

Most major hotels in town are accessible, and, of course, anything built since 1990 is. As with all tourist towns, the individually owned condos built prior to 1990 are usually not fully accessible unless the individual family has their own specific needs for such design. You may want to contact properties that are questionable, such as bed-and-breakfasts or older hotels.

Following is a list of fully accessible lodging properties with at least one ADA–compliant room. Remember during busy seasons to book in advance and request these rooms, as they are limited in number. Many properties will discount their ADA–compliant rooms upon request, especially if there are only one or two rooms available.

Vail

Marriott Mountain Resort (800-648-0720) is located in Lionshead Village, only 200 yards from the gondola, and has 14 ADA–compliant rooms, two of which have roll-in showers; bath benches are available upon request. The **Marriott** also has five accessible restaurants, ranging from pub-style American cuisine to steaks and seafood in a casual fine-dining setting. **Vail Cascade Hotel and Club** (800-453-9633) offers four ADA–compliant rooms with roll-in showers and fold-down bath benches and is also located at Lionshead. Fine American cuisine is served at their wheelchair-friendly, four-diamond restaurant **Chaps**. **The Evergreen Lodge** (800-284-8245) is located between Vail and Lionshead. They have several rooms that will work for wheelchair users, although they are not ADA compliant. **The Lodge at Vail** (800-331-5634) is one of the premier places to stay in the heart of Vail Village. They have four fully accessible rooms with step-in showers. Bath benches and handheld shower attachments are available upon request. Both restaurants are accessible, but we were most impressed with the **Cucina Rustica's** amazing Italian-style breakfast buffet. **Sonnalp** (800-654-8312) is also in the heart of Vail Village and has one accessible room. Ask about a special rate since this is their only accessible room. Along with the Lodge at Vail, we loved the convenience of being close to the ski-school meeting area.

Beaver Creek

The Charter at Beaver Creek (800-525-6660) is right cross from the Beaver Creek Golf Course. Although none of their 156 condos are 100-percent ADA compliant, they have made a great effort to make everything in the Charter doable and can install temporary grab bars, bath benches, and handheld showerheads upon request. We were very excited to find ramps to the indoor pool and hot tubs, as well as the health club, and we would definitely recommend breakfast at the **Terrace**. The **Hyatt Regency Beaver Creek** (800-233-1234) is a ski-in, ski-out hotel at the base of Beaver Creek. Choose from ten ADA–compliant rooms, four with roll-in showers and six with tubs and benches. While **Bivans** and **Vue** both looked as though they offered incredibly tasty food and the buildings looked accessible, we loved the food and atmosphere at **McCoy's Bar**. The **Pines Lodge** (800-622-3131) is a mountainside luxury hotel. There are no ADA–compliant rooms at the Pines, but all of the rooms are doable if you can do without a roll-in shower with bars. If you're eating in, the **Grouse Mountain Grill** is worth every penny. The **Inn at Beaver Creek** (800-720-5674) is the luxury hotel at the base of Beaver Creek and has one fully accessible unit with a stall shower. The rest of their rooms are doable, depending on your mobility, and they do have a shower chair available if you need one. The bar at the inn is a tasty place to hang out if you are looking for a light meal. We particularly liked the soups and salads.

Avon

The **Comfort Inn** (800-423-4374) is about a five-minute drive to Beaver Creek and a 10-minute drive to Vail. They offer two ADA–compliant rooms with tub showers but do not have bath benches available, so you will want to bring your own if you are staying here. If their free continental breakfast doesn't fill you up, there is a **Denny's** just two doors down that should do the trick.

Dining

Vail has a vast assortment of great eateries, ranging from fast food to gourmet, many of which are accessible. There are two great pizzerias in Vail Village. **Pazzo's** is very popular and usually crowded but has great pizza and pasta dishes and is worth waiting for. There is one step up to enter. **Vendetta's** is just a block away from Pazzo's and usually less crowded if you don't feel like waiting. Their specialty pizzas are fabulous. They are accessible at the back entrance, but the bathrooms are small and inaccessible. For New American cuisine, try **Sweet Basil**. The food is amazing and they are accessible by elevator. The **Ore House** is also in Vail Village and boasts some of the best steaks and seafood (with a huge salad bar) in town. They are also accessible by the back entrance. In Lionshead, **Billy's Island Grill** features American cuisine at a reasonable price and is a favorite with both locals and tourists. If you only have one night to go out to dinner, we recommend **Bagali's Italian Kitchen** in West Vail. This tiny family-style restaurant serves the best Italian in the valley at non-Vail prices. The restaurant is accessible but the bathrooms are not. If you feel like getting out of Vail to eat, **Sato**, in Edwards (15 minutes west on I-70), has fantastic fresh sushi and great Asian dishes.

    A note on dining: The restaurants listed here have accessible entryways and dining areas. Some have accessible bathrooms. We recommend calling to ask about the location of accessible parking spaces and whether or not reservations are required. All parking structures have accessible spaces available and elevators where needed. These structures should be used if dining in Vail, Lionshead, and Beaver Creek Villages.

Après-Ski

After the lifts close, Vail comes to life as it gets ready for après-ski fun and late-night music and entertainment. After you've made your last turns, check out **Los Amigos** in Vail Village for a great margarita and one of the best views of the base area. There are just a couple of steps to get in, but it's well worth it if you ask for help. **Garfinkle's**, in Lionshead, with their huge deck and live acoustic music, is another favorite. For evening fun, **The Tap Room** on Bridge St. is a great place to warm up with a martini. Once you've warmed up, you can head to one of the Tap Room's other three levels via the elevator (including a great dance floor at the top level). **The Red Lion** in Vail Village, "the place to be after you ski," is another option and offers great live music seven nights a week during the season.

Contact Information

Vail Adaptive Program
P.O. Box 7
Vail, CO 81658
Phone: 970-479-3264; TTY: 970-479-3072
Web site: www.vail.snow.com/info/mtn.adaptive.asp

Central Reservations
Phone: 888-600-2631
Web site: www.vail.rezrez.com

Ski Resort Information Booths
Phone: 970-476-9090

The visitors center is small but accessible and located on the upper level of the main parking facility, where there is accessible parking. The helpful staff will provide you with free information on Vail as well as suggest additional seasonal activities for individuals with disabilities and their families. We recommend stopping here first for an overview of the town and your options.

Winter Park—
National Sports Center for the Disabled

History
When referring to Winter Park's history, it's also necessary to talk about Fraser. The town of Fraser, along with a small construction camp known as Little Chicago, was established with the development of the railroad in the early 1920s. In 1928, the Moffat Tunnel was completed and skiers flooded into the valley. Little Chicago would later be renamed Winter Park. Located off scenic U.S. Hwy. 40, it's no doubt that settlers found its rugged peaks and open meadows an attractive place to stay.

National Sports Center for the Disabled
Winter Park is easily the most accessible town in Colorado, as the **National Sports Center for the Disabled** (NSCD) has been here for more than 30 years, assisting store and restaurant owners with upgrades and compliance. For travelers who like the ease of 100-percent accessibility and a short drive from Denver, Winter Park should be one of your first picks.

> *What kind of people take blind kids mountain climbing? The same ones that take paraplegics sailing and amputees horseback riding.*
> —*NSCD*

The NSCD was founded by Hal O'Leary in January 1970 as a ski-lesson center for young amputees from the Denver Children's Hospital. Today it is the largest outdoor therapeutic, recreational agency in the world. With 13 paid employees (six of whom are year-round staff) and more than 1,000 contributing volunteers, the NSCD plays host to some 30,000 guests annually. They are diverse enough to handle almost any disability (more than 30 in all) and offer 17 different summer and winter activities, from rock climbing to sailing to downhill skiing. Program director Christine Pufpaff started with NSCD 19 years ago as a volunteer commuting from Denver and loved it so much she moved to Winter Park and made a career of it. Her goal is to show people with disabilities the meaning of NSCD's mission statement, which is "no mountain too high."

Mountain Stats

All areas combined
Typical ski season: Pre-Thanksgiving to the second Sunday in April
Terrain: 2,886 acres
Trails: 134
Pipes and parks: Kendrick's and Rail Yard terrain parks and superpipe
Lifts: 22 lifts: 8 high-speed express quads, 4 triple chairlifts, 7 double chairlifts, and 3 magic carpets

Winter Park
Base elevation: 9,000 feet
Summit elevation: 10,700 feet
Vertical rise: 1,700 feet

Mary Jane
Base elevation: 9,450 feet
Summit elevation: 12,060 feet
Vertical rise: 2,610 feet

Vasquez Ridge
Base elevation: 9,486 feet
Summit elevation: 10,700 feet
Vertical rise: 1,214 feet

Parsenn Bowl
Base elevation: 10,348 feet
Summit elevation: 12,060 feet
Vertical rise: 1,712 feet

National Sports Center for the Disabled is the largest adaptive program in the world. Courtesy of the National Sports Center for the Disabled

Parking and Transportation

One downside to the smallness of Winter Park is the parking availability. Due to the lack thereof, parking is divided into two groups, based on need. If you are the driver, you may park in the designated lots. If the person with disabilities is the passenger, there is a drop-off area some distance away from the main parking. Unfortunately, there's nothing they can change about this; these three valleys are space limited.

Winter Park has a "**Paratransit**," and there is an ADA–services help number at 970-726-4163. Go to www.skiwinterpark.com/winter park/free_shuttle.html for schedules.

Activities

Other winter activities available to visitors with disabilities include snowmobiling, snowcat tours, dogsledding, cross-country skiing, and backcountry hut trips. For these adventurous activities, the most experienced tour companies for travelers with disabilities are **Trailblazers** (800-669-0134) and **Grand Adventures** (800-726-9247).

Ski School, Equipment, and Lift Tickets

While the typical ski instructor tends to be fairly short-term and transient, adaptive instructors tend to be more permanent. In Winter Park this is especially true. The majority of NSCD's instructors have been with the program an average of five to 10 years, with the longest tenure being 15 years. This plays a big part in a 40-percent return rate of their adaptive clients. These guests are assured of seeing the same smiling faces and getting the same great results every time they visit. The remaining large portion of NSCD's clients are either first-timers or are participants in their Denver-based school programs, adaptive camps, and other outreach programs. Astonishingly, about 60 percent of their winter visitors have never skied before. The sheer size and reputation of Winter Park's adaptive program attract people with disabilities from around the world.

The NSCD offers mono-skiing; bi-skiing; three-track, four-track, and blind skiing; and snowboarding and can accommodate between 25 and 30 adaptive lessons at once.

The equipment is updated every three years, as needed, and can even be rented without a lesson (the only adaptive program to allow this) and/or taken off-site for use. This is a great option (only $34 per day) for advanced riders and families who ski at surrounding resorts that don't offer programs of their own.

Because Winter Park is family oriented, the daily and weekly prices for everyone are nearly half of what the bigger resorts demand, and adaptive-skier and companion tickets are further reduced. This program doesn't offer a discounted "buddy" option, but for the same price as a lesson, experienced mono-skiers can certainly use their instructor as a tour guide to the best stashes on the mountain.

Adaptive Camps

Due to its small size, Winter Park's adaptive program does not offer any adaptive camps.

On-the-Mountain Information

With more than 130 ski runs, 22 lifts, and almost 3,000 skiable acres, Winter Park is a diverse mountain suitable for all levels of adaptive skiers and snowboarders (snowboarders beware of the long traverse at the top of the Olympia Express). Winter Park offers several mountains for different levels of skiers and skiing options. **Mary Jane** boasts some of North America's best bump skiing and goes by the motto "no pain, no Jane." **Vasquez Ridge** offers wide-open cruisers for beginning and intermediate skiers. **Parsenn Bowl** offers magnificent views and riding above the Continental Divide. **Vasquez Cirque** is open only to adrenaline-seeking expert skiers and backcountry fanatics. New sites at the resort include the **Rail Yard Terrain Park** for adventurous skiers and snowboarders and an increased grooming regimen at Mary Jane to attract all levels of riders, including families and mono- and bi-skiers.

The on-mountain dining facilities at Winter Park Resort are accessible to all types of disabilities. **Lunch Rock**, at the top of Mary Jane, and **Sunspot**, at the top of Winter Park, are both one level and have wheelchairs right inside the front doors. **Mary Jane** base is a split-level building, with the restrooms located on the lower level. There is a handy wheelchair phone box at the front entrance for assistance, and ramps wrap all around the building, so there is no need for an elevator. **Snoasis**, at the base of Winter Park, is also a split-level building. Each level is accessible from the outside of the building, but there is no elevator or ramp system once you're inside, so pick a level before you stop to dine.

Lodging

Again, thanks to the NSCD and its pull on tens of thousands of people with disabilities each year, the town of Winter Park has numerous accessible lodging and dining options.

The **Winter Park Central Reservations** office is very adept at handling all of your lodging needs over the phone. You can call the hotels directly yourself, but you might find Central Reservations to be more time efficient with their wealth of knowledge, resources, and experience. For a full list of accessible properties, contact their office at 800-453-2525, or call the **Winter Park and Fraser Valley Chamber of Commerce** (800-903-7425).

Most of the lodging options in Winter Park are fully or partly accessible, but we've selected a few of our favorites to recommend. The **Alpen Rose Bed and Breakfast** (970-726-5039) is a beautiful property with reasonable prices. They have a couple of doable rooms on the first floor and offer an excellent morning starter. Bed-and-breakfasts are always our favorite, when we find an accessible one. **Winter Park Mountain Lodge** (970-726-4211) has five ADA–compliant hotel rooms with roll-in showers and several others with tub setups. Although we didn't eat in the hotel, several locals we spoke with had good things to say about their family-style restaurant. For a more inexpensive option in the area, the **Super 8 Motel** (970-726-8088) has a few ADA–compliant rooms with roll-in showers and bath benches and can accommodate a wheelchair in almost any of their other rooms. Winter Park is rare in that it has condominium options for reservation as well. Central Reservations will have a current listing of all these condo options, but our favorite of the list is the brand-new **Zephyr Mountain Lodge** (877-754-8400), which has one accessible condo complete with a roll-in shower. It is a two-bedroom unit that sleeps up to six people and has a great view of the slopes. This is a full-service lodge and is barely 100 feet from the closest lift, the Zephyr lift. (The Zephyr Express is modified to accommodate 20 gondola cabins for dinner service to The Lodge at Sunspot.) With the mountain village at your doorstep, there are also plenty of places to dine.

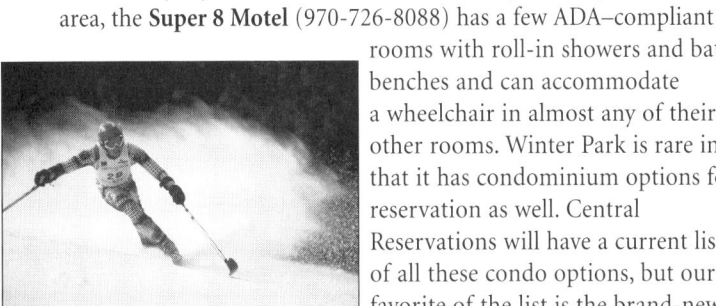

Winter Park is the long-time home of the U.S. Disabled Ski Team. Courtesy of the National Sports Center for the Disabled

Dining

Winter Park boasts nearly 100-percent accessibility for their local restaurants, so between the resort village and the town of Fraser, all visitors to the valley can find almost any kind of food desired. We've picked out a few of our favorites to get you started.

Carlos and Maria's (970-726-9674), located in Copper Creek Square, is one of our favorites for excellent Mexican cuisine and even better margaritas. **Carver's Bakery Café** (970-726-8208), also located in Copper Creek Square, is our stop for homemade pastries and fabulous eggs Benedict. **The Divide Grill** (970-726-4900) boasts large plates of steak and seafood and an excellent salad bar. **Fontenot's** (970-726-4021), located in Park Plaza, is a genuine New Orleans Cajun café serving gumbo, red beans and rice, jambalaya, and other spicy southern favorites. If you love stromboli, as we do, **Hernando's Pizza Pub** (970-726-5409) is the place to stop for a cold beer and great food. Last, **Smokin' Moes Ribhouse and Saloon** (970-726-4600) is our preferred stop for getting our hands messy with great ribs and barbecue goodies. The saloon also offers an arcade, games, and TVs, so it's a great choice for families or larger parties.

Après-Ski

The Winter Park area offers several options when it comes to winding down after a day of activities. **The Club Car**, at the base of Mary Jane, is a local favorite that offers après-ski fun, but only during the winter season. **The Kickapoo Lounge** and the **Derailer** are the best options at Winter Park base. All of these hot spots have decks and offer live music throughout the season. Although Winter Park and Fraser are definitely family towns, they are not without their nightlife. For a taste of Winter Park's handcrafted beers, go to **Moffat Station Restaurant and Brewery** at the very accessible Winter Park Mountain Lodge. They've got great views, beers, and food. **Deno's Mountain Bistro** boasts the best burgers in town and offers live music in their bar. For the biggest and best margaritas in town, head to the **Shed**, where you can listen to live music several nights a week.

Contact Information

National Sports Center for the Disabled
P.O. Box 1290
Winter Park, CO 80482
Phone: 970-726-1540
Web site: www.nscd.org
E-mail: info@nscd.org

Central Reservations
79050 U.S. Hwy. 40
Winter Park, CO 80482
Phone: 800-979-0332 or 877-266-3754
Web site: www.skiwinterpark.com

Winter Park Resort
P.O. Box 36
Winter Park, CO 80482
Phone: 970-726-SNOW
Web sites: www.skiwinterpark.com or www.winterpark-info.com

Courtesy of Adaptive Adventures

CHAPTER 5

SUMMER TRAVEL

Adaptive Activity Specialists

Adaptive Adventures

Adaptive Adventures (P.O. Box 2245, Evergreen, CO 80437; 877-679-2770; www.adaptiveadventures.org; info@adaptiveadventures.org), based out of Evergreen, Colorado, is a specialized provider and premier source of information for adaptive sports and adventure travel for people with physical disabilities. Founded during the summer of 1999 by amputee Joel Berman and paraplegic Matt Feeney, Adaptive Adventures hosts a variety of summer and winter activities.

Summer months see instructional camps on adaptive cycling, waterskiing, and wakeboarding, as well as local weekend excursions and three yearly trips to Lake Powell in Utah. Waterskiing instruction for all levels of ability is available at **Boulder Reservoir** (through **Boulder Parks and Recreation**) every Tuesday throughout the summer, while experienced and individual skiers convene at **Sloan's Lake**, just outside of downtown Denver, every Thursday. Adaptive wakeboarding is a newly adopted sport that is being pioneered by Adaptive Adventures

Adaptive riders participate in Colorado's annual Ride the Rockies.
Courtesy of Adaptive Adventures

and can be sampled on Tuesdays and Thursdays at the lake as well. We also recommend checking out the **Adaptive Water Ski and Wakeboard Festival**, usually held in July. This is a fantastic, inexpensive way to get introduced to these thrilling sports. Boating camps and weekend trips around Colorado are announced on the Web site and should be reserved in advance.

With the recent rise in popularity of adaptive water sports, Adaptive Adventures is also encouraging people to push themselves to excel by testing their skills in water-ski and wakeboard competitions. Through a combined effort with the **International Novice Tour**, they have been able to set several dates in Colorado each summer, welcoming participants of all ability levels. Those who excel have a chance to attend the national finals held in the fall.

Other summer activities include adaptive cycling and handcycling (check out the **Bicycle Tour of Colorado**), white-water rafting on the Green River, basketball, paddling, tennis, track and field, and lacrosse. These sports are available through Adaptive Adventures' special camps and youth programs during June, July, and August. Advanced bookings are recommended and can be made through the Web site.

Adaptive cycling, and, more specifically, hand-cycling, has grown in popularity during the past five years. Thanks to Adaptive Adventures, "a leader in promoting elite hand-cycle races, grassroots programs, and camps," the sport continues to expand its horizons. With their fully equipped, mobile cycling trailer, Adaptive Adventures' staff is available for clinics, demonstrations, and camps almost anywhere they are needed. Youth cycling programs were also expanded in 2003. Hand-cycling allows for an incredible amount of independence and mobility for people with disabilities. We highly recommend it.

One of the goals of Adaptive Adventures is to be a resource to other agencies and a wealth of information to locals and travelers. They have an incredible Web site that is home to more than 200 adaptive links for travelers with disabilities to Colorado and much of the country. As a nonprofit organization, they've found many donors to help make their trips and workshops inexpensive and affordable. Through partnerships with **Disabled Sports USA**, the **United States Hand-Cycling Federation**, and the **Professional Ski Instructors of America** (PSIA), they are helping to bring adaptive sports to a new level. Their Web site (www.adaptiveadventures.org) is definitely worth checking out, if you haven't already. It boasts some of the best adaptive sports photos on the Internet.

Adaptive sports give you the freedom to leave your wheelchair behind. Courtesy of Adaptive Adventures

Back Country Discovery

Perhaps one of the most innovative and progressive horse programs in the state, if not the country, is **Back Country Discovery** (BCD) (Barb Staples, Executive Director, 857 W. CR 66E, Ft. Collins, CO 80524; 970-568-3343; www.backcountrydiscovery.org; bcd@frii.com), which offers wilderness horse-packing trips for anyone with a disability. This nonprofit wilderness guiding organization works in combination with Old Glendevey Ranch, Laramie River Ranch, Crazy Horse Outfitters, and Samuelson Outfitters to provide guests with full backcountry horse expeditions all summer long. Offering several trips per summer, BCD has something for every adventurer with any ability. BCD offers scholarships to those in financial need. There are a few requirements to participate in their trips, which they can go into detail with you over the phone.

The highlight of this agency is their own invention, the pack ramp, designed by director Barb Staples. This mounting ramp travels with the group on its own horse and makes anything possible for those in need. We are glad to recommend this amazing outfitter who, against all odds, brings the backcountry to adventurers with special needs. Visit their Web site for current trips and upcoming events.

Back Country Discovery's special backcountry ramp is portable for use on wilderness trips. Courtesy of Back Country Discovery

Disabled Sports USA

Founded in 1967 by disabled Vietnam veterans, **Disabled Sports USA** (DS/USA) (451 Hungerford Dr., Ste. 100, Rockville, MD 20850; 301-217-0960; www.dsusa.org) was originally called National Amputee Skiers Association and broadened its mission in 1972 by changing its name and offering a wider scope of sports to all abilities and citizens. Changing names and missions several times before the 1990s, DS/USA finally emerged into its current status, bringing the world of sports competition to those with disabilities. Although their offices are not in

Colorado, DS/USA runs camps, clinics, competitions, and events in Colorado throughout the year.

Operating as a nonprofit organization, DS/USA is a nationwide network of community-based chapters offering snow skiing, waterskiing, sailing, kayaking, rafting, cycling, climbing, horseback riding, golf, competitions, and social activities. Their year-round online calendar displays their national and international events, clubs, and competitions. Colorado usually offers programs at ski areas during the winter and at statewide recreation areas during the summer in conjunction with the adaptive programs throughout the state.

Just for the Fun of It

Based out of the Winter Park area, **Just for the Fun of It** (Joan Handley Ogden, Bill Ogden, and Mark Mason, Certified Therapeutic Recreation Specialists, P.O. Box 161, Berthoud, CO 80513; 970-532-4032) takes people with disabilities on mini-excursions and weeklong trips around the country and the world. They offer weekend day trips twice a month from Ft. Collins to the Boulder area, three-day trips once a season on the Glenwood Springs train, to Estes Park, and to Cheyenne, Wyoming, and yearly weeklong vacations to destinations such as the Caribbean and Hawaii, Nashville, Disneyland, and more. As of yet, there is no Web site, but you can call or write to Just for the Fun of It for a full brochure.

Wilderness on Wheels

Wilderness on Wheels (WOW) (P.O. Box 1007, Wheat Ridge, CO 80034; 303-403-1110; www.wildernessonwheels. com; wow@ecentral.com) is a one-of-a-kind backcountry location made just for wheelies and other campers with disabilities who want to enjoy a woodsy location, trail, camping, and fishing all on their own terms. WOW is open between mid-April and mid-October (based on snowmelt) and reservations are required for entry. However, it is rare that you would be turned away, unless the park is reserved for a special event. No entry fee is required, but they do ask for donations, and WOW is always in need of aid, so if you enjoy your time here, be sure to send your support. WOW is located about 60 miles west of Denver on U.S. Hwy. 285. There is a map to WOW on their Web site.

Originally the Southern Narrow Gauge Railroad logging road used to transport logs for railroad ties. This unique, switchbacking, accessible boardwalk path climbs a full mile up a 12,300-foot mountain peak along the edge of the Continental Divide in Colorado.

Finished in 1993, this boardwalk took several groups of volunteers, such as the Give-a-Day Team, seven years to complete, and is now run by a volunteer host.

The trail starts at the base campground, which houses 12 campsites with elevated tent platforms along a small trout stream. Fishing is welcomed in the stream and in a stocked pond upstream, and campfire grills are provided for cooking (subject to fire restrictions). They do ask that you pack out what you pack in, as the wildlife is plentiful and trash is not good for them.

The boardwalk is 8 feet wide and accessible for all types of chairs and disabilities. Because it is a steep climb in spots, upper-body strength or assistance for manual chairs is needed. The views from above are magnificent, and the feeling of summiting your own mountain is well worth the exercise. Wildflowers and native plants bloom along the boardwalk; birds and wildlife are undisturbed and abundant. At midtrail, set back in the woods, is a secluded amphitheater for all types of parties and events.

Wilderness on Wheels offers a camping facility and an accessible backcountry trail system that is slightly more than 1 mile in length.

This area is perfect as a blissful camping retreat or even as a day stop for a workout and a good view. Visit their Web site for maps, support, and more information or reservations.

Summer Activities

Fishing

Each year the Colorado Division of Wildlife makes it easier and easier for people with disabilities and other special needs to access the outdoors. Thanks to the "Fishing is Fun" program and other state, city, and local efforts, fishing is becoming much more accessible around the state.

State parks and recreation areas are the first place to look for ADA–compliant fishing sites. In addition to the many accessible fishing piers and platforms spread throughout the Colorado state park system, there are close to 100 other great fishing spots that are easily accessible. For the complete list of all accessible fishing across the state of Colorado, visit the Colorado Division of Wildlife's Web site at www.wildlife.state.co.us. Please see the chart for favorite picks for accessible and adventurous fishing locations throughout the state.

If you have been a Colorado resident for at least six months and are totally and permanently disabled or are a disabled veteran, the state of Colorado also offers a free lifetime fishing license. For more information, visit www.wildlife.state.co.us/access ibility/#disability_fishing_license or call 303-291-7235 for an application.

Additional accessible fishing piers and platforms are being built every year.
Courtesy of the National Sports Center for the Disabled

Cold Water Fish

Name	Phone	Nearest City	Hwy.	Pier	Trail	Platform	Pads	Parking	Restrooms	Boat Ramp	Camping	Native Cutthroat	Rainbow Trout	Brown Trout	Brook Trout	Lake Trout	Kokanee Salmon	Grayling	Whitefish	Snake River Cutthroat	Stocked Trout	"Wild Trout Waters"	"Gold Medal Streams"
Animas River	970-247-0855	Durango	3rd St.		✓			✓					✓	✓	✓						✓		
Arkansas Headwaters	719-539-7289	Salida	U.S. Hwys. 24, 285, 50		✓			✓	✓		✓		✓	✓	✓						✓		
Big Thompson River	970-842-2836	Loveland	CO Hwy. 34		✓			✓			✓		✓	✓	✓						✓		
Fraser River Park	970-725-3557	Fraser	U.S. Hwy. 40		✓			✓	✓				✓	✓	✓						✓		
Fryingpan River	970-963-2266	Basalt	CO Hwy. 82		✓			✓					✓	✓	✓						✓	✓	✓
Miramonte Reservoir	970-249-3431	Norwood	CO Hwy. 145					✓	✓	✓	✓		✓								✓		
Monument Lake	719-561-4909	Trinidad	CO Hwy. 12				✓	✓	✓	✓	✓		✓		✓						✓		
North Lake	970-484-2836	Loveland	Taft Ave.	✓				✓	✓				✓								✓		
Pearl Lake	970-879-3922	Hahns Peak	CR 129					✓	✓	✓	✓	✓											
Rio Grande River	719-657-2845	Del Norte	U.S. Hwy. 160		✓	✓		✓			✓		✓	✓	✓						✓		
Roaring Fork	970-945-6443	Glenwood Springs	7th St. Bridge		✓	✓		✓			✓		✓	✓	✓						✓	✓	✓
Steamboat Lake	970-879-3922	Hahns Peak	CR 129		✓			✓	✓	✓	✓		✓								✓		
St. Vrain River	970-823-6622	Lyons	CO Hwy. 36		✓			✓					✓	✓	✓						✓		
St. Vrain River North Fork	303-823-6060	Lyons	CO 80		✓			✓					✓	✓	✓						✓		
South Platte River	303-539-3529	Fairplay	CO Hwy. 9		✓			✓					✓	✓	✓						✓	✓	✓

Warm Water Fish — Fishing Access

Name	Phone	Nearest City	Hwy.	Pier	Trail	Platform pads	Parking	Restrooms	Boat Ramp	Camping	Walleye	Yellow Perch	Crappie	Largemouth Bass	Smallmouth Bass	Channel Catfish	Northern Pike	White Bass	Bluegill	Carp	Bullhead
Arvada Reservoir	303-431-3030	Denver	CO Hwy. 93	Y			Y														
Aurora Reservoir	303-690-1286	Denver	Quincy Ave.	Y			Y			Y											
Barr Lake	303-659-6005	Denver	I-76							Y									Y		
Bear Creek Reservoir	303-271-5925	Morrison/Denver	CO Hwy. 74	Y			Y		Y		Y	Y	Y								
Bonny Reservoir	970-354-7306	Burlington	U.S. Hwy. 385				Y	Y	Y	Y	Y	Y	Y	Y	Y	Y	Y	Y	Y	Y	
Boulder Reservoir	303-441-3461	Boulder	51st St	Y			Y	Y	Y		Y	Y	Y	Y		Y			Y		
Chatfield Reservoir	303-791-7275	Denver	CO Hwy. 121				Y	Y	Y	Y	Y	Y	Y	Y	Y	Y			Y		
Eleven Mile Canyon Reservoir	719-748-3401	Colorado Springs	U.S. Hwy. 24		Y		Y	Y	Y	Y	Y						Y				
Holbrook Reservoir	719-383-3000	La Junta	CO Hwy. 266	Y			Y	Y	Y	Y	Y	Y	Y	Y		Y			Y	Y	
Pueblo Reservoir	719-561-9320	Pueblo	Pueblo Reservoir Rd.	Y	Y		Y	Y	Y	Y	Y	Y	Y	Y	Y	Y		Y	Y	Y	
Rifle Gap Reservoir	970-625-1607	Rifle	CO Hwy. 325				Y	Y	Y	Y	Y	Y			Y						
Sterling Reservoir	970-522-3657	Sterling	CR 330	Y	Y		Y	Y	Y	Y	Y	Y	Y	Y	Y	Y		Y	Y	Y	Y

Access — Fish

Golf

With each passing year, adaptive golf is spreading across the state under the guidance of **Project Gain** and the **National Alliance for Accessible Golf** (NAAG), the adaptive arms of the United States Golf Association (USGA). Compared to other programs throughout the country, Colorado is still climbing uphill to spread awareness and encourage courses to add options and carts for golfers with disabilities. While some states seem to welcome the adaptive needs, Colorado is still in the establishing stages of accessibility as a whole. In the next few years, we will see improvements toward universal acceptance, starting with the inclusion of adaptive information in the state's recreation supplement *Colorado Golf*, which is found at nearly all chamber of commerce offices in each town. As with lodging properties, it is up to the golf courses themselves to supply this information, so it has been a huge project to have this included, as there are nearly 250 courses throughout the state. You can also obtain *Colorado Golf* by contacting the **Colorado Activity Center** (CAC) directly (P.O. Box 129, Frisco, CO 80443; 800-777-8642 or 970-668-5259,). Make sure you always get the most current version of the guidebook, as Colorado golf grows yearly.

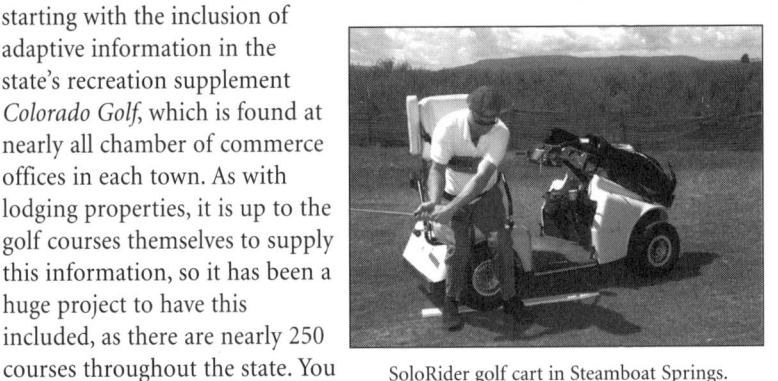

SoloRider golf cart in Steamboat Springs. Courtesy of Kathy Clarke

Slowly popping up around the state are progressive courses with adaptation on the greens and in their carts, such as with the SoloRider, which is an adaptive, full-standing cart (800-898-3353; www.solorider.com). Courses that do not offer these kinds of adapted carts do offer a cart with a red flag that signifies a golfer with disabilities with the need to drive up to the green. These are not optimal carts for wheelies, however, as the inflexibility of the seat hinders the swing. We recommend the following courses instead, mainly for their adapted individual golf carts, such as the one pictured. We also recommend calling adaptive summer programs, such as the Breckenridge Outdoor Education Center or Challenge Aspen, as they run annual camps for adaptive golf and can offer more information in their local areas.

Denver

The city's public courses share a number of SoloRiders or similar carts. The courses ask for at least a week's advance notice so they can transport the cart to the course you'll be playing on.

City Park

Known for its longstanding history and unique design, City Park (2500 York St., Denver, CO 80521; 303-295-2096) opened in 1912 and is an integral part of the history of golf in this area. City Park shares its SoloRiders with other courses, so call to reserve them in advance. Of all the city's public courses, this is the oldest and the one we recommend the most, but most of the city's public courses share the carts and are, therefore, accessible. There are more than 40 courses in the metro area, so check the current *Colorado Golf* guide for something closer to you if staying in the area.

Fox Hollow

Built in 1993 and proud to call itself fully accessible, Fox Hollow has one SoloRider for use and recommends booking it well in advance. The course and its buildings are fully accessible as well. From C-470, take Morrison Rd. east for 3 miles. The Fox Hollow entrance is on the right (13410 Morrison Rd., Lakewood, CO 80228; 303-986-7888).

Haymaker

Established in 1997, this beautiful course is set on an Audubon bird sanctuary and both its course and buildings are fully accessible. As of 2004, Haymaker is proud to bring its first SoloRider cart to its course. Located south of Steamboat Springs, at the intersection of U.S. Hwy. 40 and CO Hwy. 131 (34855 U.S. Hwy. 40, Steamboat Springs, CO 80477; 970-870-1846).

Springs Ranch Golf Club

This newer course was built in 1998 and its buildings, tees, and range are fully accessible. They do not offer single-rider carts as of yet, but do allow carts to be driven up to the greens. To get to Springs Ranch Golf Club, exit I-25 at Woodmen Rd. and go east for 6 miles. Turn right on Powers Blvd. and go 4 miles to N. Carefree Rd. and turn left (east). Take a right on Tutt (3525 Tutt Blvd., Colorado Springs, CO 80922; 719-573-4863).

Horseback Riding

Since the 1950s, people have made huge strides in understanding and developing the potential benefits of equine-assisted therapies for people with disabilities. Credit for pioneering this field goes to Liz Hartel of Denmark, who beat polio through self-rehabilitation to win a silver medal in dressage at the Helsinki Olympics in 1952. Her transition from wheelchair to horseback inspired doctors and horse experts to initiate therapeutic-riding programs across Europe. Professionals in the United States and Canada soon followed this lead and established programs in Toronto, Ontario, and Augusta, Michigan. The need for a good source to organize all of this new information was soon realized, and the first meeting to discuss formation of the **North American Riding for the Handicapped Association** (NARHA) (www.narha.org) followed in November 1969 in Middleburg, Virginia.

Today NARHA is the leader in promoting equine-assisted therapies for people with physical, emotional, and learning disabilities. Through these therapies, individuals with disabilities look forward to improving muscle tone, balance, posture, coordination, motor development, and emotional well-being. For many, this is a chance to experience activities that they never thought possible. For others, it is great way to rehabilitate injuries and take steps toward drastically improving their lives.

There are more than twenty statewide programs for therapeutic and adaptive riding.

There are many approaches to and types of equine therapy. **Therapeutic Riding** is the most common and basic equine activity for individuals with various physical, developmental, cognitive, and emotional disabilities. **Equine Assisted Psychotherapy**, or EAP, is therapy conducted by licensed psychotherapists and trained equine facilitators to help clients reach their goals. Various activities, both on the ground and mounted, are explored with the equine to address issues, elicit emotions, and provide skills for the client to apply in their life. **Therapeutic Vaulting** is similar to doing acrobatics on horseback and is usually done in conjunction with therapeutic riding. **Hippotherapy** is conducted by licensed physical, occupational, and speech therapists. Various positions of the walking horse impact the muscles and joints of the clients in a specific manner and help clients increase muscle tone, strength, and control. **Canine-Assisted Psychotherapy** is still a very new approach that uses dogs to assist in activities that can address issues, elicit emotions, and provide skills for the client to apply in their life.

Currently, there are nearly 30 NARHA riding centers in Colorado to choose from. Each of these programs is unique in its therapy options and methods to fit the needs of almost anyone. Call the program or programs that you are interested in ahead of time to see which is right for your needs. There is a lot of paperwork involved, including medical approvals and releases, that needs to be taken care of in advance, so don't wait to make your arrangements. Contact information and other related links are listed below to make your search easier.
Equine Assisted Growth and Learning Association (EAGALA): www.eagala.org
Equine Facilitated Mental Health Association (EFMHA): www.narha.org
Certified Horsemanship Association (CHA): www.cha-ahse.org

Arvada (Denver)—Hoofs 'n Paws Development Center

The mission of Hoofs 'n Paws Development Center (Renu Poduval, P.O. Box 740278, Arvada, CO 80006; 720-581-3485; www.hoofsnpaws.org; info@hoofsnpaws.org) is "Under the guidance of trained professionals, Hoofs 'n Paws Development Center will encourage the development of emotional, psychological, physical, and cognitive abilities in children and adults through safe and directed therapeutic interactions with animals. Innovative assessment and evaluation techniques will be used to ensure program participants' needs and goals are optimally met."

Hoofs 'n Paws offers several types of therapy, including therapeutic riding, equine-assisted psychotherapy, therapeutic vaulting, hippotherapy, and canine-assisted psychotherapy. Currently, the canine-assisted program is a pilot research project. They run eight-week sessions year-round with a break for Thanksgiving and Christmas. They also boast indoor and outdoor arenas, round pens, and trails around the Eveningstar Farm in Arvada, Colorado.

Broomfield (Denver)—Whistlepig Farms

Whistlepig Farms (Jeanie Clifford, 14041 Aspen St., Broomfield, CO 80020; 303-404-9858; www.whistlepigfarms.com) is an indoor/outdoor equestrian facility located in Broomfield, Colorado. Owners Tim and Jeanie Clifford opened their full-service equestran center in 2002 to cater to all equestrian needs in Broomfield, Denver, and the surrounding area. They offer riding lessons, training, boarding, and summer camps in addition to their special-needs program.

Whistlepig's special-needs equestrians offer sessions two days a week and can handle a wide range of disabilities with a focus on therapeutic riding. With more than 25 horses and access to 400 acres of trails and open space, this fast-growing center can handle all of your needs. Call ahead to inquire about one-time and part-time riding, as availability varies.

Carbondale—Sopris Therapy Services

Conveniently located just off of I-70 south of Glenwood Springs is Sopris Therapy Services (Pat Horwitz, P.O. Box 2080, Carbondale, CO 81623; 970-963-4677; www.sopristherapyservices.com; phorwitz7@comcast.net). This center offers physical and occupational therapy, cognitive retraining, speech therapy, and therapeutic riding to people of all ages and disabilities, promoting well-being through independence and hard work. This is a great program for all ability levels, and a flexible schedule allows them to offer lessons to one-time riders. Sopris is dedicated to developing the client/horse relationship rather than competitive skills, which allows them to focus on fun.

Centennial—Connections: Horses Healing Hearts

While therapeutic riding is beneficial in many ways, Connections (Cathy Stecklein, 8641 E. Dry Creek Rd. #512, Centennial, CO 80112; P.O. Box 110385; Aurora, CO 80112; 720-273-3659; www.connections-therapeutic-riding-center.com; connections@wwdb.org) focuses on dealing with psychosocial- and mental-health issues and needs such as behavior and learning disabilities. Social skills, communication, judgment, mood, and anxiety are just a few of the areas that they can improve for their clients. Through countless hours of working with psychotherapists and psychoanalysts, they are able to develop a unique and different program for each of their clients. The expert staff at Connections also works with at-risk youth and trauma victims to build self-confidence and rediscover the personal values needed to set them on a better life path.

Located just outside of Denver, this facility typically runs six-week sessions on a year-round basis. Clients ride five days per week and are encouraged to participate in consecutive sessions if they wish to continue developing and improving their skills. Cathy Stecklein, the program director, hopes to keep her program small (about 30 clients) and plans to have an indoor facility very soon. One-time and part-time riders are also welcome.

Colorado Springs—Golden Eagles

Golden Eagles (Cathleen Couchman, 3450 Hay Creek Rd., Colorado Springs, CO 80921; 719-481-3126) is a unique retreat center that offers mostly one-on-one classes designed for individual needs. Having worked with mostly the elderly since its inception, this center is equipped for all types of mobility disabilities.

There are two centers in one here at Golden Eagles, with indoor and outdoor riding options. The retreat center lies on a large, flat property with many trail opportunities for those with trail riding in mind.

Estes Park—Miracle Mount Estes Park Therapeutic Riding Center

Miracle Mount Estes Park Therapeutic Riding Center (Kay Rosenthal, Ph.D., R.N., 690 Pinewood Dr., Estes Park, CO 80517; 970-586-3472; www.optionsforhealthyliving.org; epltr@aol.com) offers recreational therapy, emotional therapy that is needed because of trauma, and mental therapy for learning disabilities. Their sessions are kept small and consist of up to five horses and riders per two or three instructors for 50-minute classes several times per week. Scholarships are available for those in need, thanks to Miracle Mount's many sponsors. Located just outside of Rocky Mountain National Park, this center has an excellent location for a day of riding before entering the park.

Ft. Collins—Front Range Exceptional Equestrians

Started in 1987, Front Range Exceptional Equestrians (Sharon Butler, P.O. Box 272452, Ft. Collins, CO 80526; 970-226-6114; rmcgavran@aol.com) is one of the older programs in the state. The program has remained small and focuses on its approximately 60 clients each year. The program offers riding for all ages and abilities, focusing mainly on cognitive disabilities and young adults. Front Range offers day and evening classes from April through September. The instructors work on improving the abilities and strength of their riders and discourage "drop-ins" for that reason.

Ft. Collins—Rancho Vista Equine Therapy Center

Rancho Vista (Ann E. Streett-Joslin, 1128 E. CR 58, Ft. Collins, CO 80524; 970-221-5522; www.ranchovista.org; info@ranchovista.org) is a thorough therapeutic program focused on promoting the physical, emotional, cognitive, and social well-being of their riders with disabilities. Located on an 8-acre complex north of Ft. Collins, Rancho Vista provides both an indoor and outdoor arena for year-round opportunity. For normal sessions, riders attend classes 8 to 10 weeks in a row, but, occasionally, Rancho Vista can offer something to visitors with limited time frames.

Longmont—Colorado Therapeutic Riding Center, Inc.

Founded in 1980, the Colorado Therapeutic Riding Center (11968 Mineral Rd., Longmont, CO 80504; 303-652-9131; www.ctrcinc.org; ctrc@ctrcinc.org) is a very busy program located just outside of Denver that runs consecutive 10-week sessions. They focus on therapeutic riding, hippotherapy, and carriage driving. In the summer of 2004, they began offering a 10-week summer camp. Colorado Therapeutic Riding Center caters to more than 500 clients each year, thanks to the help of almost 1,000 volunteers and more than 20 horses. Due to the high demand for space, they only offer riding for enrolled participants and cannot accommodate single-day riders.

Louisville—Rocky Mountain Riding Therapy

Rocky Mountain Riding Therapy (Lauren McClave, P.O. Box 909, Louisville, CO 80027; 303-494-1299; www.rmridingtherapy.org) offers their program year-round in a large outdoor arena they have access to through a lease with the City of Boulder Open Space. This small outfit of eight horses and just a handful of employees has been helping people live with their disabilities and improve their lives since 1993. At $15 per lesson, and with no intention of raising their prices anytime soon, this is a great, inexpensive program that caters to about 150 riders per year. They accept one-time and part-time riders as long as you have all of the necessary medical papers and releases.

Loveland—Hearts & Horses

Hearts & Horses (Peg Stewart, P.O. Box 2675, Loveland, CO 80537; 970-663-4200; www.heartsandhorses.org; info@heartsandhorses.org), located just south of Ft. Collins, offers a smaller, goal-oriented program for a wide range of disabilities. Their well-trained staff, with the help of 250 volunteers, focuses on therapeutic riding to challenge their clients. Outside riders may participate with the proper medical releases in place in advance. Long-term goals include adaptive trips with activities that can include the whole family. They have been running year-round sessions since 1997 and also offer a kids' summer riding camp in July.

Mancos (Durango)—The Medicine Horse Center: Therapeutic Riding and Equine Rehabilitation

Located just west of Durango in southern Colorado surrounded by gorgeous mountains and meadows is the Medicine Horse Center (Lynn Howarth, P.O. Box 1074, Mancos, CO 81328; 970-749-1266; www.medicinehorsecenter.org; howarth@rmi.net). They offer a wide range of programs covering almost any disability or special need. Therapeutic riding and hippotherapy are the focus in dealing with physical, emotional, social, and cognitive issues. They also offer equine-assisted psychotherapy for at-risk kids and abuse or trauma survivors and are consistently involved in outreach programs for children and senior citizens. When the Medicine Horse Center is not helping people, they manage to find time to help horses in need of rehabilitation.

Monument—High Point Academy and Pine Creek Foundation

One of the newer equine centers in the state, the High Point Academy (Julie Christian, P.O. Box 2885, Monument, CO 80132; 303-663-8424; www.pinecreekfoundation.org; pcfinfo@pinecreekfoundation.org) operates year-round with clients attending once a week. Their focus is on therapeutic riding as a means of empowering people to improve their lives. You must enroll for an entire session to attend, as their therapy is in high demand. They have recently joined forces with the Pine Creek Foundation in order to fulfill demands for more availability, more horses, and more space.

The Pine Creek Foundation also provides educational programs for effective communication, health, independent living, leadership, mentoring, nutrition, parenting, wellness, and at-risk-youth guidance. For more information, visit their Web site, listed above.

Palisade (Grand Junction) Desert Edge Therapy, Inc.

Located near Grand Junction on the Western Slope, Desert Edge Therapy, Inc. (Maria Frascati, 538 36 ³/₄ Rd., Palisade, CO 81526; 970-464-5274) is a small program that specializes in hippotherapy, mental health, and physical therapy and offers sessions from eight weeks to six months long. They keep all six of their horses very busy.

Parker (Denver)—Praying Hands Ranch

Located just southeast of Denver in the town of Parker is the Praying Hands Ranch (Shirley A Hanson, 4825 Daley Circle, 303-841-4043; www.prayinghandsranches.org; hansonphr@aol.com), a Christian organization of the United Way. Year-round sessions of eight weeks are typically full at this very busy equine therapy center, which sees about 100 clients per week. With this busy schedule and an ever-growing waiting list, they do not offer one-time or part-time rides, but the eight-week program is one of the best in the state, having earned high accolades from NARHA. This program has grown immensely since its inception in 1987 and now includes two outdoor arenas, a brand-new indoor arena, and large gardens to support their horticulture program.

Pueblo—Therapeutic Riding and Education Center

Therapeutic Riding and Education Center (TREC) (Virginia K. Steckman, 508 E. Idledale Dr., Pueblo, CO 81007; 719-547-8315; www.trectrax.org; steckman@aculink.net) is the first and only program of its kind in Pueblo. They offer weekly sessions on weekdays and gladly accept part-time and single-day riders with the proper doctors' releases and medical forms. Currently, the program accommodates up to 50 riders per week, handling a wide variety of physical and mental disabilities. Participants are in good hands and learn valuable life lessons through physical and occupational therapy, as well as the strengthening of family and community values. They even offer a specialty program for wheelchair users who cannot ride a horse. Make sure to call ahead to make arrangements, as they are busy all year long.

Steamboat Springs—Humble Ranch Education and Therapy Center

Tucked away in the southern hills along the Yampa River near Steamboat Springs is a small ranch aptly named Humble (Cheri Trousil, P.O. Box 776290, Steamboat Springs, CO 80477; 970-879-3443; www.humble therapy.org; cheri@humbleranch.com). Run by the Trousil family, with the help of 40 or so volunteers, Humble Ranch is an education and therapy center that caters to individuals with special needs. The main focus of the ranch is therapeutic horseback riding for locals of three neighboring counties. They are open from June to September.

Established during the summer of 2000, Humble Ranch began with 12 clients and a minimal staff. Founder and certified physical therapist Cheri Trousil began the program with a dream to provide outdoor therapy for individuals with short- or long-term illnesses. Many local Steamboat groups of all ages use the ranch during summer, usually in scheduled, weekly classes. Most of the riding is in the arena, as the trails and nearby meadows are not considered "accessible" (yet!).

Aside from its horses, the working ranch also has an accessible river trail along the Yampa with accessible fishing opportunities in its near future. It also offers accessible gardening with a horticultural therapy program with a shaded plant pavilion and two large raised planting beds.

Humble Ranch is truly a magical place, and if your family isn't set on relocating, don't worry. The Trousils do take out-of-towners too, with several weeks advance notice of course, and will either schedule you or any family members into one of the local groups or offer something on your own. If you're planning on making Steamboat a summer stop, give Cheri a call before you travel.

Telluride—Telluride Adaptive Riding Program

Telluride Adaptive Riding Program (TARP) (Candida Von Braun, P.O. Box 2254, Telluride, CO 81435; 970-728-7537; www.tellurideadaptive sports.org) is a partner of the Telluride Adaptive Sports Program and offers riding to all abilities, on a private or group basis, in one of the most beautiful parts of the state. Therapeutic riding and hippotherapy are the specialties for this new but fast-growing summer program. TARP mostly offers clinics to locals, but part-timers are welcome, with the proper medical forms, and most disabilities can be accommodated. The arena is actually located about 40 miles north of Telluride in the town of Ridgway, with incredible views of the mountains. This is truly a healing place.

Hunting

As part of the continuing effort by state and federal governments to create equal opportunities in outdoor recreation for people with disabilities, the **Colorado Division of Wildlife** (DOW) (6060 Broadway, Denver, Colorado 80216; 303-297-1192; www.wildlife.state.co.us) has created several programs to improve accessibility. The Web site listed here is literally a wealth of knowledge on hunting and other outdoor activities, including a list of shooting ranges in the state of Colorado and an entire section on accessibility. You can also subscribe to *Colorado Outdoors* magazine, a comprehensive hunting, fishing, and wildlife publication put out by the DOW.

We are not hunters, but were very impressed with the efforts put forth by the DOW to ensure equal access for hunters with disabilities. When visiting the Web site, be sure to check out the Mobility Impaired Big Game Program, the Disabled Veterans Lifetime Combination Small Game Hunting and Fishing License, and free Wildlife Recreation Permits.

Courtesy of Lisa Stern

CHAPTER 6

NATIONAL AND STATE PARKS

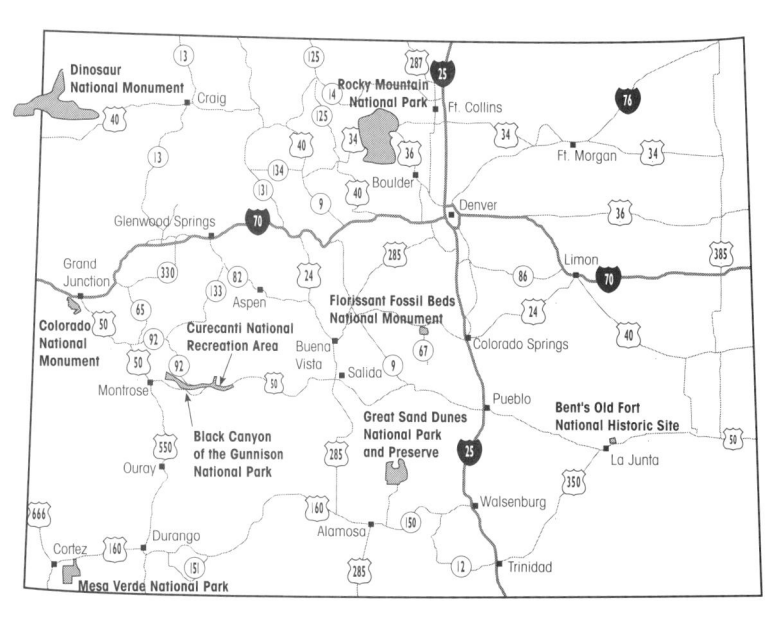

© Fulcrum Publishing

Colorado State Parks • 1313 Sherman Street, Room 618
Denver, Colorado 80203 • (303) 866-3437

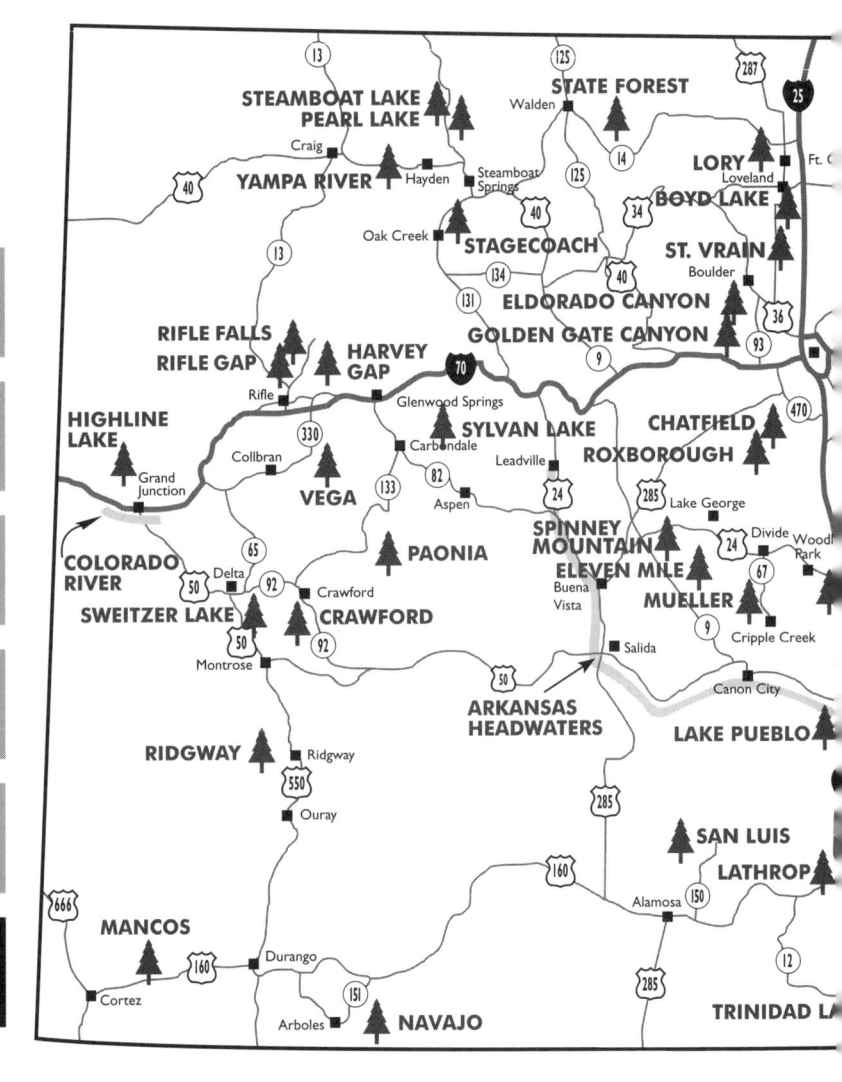

Colorado State Parks

State Parks Map

- Getting Started
- Metro Areas
- Small Towns
- Winter
- Summer
- Parks

STEAMBOAT LAKE
PEARL LAKE
Walden
STATE FOREST
Craig
YAMPA RIVER Hayden Steamboat Springs
LORY Loveland Ft. C
BOYD LAKE
Oak Creek
STAGECOACH
ST. VRAIN Boulder
ELDORADO CANYON
RIFLE FALLS
RIFLE GAP
HARVEY GAP
GOLDEN GATE CANYON
Rifle Glenwood Springs
HIGHLINE LAKE
Collbran
SYLVAN LAKE Carbondale
CHATFIELD
ROXBOROUGH
Leadville
Grand Junction
VEGA
Aspen
Lake George
SPINNEY MOUNTAIN
Divide Wood Park
COLORADO RIVER
Delta
PAONIA
ELEVEN MILE
SWEITZER LAKE
Crawford
CRAWFORD
Buena Vista
MUELLER
Cripple Creek
Montrose
Salida
Canon City
ARKANSAS HEADWATERS
LAKE PUEBLO
RIDGWAY Ridgway
Ouray
SAN LUIS
LATHROP
Alamosa
MANCOS
Durango
Cortez
Arboles
NAVAJO
TRINIDAD L

148

Camping Reservations: www.parks.state.co.us
(303) 470-1144 (Denver Metro Area) or 1-800-678-2267

State Parks Map

Getting Started

Metro Areas

Small Towns

Winter

Summer

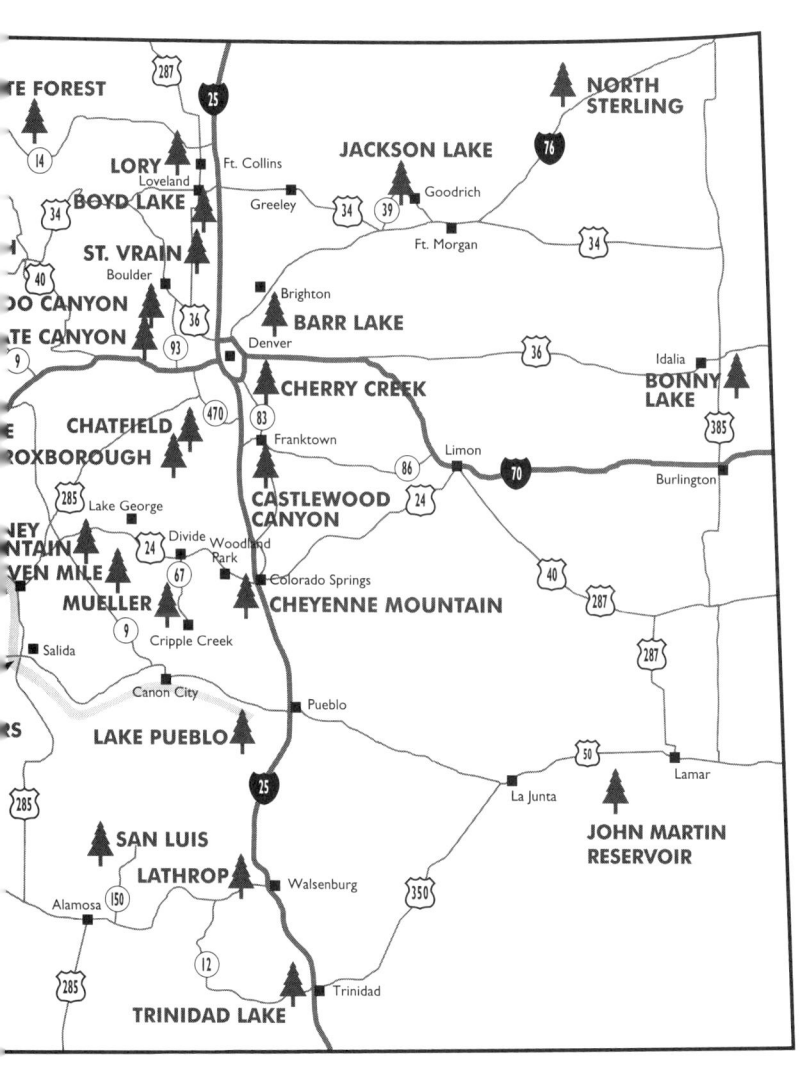

Parks

149

Courtesy of Colorado State Parks

The federal and state government–maintained parks and wilderness or water access areas are mostly accessible and have been complying with the Americans with Disabilities Act (ADA) for more than a decade now. We have found the most dependable accessibility in the visitors centers, informational buildings, public restrooms, and parking.

Passes

The federal and state governments offer several discounted and free passes to people with disabilities. The Golden Access pass is available at no cost to permanently disabled persons and is valid for life. It is easily obtained at any national park or monument.

The state parks also offer a discounted pass for residents with disabilities. It costs less than $15 and can only be obtained at one of the four regional offices. The main state park Web site (www.parks.state.co.us) or the number listed below can offer more information.

Unfortunately, so far out-of-state visitors do have to pay the full $50 for a season pass to the state parks. For more information, contact the **Denver Metro Office** (13787 U.S. Hwy. 85 south, Littleton, CO 80125; 303-791-1957).

Trails

Many of the trails in the parks are accessible for the adventurer, some with magnificent views but easy climbs, some for berry picking through woodlands, and some that have access to fishing streams. If it is at all feasible to do without disrupting the natural surroundings, most of the parks have made the effort to accommodate those with disability. Although some trails are not marked accessible, many of these are doable if you have company to assist you. Keep in mind that you may not be able to see everything, but you should be able to see most of the attractions with little or no assistance. We found most of the parks in the state to be very accommodating.

Fishing and Hunting

The **Colorado Division of Wildlife** (DOW) is also a great resource for travelers with disabilities. Their Web site (www.wildlife.state.co.us/fishing/mobility.asp) provides information on fishing, hunting, and wildlife-viewing areas around the state, which are all expanding each year.

NATIONAL PARKS, MONUMENTS, HISTORIC SITES, AND RECREATION AREAS

For additional information on all of Colorado's national parks, monuments, historic sites, and recreation areas, visit the National Park Service's main Web site, www.nps.gov, or the Colorado-specific link, http://data2.itc.nps.gov/parksearch/state.cfm?st=co.

Bent's Old Fort National Historical Site

There is about a .25-mile paved walk, or roll, to the gate of the fort, the first floor of which is accessible, which is where the accessible restrooms are located. If you are not able to walk or roll this distance, there is a shuttle service available, but it does not have a lift for wheelchairs. The documentary film shown here gives a good, quick history of the fort. Tours and demonstrations are scheduled throughout the day during the summer (June 1 through Labor Day) and twice a day during the off-season. You can also take a self-guided tour. Bent's Old Fort is an incredible journey into the pioneer days of America and should be a stop on your next visit to Colorado.

Groups are welcome with advanced booking, and special events are planned for the summer months as well. Call the park or visit their Web site for more information and reservations.

Directions
Located just northeast of La Junta, Bent's Fort can be accessed by U.S. Hwy. 50, which parallels the railroad tracks through La Junta. Coming from the east or west, head north on CO Hwy. 109, crossing the tracks and the river. Shortly after the river, take a right (east) on CO Hwy. 194, following that for about 6 miles.

Contact Information
Bent's Old Fort National Historic Site
35110 CO Hwy. 194 east
La Junta, CO 81050
Phone: 719-383-5010
TDD: 719-383-5032

Black Canyon of the Gunnison National Park

Only 20 miles from the town of Gunnison is one of the most spectacular sites in all of Colorado. The Black Canyon was formed throughout millions of years, and with 48 miles of sheer rock walls along the Gunnison River, it is the second largest of its kind in the United States. The river drops an average of 96 feet per mile here, and it drops an amazing 480 feet in one 2-mile section, making this one of the most unique canyons in all of North America. The park contains about 14 of the 48 total miles of the canyon.

The **South Rim** has the best accessibility, so make sure to stop in at the visitors center here first and ask for the accessibility information that is not included in the regular brochure. They also show a fascinating historical video and have some incredible exhibits on display.

The South Rim offers three accessible overlooks and is open year-round, with limited access during the winter. Depending on your mobility, several of the overlooks that are not marked accessible are certainly doable. We found **Tomichi**, **Pulpit Rock**, **Chasm**, and **Sunset** to be the most wheelchair friendly. We also ventured out to the Painted Rock Overlook, and, although it is sloped downward and rocky in spots, we had no problem getting to the railing. The 2,000-foot "painted wall" is worth the effort, but we recommend a strong helper and knobby tires for the return trip up to the road. The final overlook on the South Rim is at **High Point**. This is a great spot to stop and have a picnic or just relax, as it offers the only shade of all the overlooks. The picnic sites are not ADA–compliant, but a few are very doable.

Two of the 90 sites in the **South Rim Campground** are ADA–compliant, but all are doable. This campground offers accessible restrooms and is open only during the summer.

The **North Rim** of the park is much less traveled and not nearly as accessible. It is, however, worth the drive if you are coming from or heading in that direction. This drive takes about two to three hours and is closed during the winter. The only truly accessible overlook is at **Balanced Rock**. There is also an accessible ranger station on the North Rim.

The **East Portal Rd.**, also closed in winter, provides a very scenic drive on steep, winding roads. This road is a main access route into **Curecanti National Recreation Area** for fishing and eventually leads to the town of Cimarron. There is no accessible fishing in the park.

If you would rather not camp or happen to be in the park during the off-season, lodging options are available in the nearby towns of **Montrose** (www.montrosechamber.com), **Delta** (www.deltacolorado.org), **Cimarron** (www.ccccok.org), and **Crawford** (www.crawfordcountry.org). Visit their Web sites for lodging, dining, and other accessible accommodations. As always, it is a good idea to call your accommodations ahead of time to find out pertinent accessibility information related to your disability needs.

We can't believe how beautiful this park is. It may be our favorite.

Directions

There are two points of interest at Black Canyon of the Gunnison National Park: the North Rim and the South Rim. Rim Drive North follows the North Rim along a narrow and winding section that, for obvious reasons, is closed during winter months. From Crawford, take CO Hwy. 92 11 miles south and turn right (west) on Rim Drive North. The South Rim can be accessed from Montrose by taking U.S. Hwy. 50 (southeast) for about 7 miles to CO Hwy. 347 (left, or northeast), which dead-ends at the park's Rim Drive South.

Contact Information

Black Canyon of the Gunnison National Park
102 Elk Creek
Gunnison, CO 81230
Phone: 970-641-2337, ext. 205

Colorado National Monument

One of the oldest and largest included in the national parks system in Colorado, this national monument is also one of the most interesting and diverse areas in the state. Deep canyons and huge monoliths populate some 20,000 acres of arid land between Glenwood Springs and Grand Junction on the Western Slope. The views alone are worth the drive, and you are likely to see, as we did, mule deer, golden eagles, and bighorn sheep.

The visitors center is accessible, so stop here and grab a map. There is also a video to watch on the history of the monument and surrounding area. There are more than a dozen scenic overlooks within the park, three of which, **Cold Shivers Park, Independence Monument**, and **Red Canyon**, are designated as accessible. The rest are easily doable, they just lack curb cuts.

The **Devil's Kitchen** picnic area is located on the east side of the park and is fully accessible with accessible restrooms.

There is only one accessible site in the campground, which is available on a first-come, first-serve basis only. As with most parks and monuments, the rest of the campsites are not ADA compliant, but several of the sites are doable with little or no assistance. Mountain-bike tires did come in handy here, as the terrain is a little rough.

Directions

The monument is just south of Fruita, a town about 10 miles north of Grand Junction. From either town you can take CO Hwy. 340 (north from Grand Junction or south from Fruita) off of either I-70 or U.S. Hwy. 6. CO Hwy. 340 is on the west side of the Gunnison River, so make a note to cross the river. Look for Rim Rock Rd., which is about 2 miles south of Fruita, or about 10 miles north of Grand Junction. There are signs for the monument at the intersection as well. The monument is only about 2 miles up Rim Rock Rd., a very winding, switchbacking road that climbs 1,200 feet in just 2 miles.

For a four-wheel-drive, scenic, alternate route from Grand Junction, Rim Rock Rd. is a western loop off of CO Hwy. 340. This will add hours to your trip, so if you're short on time, stay on CO Hwy. 340.

Contact Information

Colorado National Monument
Fruita, CO 81521
Phone: 970-858-3617

Curecanti National Recreation Area

If you love the outdoors, and especially water sports and recreation, Curecanti is an incredible place to play. This national recreation area consists of three large reservoirs on the Gunnison River: **Blue Mesa Reservoir**, which is the largest body of water in Colorado; **Morrow Point Reservoir**, at the mouth of the Black Canyon; and **Crystal Reservoir**, at the site of the Gunnison Diversion Tunnel.

The visitors centers and campsites at **Elk Creek**, **Lake Fork**, and **Cimarron** are all accessible, complete with accessible restrooms. There are additional accessible campsites at **Steven's Creek**. Reservations are not accepted for camping.

The best views are the overlooks at **Dillon**, **Pinnacles**, and **Herman's Rest**, all of which are wheelchair friendly.

Currently, there are no accessible hiking trails or fishing within the park, so the best part of the trip for us was the fact that this park is right next to the Black Canyon of the Gunnison. Two national parks in one day was a real treat!

Directions

If you do plan to do the two parks in one day, allow more time for Black Canyon and head there first. From there, you can either take CO Hwy. 92 from the North Rim of the Black Canyon and Gunnison River or take U.S. Hwy. 50 from the South Rim. Both roads intersect at the mouth of the Blue Mesa Reservoir, the widest part of the Gunnison River. U.S. Hwy. 50 then runs along the northeast end of the recreation area, and the park's headquarters is about 10 miles past the intersection of CO Hwy. 92.

Contact Information

Curecanti National Recreation Area
102 Elk Creek Rd.
Gunnison, CO 81230
Phone: 970-641-2337, ext. 205

Dinosaur National Monument

Mostly within Colorado limits, bordering both Utah and Wyoming at the intersection of the Yampa and Green Rivers, Dinosaur National Monument is huge, and spending several days here is highly recommended. The online map (http://data2.itc.nps.gov/parks/dino/pp Maps/DINOmap1%2Epdf) will give you a great idea of how widely spread out this park is.

Dinosaur's main and most popular attraction is its **Fossil Bone Quarry**. The quarry is also a gift shop as well as a two-story dinosaur exhibit, built up against a rock wall that still encases prehistoric dinosaur bones. This is the only place in the park to view dinosaur bones, and it should be your first stop. Accessible parking is adjacent to the building; the rest of the public is shuttled from a lower parking lot, due to the high numbers of visitors. The exhibits at the quarry are an intriguing glimpse into the very distant past of the Green River, when it swept the extinct species into its waters to be fossilized forever. Accessible restrooms are upstairs and can be reached by using an elevator; ask the rangers if you need assistance. This place is great for kids.

Flight-seeing is an excellent way to view the vastness of Dinosaur National Monument and the Green River.

The **headquarters** and **visitors center** is fully accessible, including the restrooms, and both the **Crook** and **Swinging Bridge Campgrounds** also are accessible. Crook has both restrooms and grills for wheelchair users. There is an accessible fishing pier located between **Spitzie** and **Hog Lakes**, and an accessible blind for hunting waterfowl is available upon request.

The rest of the 211,000 acres of this beautiful park includes scenic drives and overlooks, including the petroglyph (ancient rock drawings) tour, fishing, rafting, flight-seeing, and camping. **Green River Campground** (a few miles past the quarry, located on the southern side of the park) is the most accessible because of its accessible tent site and adjacent restroom, but we camped in **Echo Park** for its beautiful views and remote location on the Green River at Steamboat Rock. This campground is not labeled accessible, due to its restrooms, but every campsite is doable. This was a wonderful spot for a night under the stars and well worth the long, scenic four-wheel drive to get there.

Top on our list of recommendations is flight-seeing at any opportunity. This is the most economical flying tour we've found. It costs less than $60 per person for the maximum length and offers the most spectacular views of this narrow canyon. This is really the only way to see much of the north part of the canyon, including the many waterfalls just south of Ledore. **Dinaland Aviation** (888-789-4614) leads these private trips out of Vernal, Utah, and flies as far as Browns Park in incremental-fee brackets starting as low as $30 per person. Dinaland needs one-day advance notice and reservations for two to five people. They are slightly flexible in take-off times, but, due to afternoon winds, they usually leave around 9 A.M.

The north side of the park is the **Browns Park National Wildlife Refuge** and offers amazing northern views of the Green River, the Gates of Ledore canyons, and the obvious abundance of wildlife. There are campsites on this side of the park, but no designated accessible ones, and it's a long drive for only a few sights.

Directions

There are many entrances into the park, but the three main entrances are found as follows: The north and easternmost side of the park is accessed from Maybell, Colorado, nearly two hours west from Steamboat Springs on U.S. Hwy. 40. From Maybell, go northwest on CO Hwy. 318 for 42 miles to the Gates of Ledore. Then turn left at the north entrance of the park. It's another 10 miles from there to the end.

The **headquarters and visitor center** is located about 65 miles west past Maybell, 42 miles west of Elk Springs (another not-recommended entrance), or 2 miles east of the town of Dinosaur. This is also the auto-tour road, or **Harpers Corner Dr.**, which is actually 25 miles to the park and then 10 more miles of overlooks into the canyon. The Echo Park road forks off of Harpers Corner, just before the park boundary, and it's a winding, four-wheel-drive road down to the **Echo Park Campground**, **Sand Canyon**, and the famous **Steamboat Rock**, which is at the confluence of the Green and Yampa Rivers.

The quarry is located 25 miles past the visitors center. Take U.S. Hwy. 40 to Jensen, Utah, and turn right (north) onto CO Hwy. 149. Go 7 miles north to the park entrance and the quarry. Only drivers with disabilities are allowed to drive up to the quarry (other drivers park at the lot below and take a bus). This road continues only 10 miles farther into the park to the **Split Mountain**, **Green River**, and **Josie's Cabin** sites. This is where the petroglyphs (rock paintings) are located and is a must-see.

Contact Information

Dinosaur National Monument
4545 U.S. Hwy. 40 east
Dinosaur, CO 81610
Phone: 435-781-7700

Dinosaur National Monument Headquarters
Phone: 970-374-3000

Fossil Bone Quarry
11625 E. 1500 S
Jensen, UT 84035

Florissant Fossil Beds National Monument

When scientists need answers about prehistoric life in Colorado, they look to the extraordinary and unique fossil beds at Florissant. More than 30 million years of history can be found here in the fossils and petrified redwoods that are littered about the monument. Bird-watching, hiking, and wildlife viewing are among the popular activities inside the park, which is open year-round. Hours vary depending on time of year.

The visitors center is fully accessible with exhibits and restrooms. Check out the huge pieces of petrified redwoods and pick up general information about the park before heading in.

The only trails that are wheelchair friendly are at the **Hornbek Homestead**. These trails are accessible to ADA's Challenge Level I (a supplement of the ADA), which means it takes a little extra muscle to complete the hike. We had no problem navigating these trails and enjoyed the workout.

You can also take advantage of walks to see wildflowers and the petrified forest, depending on your disability and level of mobility. Neither camping nor fishing is available at the monument. Florissant is just a short drive from Denver and the Pikes Peak area, making this an ideal and educational day trip.

Directions

The closest major town to Florissant is Colorado Springs. Take U.S. Hwy 24 for 35 miles west of I-25 through the town of Woodland Park. The town of Florissant is small enough to miss, so mark your odometer and look for signs to the monument visitors center. From this direction, turn left on Cripple Creek Florissant Rd. in the town of Florissant, and the monument will be about 2 miles south of town.

Contact Information

Florissant Fossil Beds National Monument
P.O. Box 185
15807 Teller CR 1
Florissant, CO 80816-0185

Florissant Fossil Beds National Monument Headquarters
Phone: 719-748-3253

Great Sand Dunes National Park and Preserve

Located only 80 miles south of Salida, Colorado, is one of the most beautiful national preserves in the United States and, perhaps, the world. Towering more than 750 feet in the air, these sand dunes are home to diverse wildlife and plant species alike, as well as a large population of insects found nowhere else on the planet.

The visitors center is the first place you should stop. Here you can learn about the national park and the preserve, watch a short video, and take advantage of the accessible restrooms before heading into the park.

If you are in a wheelchair, you will want to ask about borrowing one of two sand wheelchairs for navigation on the dunes. The dunes parking lot, .5 mile north of the visitors center, is the closest access to the dunes, with accessible parking right next to the access trail. While loose sand and the creek will definitely impede your progress if you are a traditional wheelchair user, the sand chair navigates these barriers fairly well. Make sure you have a helper, because you can't push yourself in the sand chair.

A view from the entrance to the recently designated Great Sand Dunes Park and Preserve.

There are two options if you plan to spend the night in the park. **Piñon Flats** has several accessible sites, and although they advertise these to be on a first-come, first-serve basis, you can call ahead and they will hold an accessible site for you until 6 P.M. Hard-packed trails, accessible restrooms, and picnic areas make this a very convenient choice. The **Sawmill Canyon Backcountry Campground** (719-378-6399), located less than 1 mile from the park, also has accessible sites with raised tent platforms, restrooms, and picnic facilities.

Wildlife sightings of elk, mule deer, coyotes, golden and bald eagles, and more are common. We saw all of these animals, as well as some bison, just outside the park. We also took tons of pictures and found that the best shots came as the sun was setting and the shadows started to creep over the dunes.

The soft, wind-swept dunes as seen from the main park road.

Summer activities include kite-flying contests, photography workshops, and concerts. The **Friends of the Dunes** (www.greatsanddunes.org) are in charge of all activities. Call the visitors center for a schedule of events.

Directions

Great Sand Dunes is equal distance between U.S. Hwy. 285 and I-25, between the Rio Grande and San Isabel National Forests. Connecting these two major highways is U.S. Hwy. 160, to the south of the park. From U.S. Hwy. 160, take CO Hwy. 150 north, about 15 miles east of Alamosa. CO Hwy. 150 dead-ends at the park, about 20 miles up from the U.S. Hwy. 160 intersection. This is flatland area, so it's hard to get lost when the road stretches out for miles in front of you.

Contact Information

Great Sand Dunes National Park and Preserve
11999 CO Hwy. 150
Mosca, CO 81146
Phone: 719-378-6399

Mesa Verde National Park

Your first stop inside the park should be the **Far View Visitors Center**, open from June to October. If you are visiting outside of the peak season, the museum at the top of the **Chapin Mesa** serves as the visitors center and is a must-see. The displays are incredible, and the center shows a short, historical video about the park and its ancient inhabitants.

There are two main "finger" mesas to visit once inside the park. Chapin Mesa is the easiest for people with disabilities to get around and is open year-round to visitors. Paved, accessible walkways make it easy to see more than a dozen mesa and cliff dwellings along the **Mesa Top Loop Rd.**, and accessible restrooms are available throughout the park. We recommend this loop. It will take most of the day to see.

The **Wetherill Mesa**, open only during the summer, has only one accessible overlook. The **Badger House Community Overlook** is at the end of a .75-mile paved trail and is worth the hike. Accessible restrooms and parking are available.

Camping within the park is accessible with minimal assistance. The best sites, complete with accessible restrooms and paved walks or hard-packed gravel trails, are at the **Morefield Campground**. There are also marked accessible sites on the **Navajo Loop**. This campground is the largest in the park, but we still recommend calling in advance to hold a spot.

The nation's largest archaeological preserve, originally home to thousands of people, is an incredible journey into the past and into the lives of our country's native heritage. The views alone were worth the trip for us, but rolling between the ancient dwellings and imagining what the people and the lives they led were actually like was an experience that we will never forget.

The Anasazi's ancient home structures in Mesa Verde National Park.

Directions

Mesa Verde is one of the easier parks to find, located between the towns of Cortez and Mancos in the far southwest corner of the state. Out of both of these two towns runs U.S. Hwy. 160, from which you will see signs for the park directing you to head south on Mesa Verde Loop. The park headquarters are about 4.5 miles in.

Contact Information

Mesa Verde National Park
P.O. Box 8
Mesa Verde, CO 81330
Phone: 970-529-4465

Rocky Mountain National Park

Rocky Mountain National Park boasts more than 60 peaks that are more than 12,000 feet tall, providing visitors with unbelievable, jaw-dropping scenery. Trail Ridge Rd., which cuts through the heart of the park and is open from Memorial Day through late fall, is at more than 12,000 feet in elevation and is the highest paved road in the country. This park is huge and has many accessible options and activities for people with disabilities, so plan a couple of days to really explore here.

Don't forget your camera and plenty of extra film, because you may never have a chance to take pictures like this again!

There are five visitors centers inside the park. All provide information on the park and the surrounding area. Be sure to ask for the detailed accessibility brochure at any of these locations. This will make your day much easier to plan. You can also call ahead (970-586-1206) to have a copy of the brochure mailed to you. All of the visitors centers have accessible restrooms.

Topping out at 12,183 ft., Trail Ridge Rd. is the higest road in the United States and is only open during the summer.
Courtesy of Christopher Jehn

The **Alpine Visitors Center** is located at the junction of Trail Ridge and Old Fall River Roads and is closed during winter. This is mostly an informational stop, with ranger programs and alpine tundra exhibits.

Beaver Meadow Visitors Center is located on U.S. Hwy. 36, 3 miles from the town of Estes Park, at the park entrance. It is open year-round from 8 A.M. to 5 P.M. There is a huge topographical map of the entire park on the upper level, which is considered moderately accessible. There is also a small bookstore here. An introductory park film is shown in the auditorium on the lower lever, which is considered marginally accessible. Access to the lower level is through the back of the building via a fairly steep ramp that may require some assistance.

The **Fall River Visitors Center** is located on U.S. Hwy. 34, 5 miles west of the town of Estes Park, at the **Fall River Entrance** to the park. It is open year-round, with weekend hours only after November 2 and special holiday hours. An elevator connects the upper and lower levels, and there are amazing, lifelike wildlife displays along with an educational children's room. The restaurant and gift shops are right next door.

One mile north of the town of Grand Lake on U.S. Hwy. 34 at the entrance to the park is the **Kawuneeche Visitors Center**. It is open year-round, with daily hours from 8 A.M. to 4:30 P.M. They offer maps and displays similar to the center at Beaver Meadows. This is also where people venturing into the backcountry will want to check in.

Lily Lake has a visitors center on CO Hwy. 7, 6 miles south of the town of Estes Park, which is open only during summer months. Accessible parking is in the upper lot at the side of the visitors center. You will also find ranger programs and an information desk here. There is a great nature trail that wraps around the lake that is very wheelchair friendly.

There are five campgrounds to choose from when planning your stay in the park. **Glacier Basin**, **Moraine Park**, and **Timber Creek** are the most accessible. All three have accessible restrooms, picnic tables, and fire rings. **Aspenglen** and **Longs Peak Campgrounds** do not offer accessible sites. Some backcountry sites are also accessible at **Sprague Lake Camp**. None of the campgrounds offer showers, electricity hookups, or sewer facilities. Reservations can be made only for Glacier Basin and Moraine Park campgrounds.

Glacier Basin is open through the summer, starting around May 25, and is located off of the Bear Lake Rd., 7 miles west of the Beaver Meadows Visitor Center. This is a gorgeous campground, with four ADA–compliant sites and a moderately accessible amphitheater. Group sites are also available.

Moraine Park is open year-round and is located off of the Bear Lake Rd., 2.5 miles from the Beaver Meadows Visitor Center. The campground offers four ADA–compliant sites for individual and family camping. We thought the views here were the best. Our campsite overlooked all of Moraine Park. Reservations are accepted from May 20 through September 30 and, again, are strongly recommended.

Timber Creek is also open year-round and is located just south of the Colorado River Trailhead on the west side of the park. The four ADA–compliant sites here are offered on a first-come, first-serve basis only. The amphitheater is only marginally accessible, as it is accessed via a steep ramp.

Sprague Lake Camp is the only backcountry campground that is accessible. A paved trail starting at the Sprague Lake parking area leads to a 12-person camping area complete with picnic tables, fire pit, and grill. You absolutely must make reservations for this area and you must obtain a backcountry permit. Permits are available at park headquarters as well as the Beaver Meadows and Kawuneeche Visitors Centers. You will also find a .5-mile hard-packed gravel trail encircling the lake, which has several accessible fishing platforms.

There are many overlooks and trailheads located along Trail Ridge Rd., several of which are accessible. Many of these accessible overlooks do not have accessible parking spaces, but you should have plenty of room to load and unload from your vehicle.

As you are traveling from east to west through the park, the first stop to check out is the **Beaver Boardwalk**. There aren't any accessible parking spaces here, but a moderately steep ramp allows access to a wooden boardwalk that takes a quick trip through a deserted beaver village. **Bear Lake**, at the end of the Bear Lake road, has a .5-mile moderately accessible trail that is worth checking out. The **Hidden Valley Snowplay and Picnic Area** is the next stop. Brand-new, accessible restrooms and parking and picnic facilities are available here. **Many Parks Curve Overlook** has two parking areas and provides great views of Longs Peak and the Estes Valley. The trail that connects the two lots is moderately accessible. **Rainbow Curve Overlook** has a curb cut and paved sidewalk to the viewpoint overlooking the **Mummy Range** and **Horseshoe Park**, and it is definitely jaw-dropping scenery. There is also an accessible restroom here. **Forest Canyon Overlook** does have accessible parking spaces. The paved trail from the parking lot to the overlook is considered marginally accessible, as it has a couple of steep inclines and is somewhat uneven. Adventurous wheelers shouldn't have any problem, while others may want to bring a helper. **Rock Cut and Tundra Nature Trail** is a good spot to stop for accessible restrooms, but the paved trail here is pretty hairy, as it is very uneven and very steep; I was glad to have my partner with me. The parking lot at **Milner Pass** provides accessible restrooms and accessible parking and offers a great look at the Continental Divide and Poudre Lake. **Lake Irene** also has accessible restrooms and parking. The picnic area here is doable if you're not in a power chair, and the trail to the lake is not accessible. The **Colorado River Trailhead** has accessible restrooms, but the trail to the river is not very accessible, although we made it down to the river and back with some extra effort. The fishing access along the river is doable, but not great. A strong helper is necessary for both. **Timber Lake Trailhead** offers accessible restrooms, but the trail is not accessible. **Bowen-Baker Gulch Trailhead** also has accessible restrooms. We found the gravel road leading into the national forest to be very strenuous for wheelchair users and don't recommend it. **Coyote Valley Trailhead** provides accessible parking, restrooms, and picnic tables. The moderately accessible, 1-mile-long trail from the parking lot crosses the Colorado River and was a great workout for both of us. **Green Mountain, North Inlet, and East Inlet Trailheads** all have accessible restrooms, but the trails are not accessible.

For an accessible, historical look at the park, you can visit the **Moraine Park Museum**, which is located just 1.5 miles from the Beaver Meadows Entrance on the Bear Lake Rd. This museum is only open in summer months, but it offers full facilities for people with disabilities, including restrooms, a bookstore, and a .5-mile nature trail. The first and second floors are connected by a wheelchair lift.

Accessible restrooms are on the first floor, as are an information desk, bookstore, and art gallery. Historical exhibits are on the second floor.

You can also check out the **Holzwarth Historic Site**, which is on U.S. Hwy. 34, about 7 miles north of the **Grand Lake Entrance Station** on the **Never Summer Ranch**. Access to the historic lodge and nearby buildings is via a rough, .5-mile trail that is considered moderately accessible, but the buildings themselves are not accessible. Guided tours are offered during summer months while the site is open.

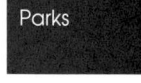

Camping at Rocky Mountain National Park.

It is common to see elk, mule deer, moose, bighorn sheep, black bears, coyotes, cougars, eagles, hawks, and much more along the way. In fact, we were held up for more than an hour, thanks to a herd of bighorn sheep that decided to make themselves comfortable in the middle of the road. Obviously, the animals in the park have the right-of-way, so make sure to allow the entire day to enjoy this drive.

For planning your trip around the scenery, the wildflowers are at their peak of color between mid-June and early July and light up the hillsides with their splendor. The fall colors brighten in mid-September, and the highlight at this time is the famous elk-mating rituals and bugling.

If you are planning to camp, you will want to make your arrangements well in advance, as this is a very popular camping destination. Fully accessible sites are available with accessible restrooms. If you aren't planning to spend the night, you can end your day in **Estes Park** (www.estesparkresort.com), on the east side of the park, or **Grand Lake** (www.grandlakechamber.com), on the west side of the park.

Directions

Without a doubt the largest park in the state, Rocky Mountain has three entrances: one from the west, at Grand Lake, and two from the east, past Estes Park. U.S. Hwys. 36 and 34 parallel each other out of Estes Park, so don't let these two entrances fool you; they intersect again when the road starts to climb into the steeper terrain. U.S. Hwy. 34, otherwise known as Trail Ridge Rd., runs the length of the park, offering the most amazing stretch of scenery your eyes will ever see.

Contact Information

Rocky Mountain National Park
1000 U.S. Hwy. 36
Estes Park, CO 80517
Phone: 970-586-1206
TDD: 970-586-1319
Campground Reservations: 800-365-2267

Estes Park Convention and Visitors Bureau
Web site: www.estesparkcvb.com

STATE PARKS

General Colorado State Parks Contact Information

Colorado State Parks General Information: 303-866-3437
Colorado State Parks Central Reservation Office
Denver area: 303-470-1144
Toll-free: 800-678-2267
For additional information on all of Colorado's state parks, visit the Colorado state parks Web site, www.parks.state.co.us.

Arkansas Headwaters State Park

Stretching nearly 150 miles along the scenic Arkansas River, this recreation area is one of the most beautiful in the country. The U.S. Bureau of Land Management and Colorado State Parks combined efforts to create and maintain this incredible area. Thanks to this partnership, visitors from around the world enjoy all kinds of summertime activities, such as fishing, world-class rafting, kayaking, picnicking, hiking, camping, mountain biking, and sightseeing. Wintertime also offers several activity options, including skiing, snowshoeing, snowmobiling, and camping (for the hearty traveler).

A view from the shore of the Arkansas River.
Courtesy of Jack Lenzo

Camping, boating, and snowmobiling registration can be done very easily online and should be done in advance. The park neighbors seven Colorado towns (Leadville, Buena Vista, Poncha Springs, Salida, Cañon City, Florence, and Pueblo), providing guests every opportunity to dine, shop, and play. Lodging accommodations are available in these towns as well. Visit the following links to find out more about each town: www.2chambers.com/pueblo.htm, www.2chambers.com/ canon_city,_colorado.htm and www.2chambers.com/ salida,_ colorado.htm, and www.2chambers.com/leadville,_colorado.htm.

We really liked that there is a fully accessible restroom facility at each of the five developed campgrounds. Each campground also has at least one fully accessible campsite. With the number of sites obviously limited and the summer months attracting more than 200,000 visitors per year, it is important to plan ahead and reserve a site well in advance.

Unfortunately, the trails within the park are forest service trails, so they are not paved surfaces and can be difficult for wheelchair access. Any fishing you are planning to do will have to be from the shore. For up-to-date fishing information and conditions, visit www.arkanglers.com or contact the DOW for their fishing report at www.wildlife.state.co.us/dowfish.

Directions

Depending on what part of this enormous park you choose to visit and what direction you're driving from, it's best to look at the map provided on the state parks' Web site above. For most of the northern section of the park, access is via U.S. Hwy 24. South of Buena Vista, access is via U.S. Hwy. 285. From Poncha Springs, access is via U.S. Hwy. 50.

Contact Information

Arkansas Headwaters State Park
307 W. Sackett
Salida, CO 81201
Phone: 719-539-7289
E-mail: ahra@state.co.us

Barr Lake State Park

Just a few miles northeast of Denver is a special treat for wildlife enthusiasts: Barr Lake State Park. Home to the **Rocky Mountain Bird Observatory**, this park features some 300 species of birds, including a family of bald eagles and blue herons. With its convenient proximity to the capital and half of the park designated as a protected wildlife refuge, it is a perfect place for a day of fishing, bird-watching, or just appreciating nature. Boats are permitted on the lake, but motors must be 10 horsepower or less. The fact that Barr Lake is day-use only and offers no camping facilities has helped to preserve the beauty of the area. For reservations and fee schedules, call the number listed below or visit the state park Web site. Always remember to ask if there are any discounts for people with disabilities.

The gazebo boardwalk is accessed only by a hiking trail that is also used for bicycles and horses. The **Eagle Express** can take visitors to the boardwalk, but you will need assistance into the shuttle (there is no lift). Accessible restrooms are available in the park.

We loved how peaceful and relaxing this little park was. The lack of loud motors and mobs of people was a nice change, even from our quiet haven in Steamboat. On a clear day the view of the mountains is spectacular.

Directions

From Denver, take I-76 along the east side of Barr Lake and exit at the north end at Bromley Ln. Less than .5 mile to the east, turn right on Picadilly Rd. The park entrance is in about 1.5 miles.

Contact Information

Barr Lake State Park
13401 Picadilly Rd.
Brighton, CO 80603
Phone: 303-659-6005
E-mail: barr.lake@state.co.us

Bonny Lake State Park

After miles and miles of driving through endless prairie, Bonny Lake is an astonishing and welcoming site. Spanning some 1,900 surface acres, this state park is, obviously, best known for its water recreation opportunities. The fishing here is fantastic, thanks to year-round warm water temperatures. Windsurfing and waterskiing are permitted and popular here, thanks to dependable winds and those same warm waters, with camping, hunting, and hiking also helping to attract the thousands of visitors that the park sees each year. Conditions permitting, ice fishing is a great wintertime option.

Three of the campgrounds here have one fully accessible site each, and the **Wagon Wheel Campground** also has coin-operated accessible showers. There are not accessible trails, so on-the-water activities are your best bet. For reservations and fee schedules, call the number listed below or visit the Web site. Always remember to ask if there are any discounts for people with disabilities.

If you are planning to do any fishing, you'll want to fish from a boat. While there is plenty of shore to fish from, there aren't any accessible platforms available. You can, of course, bring your own boat, or you can rent one from the **Bonny Marina and Store** (970-354-7339). Call ahead if you are planning to rent. Waterskiing is also an option, but you will need to bring your own equipment.

Directions

This is the easternmost park in Colorado, located almost three hours east of Denver just before the borders of Nebraska and Kansas. The fastest way to get there is to take I-70 east all the way to Burlington (about 160 miles). Once you arrive in Burlington, you can stop at the welcome center for more information or continue to the park. In Burlington, turn left at the Kit Carson Carousel onto U.S. Hwy. 385 and head north for about 23 miles. Then turn east at CR 3 and continue 3.5 miles to the entrance.

Contact Information

Bonny Lake State Park
30010 CR 3
Idalia, CO 80735
Phone: 970-354-7306
E-mail: bonny.lake.park@state.co.us

Boyd Lake State Park

Dubbed "the most modern water-sports facility in northern Colorado" by Colorado's state government, Boyd Lake is a great family getaway in the Rocky Mountains. Sailing, fishing, windsurfing, and waterskiing are among the favorite activities enjoyed on the lake, while sunbathers populate the beach. There are also plenty of camping and hiking opportunities. Seasonal events include regattas and hydroplane races.

Since 1981, thanks to monies generated by the Colorado lottery, Boyd Lake has seen more than $4 million in upgrades and improvements. There are five restrooms scattered throughout the park; all are accessible. There are also four fully accessible campsites available.

A concrete walkway that stretches along the west side of the lake is perfect for wheelchair users. This path is also great for adaptive cycling, and it connects the lake to the City of Loveland trail and park system. We recommend spending a few days here to really enjoy all that the park has to offer.

The park is useable during the winter, but access and fishing opportunities depend on weather and conditions.

Directions
Boyd Lake is located just north of Loveland and south of Ft. Collins, between I-25/U.S. Hwy. 87 and U.S. Hwy. 287; both are north-south highways. Although there are several routes to get you there, the easiest is from U.S. Hwy. 34, an east-west highway that intersects with both I-25 and U.S. Hwy. 287. In Loveland, take Madison Ave. north from U.S. Hwy. 34. Eventually, the road curves right, about 1.5 miles in, turning toward the lake. From there the park and lake parallel CR 11-C.

Contact Information
Boyd Lake State Park
3720 N. CR 11-C
Loveland, CO 80538
Phone: 970-669-1739
E-mail: boyd.lake@state.co.us

Castlewood Canyon State Park

Directly south of Denver, in the middle of the Black Forest, is Castlewood Canyon State Park. This day-use-only park is used by bird-watchers, hikers, and picnickers and offers photographers remarkable and unique photo opportunities as well. The steep, incredible canyon walls also make it ideal for rock climbing.

Castlewood Canyon State Park is fully equipped with accessible restrooms throughout. The visitors center has the best facility.

There are several options for accessible hiking as well. The **Canyon View Trail** is a 1.2-mile paved pathway starting at the east entrance of the park. There are concrete access trails to the Canyon View Trail from the **Juniper Rock** and **Canyon Point** parking lots. This trail gives great views of the canyon right beside Cherry Creek. The upper deck of the **Bridge Canyon** overlook is also accessible for a great view above the canyon.

The park is only open from 8 A.M. until sunset daily, and camping is not allowed. The area is also used for snowshoeing and cross-country skiing during the winter. If you have an adaptive cross-country setup or are into skijoring or other adaptive winter activities, you can use the canyon year-round.

Directions

Castlewood Canyon State Park is close to the town of Castle Rock, about 25 miles south of Denver on I-25. From I-25, head east (left) on CO Hwy. 86 for about 7 miles to Castlewood Canyon Rd., or CR 51. If you get to Franktown or CO Hwy. 83, you've gone too far.

Contact Information

Castlewood Canyon State Park
2989 S. CO Hwy. 83
Franktown, CO 80116
Phone: 303-688-5242
E-mail: castlewood.canyon@state.co.us

Chatfield State Park

Chatfield is, by far, the most convenient recreational resource in the Denver metro area. Located just minutes from the capital right off of CO Hwy. 470, this important reservoir provides more than 1.5 million annual visitors with endless outdoor fun and activities. Guests can enjoy hiking, biking, swimming, boating, camping, and wildlife viewing, to name a few. The park is also equipped with a full livery for people wanting to do some horseback riding. You can rent horses from the livery or bring your own. If you are bringing your own, you can corral them overnight only if you are camping, and you must provide your own feed, as grazing is not allowed. Although there is a full-service livery here, there is not an adaptive program to take special-needs guests riding.

The majority of the 18 miles of trails in and around the park are wonderfully accessible. Even the few that are not paved are doable for most wheelchair users. There are plenty of accessible restrooms available in the park as well.

Camping is available within the park. There are seven fully accessible sites that should be reserved in advance, and there is also an accessible fishing platform for the avid fisherman. In addition to the channel catfish, yellow perch, crappie, bluegill, sunfish, and carp that populate the reservoir, the Colorado DOW periodically stocks

A hot air baloon floats above a fishing boat at Chatfield Reservoir. Courtesy of Jack Lenzo

Chatfield with rainbow trout. The best trout fishing is in the fall, when the temperatures start to drop but before the reservoir freezes.

If you are adventurous, as we are, you can take a breathtaking hot air balloon ride for the best view of the mountains from the Denver area. Make sure you call ahead to make arrangements. A folding chair with a couple of pillows to sit on and two strong people to lift was all it took for me. This was well worth it!

Ice-skating, ice fishing, and ski touring are activities available during the wintertime. Call 303-791-7275 for recent ice and snow conditions.

Directions

Located on the southwestern tip of Denver, Chatfield Lake lies just south of CO Hwy. 470 between CO Hwy. 121 (Wadsworth Blvd. and S. Platte Canyon Rd.) and U.S. Hwy. 85 (S. Santa Fe Dr.). Although there is access from all three highways, the main Dear Creek entrance and check-in are off of CO Hwy. 121. There is a great map of the park on the Web site, so check out the accessible locations prior to arrival.

Contact Information

Chatfield State Park
11500 N. Roxborough Park Rd.
Littleton, CO 80125
Phone: 303-791-7275
E-mail: chatfield.park@state.co.us

Cherry Creek State Park

Surrounding the 880-surface-acre Cherry Creek Lake is a beautiful state park that offers something for everyone. Camping, boating, bird-watching, group picnics, cycling, and just enjoying the views of the Rockies are few of the available activities.

Most of the trails in the park are accessible to wheelchair users. There are several that are paved, including one to the beach and some throughout the campgrounds. The newly renovated campgrounds offer several fully accessible sites that are complete with water, electric hookups, and accessible restrooms.

There are two accessible fishing platforms in the park for avid or novice anglers, one on the east side and one on the west side. There is also a small wetlands preserve in the southeast corner of the park.

The winter season provides options such as wildlife viewing, cross-country skiing, and ice fishing and skating, depending on ice conditions. Access to these trails and activities is heavily dependent on your level of ability and amounts of standing snow.

Directions

On the southeastern tip of Denver lies Cherry Creek Lake, between CO Hwy. 470, I-225, and CO Hwy. 83. There are two official entrances to Cherry Creek Lake: the west entrance off of E. Union Ave. (take I-225 to S. Yosemite St. to E. Union Ave.) and the east entrance off of S. Parker Rd. (CO Hwy. 83, also off I-225). The marina is just north of the west entrance, but Lake View Rd. wraps around the south side of the lake, connecting all aspects.

Contact Information

Cherry Creek State Park
4201 S. Parker Rd.
Aurora, CO 80014
Phone: 303-699-3860
E-mail: cherry.creek.park@state.co.us

Cheyenne Mountain State Park

Located just west of Colorado Springs, Cheyenne Mountain is the newest in the state park system. Since the acquisition of the land in 2000, the planning process has been in high gear. It is anticipated that final minor construction on amenities will be complete by late 2005. More than 13 miles of trails have been constructed, including a technical single-track for mountain biking.

Directions

Cheyenne Mountain State Park is not yet open to the public. Please refer to the Colorado State Parks Web site for updated information.

Contact Information

Cheyenne Mountain State Park
4255 Sinton Rd.
Colorado Springs, CO 80907
Phone: 719-227-5256
E-mail: cheyenne.comments@state.co.us

Colorado River State Park

The park's five sections are all located along the gorgeous Colorado River. Thanks to this unique setup, visitors can engage in almost any kind of outdoor activity imaginable. Camping, fishing, picnicking, hiking, biking, swimming, and wildlife viewing are a few, but the list goes on. Accessible restrooms and shade shelters are located throughout the park.

Corn Lake features 2 miles of paved trails that are perfect for wheelchair users and are great for cycling, jogging, in-line skating, or just taking a quiet stroll. There is also a 1-mile hard-packed gravel surface trail that is doable with a little effort.

Connected Lakes offers almost 6 miles of trails connecting the three lakes. The first 2 to 3 miles are a brand-new, 10-foot-wide concrete path. The trail then turns into an older blacktop surface for 2 miles and finishes on a gravel road surface that is definitely rough and may require assistance to navigate.

Fruita has a .25-mile hard-packed trail between the river and the lake that is doable as well.

If you are camping, you'll want to reserve a site either in the **Island Acres Campground** or at Fruita. Of the 80 sites at Island Acres, there are three ADA–compliant and accessible campsites in the A Loop, one in the B Loop, two in the C Loop, and one in the D Loop. There are also accessible pay showers located here, with adaptive showerheads obtainable upon request. Fruita has one site that is truly ADA compliant, but almost all of the sites are very doable.

The easiest access for fishing is either at Corn Lake, where there is a floating dock, or at Connected Lakes, where there are five paved trails with access to concrete fishing piers, complete with safety railings and rod holders.

The picnic areas are located within the park at Connected Lakes, Corn Lake, Fruita, and Island Acres. All have barbeque grills, nearby water, and shade shelters, although Fruita is the least shady of the five.

Directions

This park stretches along the Colorado River from Fruita to the east of Grand Junction, paralleling I-70, the railroad, and the river. There are five main areas from which you can enter. The roads in Grand Junction are mostly decimal numbers and letters, so it takes some getting used to, as we were easily misguided because of this.

The westernmost entrance is called Fruita, the same as the town, and is accessed off exit 19 of I-70, .25 mile south on CO Hwy. 340 or 17.00 Rd.

Heading east, the next entrance is Connected Lakes/Walker State Wildlife Area, adjacent to CO Hwy. 340 just north of Broadway Rd. on Dike Rd.

Next is Colorado River Wildlife Area, south of D.00 Rd. on 30.25 Rd. just south of where U.S. Hwy. 6 intersects the business loop of I-70.

Corn Lake neighbors Colorado River Wildlife Area, also south of D.00 Rd. on 32.00 Rd.

Last and farthest east is Island Acres, at exit 47 of I-70, which is nearly 15 miles from Corn Lake and about 3.5 miles from where U.S. Hwy. 6 joins I-70.

Contact Information

Colorado River State Park
P.O. Box 700
Clifton, CO 81520
Phone: 970-434-3388
E-mail: colorado.river.park@state.co.us

Colorado State Forest State Park

Colorado State Forest State Park is very spread out, offering four campgrounds on a 5-mile stretch of CO Hwy. 14: **Ranger Lakes**, **The Crags**, **North Michigan Reservoir**, and **Bockman Campgrounds**. Of these, North Michigan is considered the most accessible, offering one fully accessible cabin (number 4) for rent, and a bigger, hardened cement pad at campsite number 207. The four cabins along the shore of North Michigan Reservoir sleep up to six people, and two larger ones sleep up to 20. Three have propane stoves (numbers 1 through 3), and three have wood-burning stoves (numbers 4 through 6). They all have fire grills and tables outside, as well as tables, benches, and bunks inside, but no electricity, running water, or bedding. These are popular and require a small, nonrefundable portion of the fee in advance.

Most of the campsites in North Michigan and Bockman are flat and accessible, as well as some in Ranger Lakes. Ranger Lakes offers a fully accessible fishing pier and four tables and grills for picnicking. The **Moose Visitors Center** is fully accessible and is located off of CO Hwy. 14.

North Michigan and Bockman are located behind the KOA Campground, so don't be fooled by their sign. The KOA is also partly accessible, offering camping and restrooms for those with disabilities.

Of the four park campgrounds, The Crags is the most inaccessible, even for low-to-the-ground or larger vehicles with trailers. The winding camp road is rocky and steep in spots, but does have the best views of The Crags and did pass our adventurous test when we spent one night up in these cold mountains. The forest here offers 75 miles of four-wheel-drive trails, so it is possible to spend a few days up in this beautiful area.

Although winter activities are encouraged up here, please note that narrow and winding **Cameron Pass** is sometimes inhospitable during the winter months, but usually well maintained once storms pass.

Directions

You can get to this park from Steamboat Springs or from Ft. Collins, but it is a closer drive if you are heading west from Ft. Collins. Follow CO Hwy. 14 over Cameron Pass toward the town of Walden, approximately 80 miles. The park is located at the base of the pass on the western side and is hard to miss as it sits right on CO Hwy. 14.

If you are coming from the Steamboat direction, the park will be on your right, about 15 miles east of Walden.

Contact Information

Colorado State Forest State Park
56750 CO Hwy. 14
Walden, CO 80480
Phone: 970-723-8366
E-mail: state.forest@state.co.us

Crawford State Park

With the **Black Canyon of the Gunnison** and **Blue Mesa Reservoir** close by, this park is easily overlooked. The views here are spectacular, in a serene setting with access to fishing, hiking, and other recreational water activities. There is a brand-new park headquarters located at the Peninsula day-use area that should be your first stop for the great displays and fully accessible restrooms.

There are seven fully accessible campsites available between the **Iron Creek** and **Clear Fork Campgrounds**. Both campgrounds feature accessible hot showers and flush toilets. Iron Creek also has RV hookups and an accessible wildlife kiosk. Clear Fork does not have hookups but drinking water is available. There are also several places to picnic in the park. The **Peninsula** day-use area has the most accessible site and can also accommodate groups. This is also where you will want to swim.

There is a 1-mile-long ADA–accessible trail on the east side of the park that has a hard-packed granite surface that is great for wheelchairs. There is also a trail on the west side, but it is not accessible.

Fishermen catch a large variety of fish at Crawford State Park. Perch, crappie, and largemouth bass are the most abundant, and huge northern pike are being caught more and more frequently. Information on guidelines and limits is available at the park office or online.

Waterskiing and scuba diving can also be enjoyed here until mid-August, when the water temperatures drop significantly. During the winter, ice fishing, ice-skating, and snowmobiling are popular.

Directions

Just north of the Black Canyon National Park lies the town of Crawford, west of Delta and south of Hotchkiss. CO Hwy. 92 is the major thoroughfare, and Crawford Reservoir lies east of it, 1 mile south of Crawford. The main entrance is on the Peninsula, but accessible camping is on Iron Creek.

Contact Information

Crawford State Park
P.O. Box 147
Crawford, CO 81415
Phone: 970-921-5721
E-mail: crawford.park@state.co.us

Eldorado Canyon State Park

Known best for the wealth of technical rock climbing, the park also offers picnicking, fishing, hiking, and plenty of wildlife viewing. There are more than 500 different routes open to rock climbers. This beautiful canyon is open for day-use only, but is a great stop to just relax and enjoy nature. If you like to take pictures, you won't want to forget your camera to capture the truly picturesque landscape.

There is one large picnic area in the park, with 40 sites available on a first-come, first-serve basis. It is located along the banks of **South Boulder Creek**, and all sites have tables and grills. Expect this area to fill up by noon between Memorial Day and Labor Day, and remember they will not accept reservations.

Approximately the first 300 feet of the .5-mile-long **Streamside Trail** and the first half of the .7-mile-long **Fowler Trail** are accessible to wheelchairs. The rest of the trail system is considered moderately difficult and not accessible.

While we didn't think this park offered a lot for people with disabilities, it is certainly worth the stop for the picnic area or just to use the accessible restrooms, if you're in the area.

Directions

Eldorado lies in the foothills of the Rocky Mountains, 2 miles south of Boulder and 15 miles north of Golden. CO Hwy. 93 connects these two foothill towns, and Eldorado Springs Dr. (CO Hwy. 170) will take you to Eldorado Springs. Continue 1 mile past town to the park, and as you enter the canyon at Eldorado Springs, you can take in Eldorado Mountain to the south (left) and South Boulder Peak to the north.

Contact Information

Eldorado Canyon State Park
9 Kneale Rd., Box B
Eldorado Springs, CO 80025
Phone: 303-494-3943
E-mail: eldorado.park@state.co.us

Eleven Mile State Park

Eleven Mile State Park, one of Colorado's largest reservoirs, is known as one of the elite fishing destinations in the state. Avid fishermen pull rainbow, brown, and cutthroat trout, as well as salmon, northern pike, and smallmouth bass from the pristine waters of this reservoir.

Eleven Mile is incredibly spacious compared to many state parks. Campsites are right at water's edge, and the scenery is incredible. Wind conditions and water temperatures happen to be ideal for sailing and windsurfing here also. The park is open year-round.

Eleven Mile State Park has 15 well-maintained picnic sites to accommodate day-use visitors. These sites are located primarily in the **North Shore** area. A universal access picnic site is located at the **North Shore Amphitheater** parking lot, complete with a concrete pad. There are also a couple of accessible sites at the nearby **Spinney Mountain State Park**.

With plenty of space, anglers are often alone with the birds.
Courtesy of Jack Lenzo

The trail system here is all backcountry hiking, biking, and horseback riding. None of the trails are suitable for wheelchair users.

Your best bet for fishing at Eleven Mile is to rent or bring your own boat. There is not an accessible fishing platform here yet. Fishing equipment and boat rentals are available at **11 Mile Sports**. For more information on rentals, visit their Web site (www.11milesports.com).

The first two campsites in the **Rocky Ridge** campground are ADA accessible, as is one site in the **North Shore Campground**. If you're looking for shaded sites with trees and cool landmarks, such as the nearby jagged crags, reserve a spot at Rocky Ridge. North Shore's accessible site is on the waterfront.

The **Eleven Mile General Store** is located right outside the park entrance and carries firewood and other camping necessities. The towns of **Florissant**, **Divide**, and **Woodland Park** are also nearby if you are feeling like getting out of the campsite for a while.

Royal Gorge is the world's highest suspension bridge and happens to be only 35 miles from Eleven Mile State Park. The Arkansas River rages through the canyon more than 1,000 feet below, providing unbeatable views.

Pikes Peak (14,110 feet), which can be seen from the park on a clear day, is only about an hour's drive away. The spectacular, scenic drive through **Pike National Forest** to the peak is a great half-day detour.

Gold Belt Scenic Byway Tour is another half-day drive, starting in Florissant. This is a great way to take in the beauty of the **Royal Gorge** and the **Beaver Creek Wilderness Area**. Also on the loop are the historic towns of **Cripple Creek** and **Victor**.

For additional activities and information, check out the nearest chamber of commerce at www.2chambers.com/woodland_park,_colorado.htm.

Directions

West of the Florissant Fossil Beds National Monument and located on U.S. Hwy. 24 is the small town of Lake George and the turnoff for Eleven Mile Canyon Reservoir. The second left out of town is CR 90. Take this south for 6 miles, to CR 92, which leads to the park, 5 miles down the road.

Contact Information

Eleven Mile State Park
4229 CR 92
Lake George, CO 80827
Phone: 719-748-3401
E-mail: eleven.mile.park@state.co.us

Golden Gate Canyon State Park

Just a short distance from Denver the densely forested 12,000 acres of Golden Gate Canyon State Park are exploding with outdoor opportunities. Endless meadows of wildflowers and incredible views of more than 100 miles of the Continental Divide display Colorado's natural beauty. **Panorama Point** is a perfect place to enjoy the surroundings. The backcountry also provides unlimited access to hiking, mountain biking, and horseback riding trips.

Thanks to a recent construction project at **Reverend's Ridge Campground** (97 total sites), all roads and parking sites are paved and very accessible. Concrete high-use pads and walkways were also installed to improve accessibility for the cabins, yurts, and to the showers and bathroom facilities. The 11 ADA–compliant sites each include a grill, table, and walkways to the accessible bathrooms and showers. Campsites can and should be reserved.

Almost 300 picnic sites can be found along **Ralston Creek**. **Bridge Creek**, **Kriley Pond**, and **Slough Ponds**. All have accessible picnic sites with paved pathways, raised grills, and accessible restrooms. Panorama Point also has a paved path with access to the two upper levels of the observation deck. **Bootleg Bottom** and **Ole' Barn Knoll** are doable with a little assistance. You can also reserve the **Red Barn Group Picnic Area** for groups of up to 150 people by calling 303-582-3707.

While regulations allow you to fish any stream or pond within the park, the best spot for wheelchair users is the accessible fishing platform at **Kriley Pond**. All Colorado DOW regulations apply.

Directions

Close to Nederland, Golden Gate is 2 miles east of CO Hwy. 119, between Nederland and Idaho Springs on Golden Gate Canyon 2 Rd./Gap Rd. If traveling from Golden or Denver, you could also take scenic Golden Gate Canyon Rd. (CO Hwy. 46) for 13 miles from CO Hwy. 93. Past Kriley Pond, take Golden Gate Canyon 1 Rd. north (right) for 2.5 miles to the park.

Contact Information

Golden Gate Canyon State Park
92 Crawford Gulch Rd.
Golden, CO 80403
Phone: 303-582-3707
E-mail: golden.gate.park@state.co.us

Harvey Gap State Park

Harvey Gap State Park is known as a quiet, out-of-the-way park with fantastic fishing and windsurfing opportunities. Boaters are limited to motors with 20 horsepower or less. Visitors can also hike, picnic, swim, and scuba dive, but camping is not allowed. For nearby camping options, see the information on **Rifle Gap** and **Rifle Falls** State Parks on pages 204–5.

All fishing here is either from the shore or boat, so be prepared with your equipment if you want to catch some fish.

Thirty picnic sites with grills are available. Some sites line the reservoir and others sit on an overlook above the lake. There is one ADA–compliant parking spot with a paved path to a picnic table and grill.

Directions

Harvey is accessed by the north or south ends of the lake on CR 237. The south entrance is about 4 miles north of I-70 at Silt at exit 97, but in our opinion, there's no straight (easy) way to get there. Off the I-70 exit, head north on 9th St. across the train tracks toward Silt for a block. Take a left (west) on U.S. Hwy 6. and continue for 8 blocks, then take a right (north) on CR 231. Follow this for about a mile to CR 233/Silt Mesa Rd. Continue for .5 mile and take a right on Rainbow Dr., which dead-ends at Harvey Gap Rd., where you'll take a right again.

Whew! It's much easier to get to from the north, but it's doubtful that you'll be coming from that way unless you're visiting **Rifle Gap** or **Rifle Falls State Parks**. CO Hwy. 325 connects these two other parks, and CR 225 will take you right from that highway to CR 237/Harvey Gap Rd.

Contact Information

Harvey Gap State Park
c/o Rifle Gap State Park
5775 CO Hwy. 325
Rifle, CO 81650
Phone: 970-625-1607
E-mail: rifle.gap.park@state.co.us

Highline Lake State Park

Highline Lake State Park offers all kinds of outdoor fun on two beautiful lakes. **Mack Mesa Lake** is strictly for fishing and wakeless boating, while **Highline Lake**, which is now one of the most popular water recreation areas on the Western Slope, is open for waterskiing, Jet Skiing, and boating.

Camping is available year-round at the **Bookcliff Campground**. Of the 27 campsites, only one (19) is ADA compliant, and the campground routinely fills up during the summer months, so call ahead to reserve this spot. ADA–compliant showers and restrooms are available.

There are two main trails in the park. The **Highline Lake Trail** is a 3.5-mile gravel-based loop that is fairly easy for wheelchairs and is great for wildlife viewing. The **Mack Mesa Trail** is also wheelchair friendly and is only .5 mile in length.

Mack Mesa Lake offers an accessible fishing pier and a waterfowl overlook to view the large waterfowl that migrate here, such as white pelicans and great blue heron.

Most of the 40 or so picnic sites at Highline Lake are accessible and provide plenty of shade and grills lakeside. There is also a group picnic area, which can handle up to about 150 people and features a large grill and a covered picnic area. Accessible restrooms are nearby.

Power boating, Jet Skiing, and waterskiing are only allowed on Highline Lake from March 1 through September 30. During summer days, the boat capacity limit is often reached, so get there early.

The swimming area and beach are open from Memorial Day through Labor Day, and water temperatures can hover in the 80s, making Highline Lake ideal for swimming.

Directions

Highline Lake is 6 miles north of Loma. From I-70 west, take exit 15 at Loma. Head north (right) on CO Hwy. 139 for 6 miles to Q Rd. and take a left. You'll see signs at this point to the park, but take a right on 11.8 Rd., which dead-ends at the park a mile up.

Contact Information

Highline Lake State Park
1800 11.8 Rd.
Loma, CO 81524
Phone: 970-858-7208
E-mail: highline.park@state.co.us

Jackson Lake State Park

Very popular for its warm water, Jackson Lake State Park welcomes all types of water enthusiasts to its sandy beaches during both summer and winter months.

Camping sites for tents and trailers are available in the park, which boasts more than 250 sites total. There is one accessible site located in the **Lakeside Campground** (number 35), along with accessible restrooms, laundry facilities, and pay showers. All of the trails around the park have a hard-packed gravel road base and are doable with little or no assistance.

Early springs and falls bring lots of anglers to Jackson Lake. There is not a designated ADA–compliant platform, but the end of the concrete pier located near the boat launch on the west shore of the lake is an accessible fishing option that should be taken advantage of. The weekends can be hectic with boat traffic, making the fishing challenging, but we visited during the week and there was nobody there. Fishing is not allowed near the beaches or during hunting season. Boats can be rented from the **Shoreline Marina** (970-645-BOAT).

The marina also rents Jet Skis, ski boats, and paddleboats, and warm, shallow, crystal-clear waters make for superb swimming. We recommend calling ahead to make arrangements.

Picnic sites at Jackson are limited and can be reserved in advance. Most are doable, although they are not up to ADA code. The most accessible site is the group picnic area. This requires reservations. Call 970-645-2551 for more information.

Directions

About 70 miles northeast from Denver, into the plains and up near the Nebraska border, is Jackson Reservoir. It's about 14 miles west of Ft. Morgan off of CO Hwy. 144. Fairly easy to get to from either U.S. Hwy 34 or I-76, CO Hwy. 144 intersects both these highways in Ft. Morgan. From CO Hwy. 144, follow signs to Goodrich, then go west on CR 5 for 2.5 miles until you reach the park.

Contact Information

Jackson Lake State Park
26363 CR 3
Orchard, CO 80649
Phone: 970-645-2551
E-mail: jackson.lake@state.co.us

John Martin Reservoir State Park

John Martin Reservoir State Park is one of the newest in the park system and recently saw a major renovation to the tune of almost $5 million. People travel from all over Colorado to take advantage of this modern and uncrowded haven, and the camping, boating, and fishing here are some of the best in the state. As avid birders, we brought our binoculars and zoom lenses to camp out at this famous haven for bald eagles and managed to catch a glimpse of quite a few species of hawks and eagles.

The **Lake Hasty Campground**, open year-round, is best for accessibility and offers lots of shade from hot summer sun. There are two ADA–compliant sites here (numbers 59 and 60) with accessible restrooms and showers in the camper-services building right next door. Most of the sites here are doable, with a gravel road base surface to access them. The **Point Campground** overlooks the reservoir, but there are no ADA–compliant sites here. The sites are doable, but services are limited to vault toilets. It is a good idea to reserve sites in advance, even though the campgrounds rarely fill up.

Hiking is not as popular at this park, although there is one 4.5-mile trail that is great for bird-watching and taking pictures. This trail is not wheelchair friendly, however. If you are not limited to a chair, this trail is perfect for wildlife viewing and searching for ancient pictographs and other Native American drawings.

Thanks to the modern improvements made in 2001, there is an ADA–compliant fishing pier below the dam at Lake Hasty. The lake is stocked with trout, bass, bluegill, and catfish.

As with most state parks, we found all of the picnic facilities at John Martin fairly easy to access. The paved lot near the fishing pier has an ADA–compliant site right at the water's edge, with a paved pathway. This site is also very close to the swimming beach.

One of the largest reservoirs in the state, this park is very popular for the water recreation enthusiast, and all types of water play are allowed, but you must bring your own motorized toys as there is no marina to rent from.

Directions

On the eastern plains of Colorado east of Bent's Old Fort National Monument and 5 miles east of the town of Las Animas lies the western mouth of the John Martin Reservoir. Just south of U.S. Hwy. 50, and most easily accessed from the town of Hasty, the reservoir actually stretches more than 12 miles in length, so there are many entrances. The main area, marina, and accessible fishing pier are at the eastern end of the lake, south of Hasty and adjacent to Lake Hasty, which is also included in the park. From U.S. Hwy. 50 in Hasty, take CR 24 south and follow signs for the park, which is only about 2 miles down.

Contact Information

John Martin Reservoir State Park
30703 CR 24
Hasty, CO 81044
Phone: 719-829-1801
E-mail: john.martin.park@state.co.us

Lake Pueblo State Park

Lake Pueblo State Park is a huge recreation area, offering almost 10,000 acres to enjoy any outdoor activity imaginable. There are two full-service marinas on the lake to take care of your water-activity needs, as well as a five-story waterslide, bumper boats, and paddleboats. Swimming, fishing, camping, and hiking are also very common. This area is also surrounded by mountains, so the views are spectacular. The visitors center at Arkansas Point offers area information, displays, and a gift shop.

Lake Pueblo has a staggering 401 campsites available. There are 14 ADA–compliant sites spread out over the three main campgrounds: **Northern Plains**, **Arkansas Point**, and **Juniper Breaks**. Accessible restrooms and showers are located near all three. We consider all of the sites within the park doable, as they all have paved parking spots, covered picnic tables, and fire pits. Northern Plains also has a small trail system that is very doable for wheelchairs. This is a very popular park with heavy traffic in the campgrounds. Make sure to call ahead and reserve a spot, as the weekends during summer months are often sold out (719-561-9320, ext 0).

Fishermen get in a full day as dusk approaches at Lake Pueblo. Courtesy of Jack Lenzo

There are more than 30 miles of trails in the park open to hiking, biking, and horseback riding. The **Dam Trail** is a 16.5-mile paved trail that connects all parts of the park, even by wheelchair. This trail is at least 20 years old and does have a few steep inclines, so it's good to have a helper. Visitors are treated to regular wildlife sightings. In the short time that we spent here, we saw several red-tailed hawks as well as a deer, a fox, and two raccoons. The **Arkansas Point Trail** is much newer and ADA compliant. This trail accesses the bluffs at the south end of the park and is slightly less than 1 mile in length.

If you are an avid fisherman, make sure to bring your gear to **Lake Pueblo**. You can catch trout, walleye, large- and smallmouth bass, crappie, channel catfish, wiper, bluegill, and yellow perch from the accessible pier at **Anticline Pond**. Shore fishing can be done below the dam, but only when water levels are low. Shade and accessible restrooms are nearby, as is the playground if you are traveling with children.

A large portion of the day-use area's picnic facilities are accessible, and Lake Pueblo also offers five fully accessible group picnic sites, complete with electricity, water faucets, large barbecue grills, private parking, volleyball, horseshoe pits, and restroom facilities. Reservations are required and can be made at the park office.

Thanks to very warm water temperatures throughout the summer, we love this area for swimming and waterskiing. The marinas offer slip rentals, gas pumps, minor boat repair, marina stores, and snack foods; people swarm here for the fun and the convenience. For more information visit their Web site www.thesouthshoremarina.com.

Directions

Pueblo Reservoir is 3 miles west of Pueblo and easily accessed on CO Hwy. 96 by following the user-friendly signs to the lake. If you are not already in Pueblo, U.S. Hwy. 50 will also get you to the north side of the lake. Take either Marina Access Rd. or Recreation Access Rd. (both lead south to the lake from U.S. Hwy. 50).

Contact Information

Lake Pueblo State Park
640 Pueblo Reservoir Rd.
Pueblo, CO 81005
Phone: 719-561-9320, ext. 0
E-mail: lake.pueblo.park@state.co.us

Lathrop State Park

With 14,000-foot peaks all around you and plenty of camping, fishing, and water sports available, Lathrop State Park is one of the state's less-traveled-to parks and a worthwhile spot to visit. There are two lakes to choose from and a nine-hole golf course if you feel like hitting the links. The brand-new, accessible visitors center displays local art and offers information on the area.

Piñon Campground added ADA–accessible sites in 2004, but all of the sites are paved and were doable for us. There are also modern toilets, laundry facilities, and a playground. A new, accessible shower building was also one of our favorite highlights. **Yucca Campground** is much smaller and less wheelchair friendly but is very beautiful. If you are traveling without a wheelchair, we recommend this spot.

The **Cuerno Verde Trail** is a paved, accessible path that wraps around Martin Lake. Martin Lake is about 3 miles around and is open to bikers, walkers, and wheelers. **Cuerno Verde Picnic Area** is also accessible, with a concrete ramp leading to two ADA–accessible sites.

The accessible fishing access area, complete with ramp and concrete pier, is located on the west side of Martin Lake. Both lakes are stocked with rainbow trout, channel catfish, bass, walleye, bluegill, crappie, and wipers. There is also a fishing pond for kids (15 and under) near the dam on Martin Lake that gives young anglers a better chance at a good catch.

Martin Lake and **Horseshoe Reservoir Picnic Areas** are both accessible, with tables, grills, and accessible restrooms. The group picnic area is open for use by reservation only.

Directions

Lathrop lies about 45 miles south of Pueblo off of I-25 near the town of Walsenburg. Coming from Pueblo, take I-25 to Walsenburg and then head west on U.S. Hwy. 160 for only 2 miles. This road runs along the southern border of Colorado, so it can be taken east if traveling from Alamosa, for example. The park is just north of the highway, and there are plenty of signs to both lakes.

Contact Information

Lathrop State Park
70 CR 502
Walsenburg, CO 81089
Phone: 719-738-2376
E-mail: lathrop.park@state.co.us

Lory State Park

This beautiful area is lush with birds, mammals, geology, and flora and is well-known for its longer hunting season, extensive trail system, and fishing on the reservoir.

This park is wonderful for groups, as the picnic areas are large and can accommodate up to 50 people. There are fees for reserving these sites, but they offer magnificent views of the reservoir, covered tables, grills, horseshoes, and shaded cover. Because the park is fairly close to Ft. Collins, we recommend making reservations early. All of the camping at Lory is backcountry, so none is accessible.

Lory State Park offers 20 miles of hiking trails, ranging from easy to difficult, and they can be used for short or long hikes, jogging, mountain biking, and horseback riding. There is a flat, self-guided, nature trail loop with informational stops; a brochure is available at the main center. However, all of their trails are single-track trails and may not be suitable for wider wheelchairs.

Directions

Lory is at the north end of Ft. Collins's largest lake, Horsetooth Reservoir, which lies due west and stretches the entire length of the city. Paralleling the lake is CR 23, running along the entire eastern shore. From Ft. Collins, nearly all major east-west running roads will get you in that direction, but the main entrance is on the northern shore and the sure way to get there is through the town of Bellvue just north of Ft. Collins. Take CR 54G out of the city to Bellvue and then head south on CR 23. About a mile up, turn right onto CR 25G, which leads to the entrance of the park.

Contact Information

Lory State Park
708 Lodgepole Dr.
Bellvue, CO 80512
Phone: 970-493-1623
E-mail: lory.park@state.co.us

Mancos State Park

Mancos passed our accessibility test with flying colors. They not only offer two picnic sites and a campsite up to ADA–accessible standards, but one of their yurts is fully accessible as well—a rare find!

The park has 10 picnic sites, each with its own grill, as well as a volleyball court (net and ball provided) and two horseshoe pits.

There are approximately 5.5 miles of widened trails for hiking, biking, and horseback riding, and these connect to the **Durango-Denver Colorado Trail**. Most trails are dirt and somewhat accessible, although none is fully so. There are plans in the works to establish an accessible loop. There is a pedestrian bridge over the inlet.

The reservoir offers fishing and wakeless boating only, as waterskiing, Jet Skiing, and swimming are prohibited here to maintain the park's high standards of safety and preservation.

There are 32 campsites total, one (number 24) that is fully accessible, on the south side of the reservoir, and some others that are doable. The restrooms are also accessible here and adjacent to the accessible campsite. Additional information can be obtained from the rangers at the park entrance.

Mancos also offers two new yurts, at sites 22 and 24. These can and should be reserved in advance; yurt 24 is ADA accessible and 22 is doable, it just has one step up to the front deck. The yurts sleep up to six people on two bunks and two futons, but bedding is not provided. There is a deck, a picnic table, and a barbecue and campfire ring outside for those who like to camp but don't like to rough it.

There are fees for all services at Mancos. All questions can be directed to their reservations line (800-678-2267 or 303-470-1144).

Directions

Between Durango and Cortez is the tiny town of Mancos, which is just south of its namesake state park. U.S. Hwy. 160 will get you to Mancos, and then CO Hwy. 184 and CR 42 will take you north to the park, which is about 4 miles north of Mancos.

Contact Information

Mancos State Park
42545 CR N
Mancos, CO 81328
Phone: 970-533-7065
E-mail: mancos.park@state.co.us

Mueller State Park

Nestled at the base of famous Fourteener Pikes Peak, Mueller State Park is known for its panoramic views of the Rocky Mountains, aspen groves, and wildlife.

Mueller offers 132 campsites total, including 22 walk-in tent sites and an RV campground as well. The services building offers restrooms, showers, and laundry, and all sites except the tent campsites offer electric hookups. There are fees for the sites, and the season for camping is May through Labor Day.

Mueller is also home to more than 50 miles of scenic trails, used for hiking and horseback riding in the summer months and cross-country skiing and snowshoeing during winter. Wildlife is plentiful here and sightings are frequent. The trails vary from short, easy walks to full-day backcountry hikes. The most accessible is the **Wapiti Nature Trail**; self-guided brochures for this trail can be picked up at the visitors center.

The fishing is all backcountry and accessed by trails only, so without help or horseback, it's not considered accessible.

The park has more than 40 picnic tables with raised grills in four sites: **Preachers Hollow**, **Outlook Ridge**, **Bootlegger**, and **Lost Pond**. The latter three have drinking water and vaulted toilets available, and all but Bootlegger are at trailheads.

Directions

Mueller is 3.5 miles south of the tiny town of Divide, which is 25 miles west of Colorado Springs. Divide is easily missed if you aren't looking for it, so if you're traveling from The Springs, you may want to mark your odometer. Look for CO Hwy. 67 in Divide and take that south for 3.5 miles until you see signs for the state park. If you get to Midland, you've gone too far.

Contact Information

Mueller State Park
P.O. Box 39
Divide, CO 80814
Phone: 719-687-2366
E-mail: mueller.park@state.co.us

Navajo State Park

Because of all its water, Navajo offers fairly accessible beachfront activities, although the sand can be an obstacle. However, as of 2004, the park has a brand-new, fully accessible fishing area, including a dock and parking for those with special needs. Call ahead for reservations or book online.

Waterskiing, sailboarding, and Jet Skiing are all allowed on the reservoir, which has enough water for recreation even during drought years. The park also offers one of the longest boat ramps in the state and offers marina services and rentals (970-883-2208).

They have an extensive picnic area with 10 sites at **Windsurf Beach**, with plenty of accessible parking and shelter.

Navajo offers a three-piece campground, with 113 sites for both tents and RVs, including full hookups. The campground offers several fully accessible sites as well as restrooms, showers, and laundry.

Directions

Navajo Reservoir is between Pagosa Springs and Durango, which are connected by U.S. Hwy 160. From U.S. Hwy. 160, CO Hwy. 151 will take you there, but there is no landmark or town to look for at this intersection. There are signs, however, to Chimney Rock Archeological Area, which is about 2 miles down CO Hwy. 151 on the way to the reservoir, so look for those. The intersection is 17 miles west of Pagosa Springs and 40 miles east of Durango, so you can also use your odometer, depending on which city you're coming from. Follow CO Hwy. 151 south for 18 miles to Arboles, where you'll turn left on CR 982, which wraps around the western shore of the lake. The lake borders New Mexico, so this is your chance to sit in a two-state body of water!

Contact Information

Navajo State Park
1526 CR 982 (Box 1697)
Arboles, CO 81121
Phone: 970-883-2208
E-mail: navajo.park@state.co.us

North Sterling State Park

Sterling's 3,000 total acres of water are mainly used for boating . The local marina offers rentals, supplies, and three boat ramps. Swimming, waterskiing, fishing, and gasoline boats are all allowed here.

One of our favorite spots for swimming is at the **Cottonwood Cove** beach, just a short walk and roll from the **Chimney View Campground**, but note that there are no lifeguards for safety, so keep an eye on the children. The campground has great accessible showers and bathrooms, as well as a picnic pavilion and a playground.

Sterling's 6-mile trail system around the reservoir includes a 130-foot pedestrian bridge over one of the inlet canals and is another one of the park's highlights, for wildlife viewing. The surface is compacted rock and fairly accessible and flat. North Sterling also offers something unique with **Star Park**, created with help from local junior colleges. This observatory and astronomy center offers gazing without light pollution for panoramic views and education. This area was chosen for its accessibility and darkness and the center is a must-see if you're in the area at night, for there's nothing else quite like this here in Colorado. Sometimes even the northern lights are visible from here. More information about the observatory can be obtained through the main park phone number.

Directions

Sterling is in the far northeast corner of Colorado more than 100 miles northeast of Denver on I-76. Get off the highway at exit 125 and head north across the river and railroad tracks to U.S. Hwy. 6. We found that taking U.S. Hwy. 6 north of Sterling was the easiest route. Then take CR 43.5 in Ackerman north for 6 miles to CR 46. Sterling's roads are set up like a grid, so any of the roads running north-south will get you to CR 46. If you pass Ackerman, you can also take CR 46 west from Iliff.

Contact Information

North Sterling State Park
24005 CR 330
Sterling, CO 80751
Phone: 970-522-3657
E-mail: ling.park@state.co.us

Paonia State Park

Paonia's main attractions are the water and the camping. The park offers no formal hiking trails, but there is plenty of land for exploring by horse or skis for the more adventurous souls.

There are two campgrounds here, **Spruce** and **Hawsapple**, both offering one accessible campsite each. All sites have a picnic table and fire ring, and both campgrounds have vaulted toilets but no fully accessible restrooms. There is also no drinking water available here, so plan ahead. Don't let the reduced accessibility at Paonia stop you from visiting, however. It's one of the more secluded parks, and we didn't see a soul the entire time we were here, but we saw plenty of wildlife, including many birds of prey and a herd of elk.

Directions

The town of Paonia is about 30 miles west of Delta on CO Hwy. 133, and the park is another 16 miles northeast of town, right off the highway on Paonia Reservoir. Our favorite campsite is south of the reservoir, so we'd recommend coming from this way. However, you may also drive south of Glenwood Springs on CO Hwy. 82 to Carbondale, where CO Hwy. 133 intersects.

Contact Information

Paonia State Park
P.O. Box 147
Crawford, CO 81415
Phone: 970-921-5721
E-mail: crawford.park@state.co.us

Pearl Lake State Park

Pearl Lake State Park is tucked deep into the Sawtooth Mountain Range and offers much more privacy than can be found at its neighboring park, Steamboat Lake. There are 38 campsites, including two new popular yurts, more than 100 miles of backcountry trails, and all-season fishing, boating, picnicking, and hunting. Due to 300 inches of annual snowfall in the area, the park is only open by foot and snowmobile during the winter, offering even more privacy than during the summer.

The campground is mainly gravel, and although no campsites are fully accessible, there are several that are doable, including the yurts, which are on raised platforms but have widened doors, very open interiors, and several beds (without bedding). All campsites have level parking areas and fire rings. For showers, laundry, and garbage dumping, you have to use the facilities at neighboring Steamboat Lake. Yurts and campsites have fees. Reservations are available and recommended.

Although there is no fishing platform, fishing can be done from canoe. Fishing is designated here as "gold medal" by the DOW for the abundance of cutthroat trout, with occasional browns and graylings as well.

As for wildlife, well, these mountains are full of it. Visitors report sightings of mule deer, elk, red fox, beaver, and smaller mammals, such as pine martens and snowshoe hares. Sandhill cranes and other large bird species nest here as well, but visitors are asked to keep their distance to preserve the natural habitats.

Directions

From downtown Steamboat Springs, follow U.S. Hwy. 40 west for 2 miles and turn right at the last stoplight out of town onto Elk River Rd. (CR 129). Follow this road for about 25 miles through the small town of Clark and turn right at CR 209. From here, follow the right-hand forks and signs to the lake.

Contact Information

Pearl Lake State Park
P.O. Box 750
Clark, CO 80428
Phone: 970-879-3922
E-mail: steamboat.lake@state.co.us

Ridgway State Park

Where to begin with Ridgway? The trail system alone is elaborate enough to keep you busy photographing for days. The reservoir is very large. There is a section below the dam where the campgrounds are located, as well as an accessible camper-services building and picnic areas.

One of the major highlights for travelers with special needs at Ridgway are the 3 miles of concrete trails, including a 1-mile section along the shoreline in the main cove, and the **Forest Discovery Nature Trail**, for those who enjoy self-guided tours through the forest.

The reservoir is stocked for good fishing and the park offers a full marina for boaters, which allows for all kinds of water activities, from Jet Skiing to swimming. There are two accessible fishing platforms, one down at the ponds at the **Pa-co-chu-puk Campground** and one by the main marina.

Ridgway offers 280 campsites broken into three loops of campgrounds, offering tent sites or full RV hookups, accessible restrooms and showers, laundry, and the ever-popular home-away-from-home yurts. The accessible sites are numbers 230, 280, and 281. This park has three yurts, one of which has a ramp up to its raised platform, and all are available to rent year-round.

Because of this park's popularity, we recommend booking the accessible yurt or campsites in advance.

Directions

Very easy to find, Ridgway is located about 22 miles south of the city of Montrose on U.S. Hwy. 550. The park's entrance will be on your right.

Contact Information

Ridgway State Park
28555 U.S. Hwy. 550
Ridgway, CO 81432
Phone: 970-626-5822
E-mail: ridgway.park@state.co.us

Rifle Falls State Park

The camping facilities are modest, with only 19 total sites along the **East Rifle Creek**. Ten sites are drive-in, and all of these are considered accessible, though there is one raised tent bed at site number 2. The remaining nine sites are walk-in.

There are nine picnic sites close to the falls and two slow-incline trails with a hard-packed surface for fair accessibility. We had no problem navigating the trail and absolutely loved the waterfall. This park is a must-see for waterfall lovers like us and photographers alike. Campers can get a sense of adventure without working too hard for it here.

Neighboring **Rifle Gap State Park** has enough to offer outdoor enthusiasts, whereas Rifle Falls has the peace and tranquility of wilderness.

Directions

The town of Rifle is located just off I-70 about 50 miles east of Grand Junction. **Rifle Gap** (see listing below) and **Rifle Falls** state parks are north of the town of Rifle. Rifle Falls is just beyond Rifle Gap: From I-70, get off at the Rifle exit and take CO Hwy. 13 north for 3 miles. Then take a right (northeast) on CO Hwy. 325 for about 4 miles until you see the reservoir. For Rifle Gap, take a left on CR 219 (signs will lead you to either park) for 1.5 miles to the park's entrance. For Rifle Falls, you will head right at the reservoir, which continues on CO Hwy. 325 for about 6 miles to the entrance of Rifle Falls State Park.

Contact Information

Rifle Falls State Park
5775 CO Hwy. 325
Rifle, CO 81650
Phone: 970-625-1607
E-mail: rifle.gap.park@state.co.us

Rifle Gap State Park

Another one of our favorite parks, Rifle Gap offers something unique that you don't normally see at a state park: An 18-hole golf course neighbors this beautiful, 1,300-acre area. Also nearby is the **Glenwood Hot Springs**, if you feel like a soak afterward. We have found this park to be quite busy in the summer months, filled with water enthusiasts of all kinds, even including scuba divers. The swimming here is great! Though the water isn't warm, it is crystal clear, and the west-side beach is shallow and warmer.

There are four campgrounds here that offer a total of 46 sites for tents, trailers, and a few larger RVs. Picnicking is also available, and the good news is that the campgrounds are rarely full. **Cottonwood Campground** is the most recently updated of the four and has the best options for accessibility. Site number 3 has a raised tent bed, but we found the rest to be easily doable and flat. All of their picnic tables have the extended ends, and their bathrooms are accessible and quite spacious.

Don't miss neighboring **Rifle Falls** if you have the time to visit a photographer's dream.

Directions
Please see directions to Rifle Falls State Park, above.

Contact Information
Rifle Gap State Park
5775 CO Hwy. 325
Rifle, CO 81650
Phone: 970-625-1607
E-mail: rifle.gap.park@state.co.us

Roxborough State Park

Recently designated a natural archaeological district and national natural landmark, the area's diversity offers something for the geologist as well as the naturalist, from 500 million-year-old rock formations to abundant wildlife.

We love Roxborough State Park for its unique ride system for visitors with disabilities, the **Roxborough Ride**. This lengthened golf cart–tram offers a naturalist guide, with donations requested but not required and reservations recommended. This is a wonderful way to see the magnificent views of the 2.3-mile Fountain Valley Trail loop. There is quite a vast trail system at this park, but we found them to be quite rocky in spots and too narrow for a wheelchair. If you are without a wheelchair, however, we recommend **Willow Creek Trail** in the summer months for wildflower enthusiasts.

The visitors center offers accessible bathrooms and benches but no picnic facilities.

Directions

Roxborough State Park lies 4 miles south of **Chatfield State Park** on the very southern tip of the city limits of Denver. It's hard to get to this park without going around Chatfield Reservoir, flanked by CO Hwy. 121 and U.S. Hwy. 85. We've found that the easiest route is via CO Hwy. 121 (or Wadsworth Blvd.) south from the city. Go around Chatfield Reservoir and turn left (east) onto Waterton Rd., which is over Platte Canyon Reservoir. CO Hwy. 121 dead-ends here, just before the entrance to Lockheed Martin. Once over the second reservoir, the road will end again at N. Rampart Range Rd., where you will turn right (south) and go until you get to Roxborough Rd., which is about 4 miles down. At this point, all roads lead you to the park, but the entrance is on Roxborough Rd.

Contact Information

Roxborough State Park
4751 Roxborough Dr.
Littleton, CO 80125
Phone: 303-973-3959
E-mail: roxborough.park@state.co.us

San Luis State Park and Wildlife Area

The largest attraction here is San Luis Lake, a popular tourist spot for water sports since the early 1900s. Waterskiing, boating, fishing, sailing, and windsurfing are all allowed here. The only main restrictions are on the north end of the lake, as a wildlife area exists and nesting habitats are protected by a buoy line.

San Luis Lake is stocked with rainbow trout fairly regularly, and the fishing can be very good here when water levels are up to par. When the levels are normal, wheelchair users can fish very comfortably from the boat ramp's pier. We strongly recommend calling ahead to check, as the water levels have been extremely low in the past few years.

There is also a pool facility within a few miles of San Luis Lake. The **Sand Dunes Pool** (719-378-2807), or **Hooper Pool**, is located about 15 miles north of the lake on CO Hwy. 17 in the town of Hooper. The main pool ranges from 3 to 10 feet deep, and they have a separate pool for kids. They also have one therapy pool. This pool is kept between 108° and 110° F and has jets just like a hot tub. This is your oasis in the middle of the desert, and the building, pools, and restrooms (including showers) are all accessible with minimal assistance.

The **Needles Picnic Area** is located at the swim beach with accessible restrooms and large picnic areas for groups.

San Luis offers camping with amazing views of the lake and the sand dunes, a wonderfully accessible bathhouse with restrooms, showers, and laundry, and elaborate sites with hookups, sheltered tables, fire grates, drinking water, and a dump station. Camping here just isn't what it used to be! We felt thoroughly pampered at San Luis.

Picnic tables overlook San Louis Lake and the Great Sand Dunes.
Courtesy of Jack Lenzo

The trails around the lake are hard-packed surfaces and welcome hikers of all abilities, including those in wheelchairs. However, the trails along the dunes are sandier, and we found them to be much less accessible.

If you are visiting the neighboring **Great Sand Dunes National Park and Preserve**, take an extra day to dip in the cool waters of San Luis during the summer or take advantage of the winter activities here. Snowshoeing, ice fishing, ice-skating, and cross-country skiing are welcomed during snowy months or, if driving through, stop by to view the nesting bald eagles.

Directions

Located just southwest of the Great Sand Dunes National Park and Preserve, San Luis Lake State Park are off of Six Mile Ln., which is a right-hand turn 7 miles south of the national park off CO Hwy. 150. Coming from the south on U.S. Hwy 160 from Monte Vista or Walsenburgh, head north on CO Hwy. 150 for 13.5 miles and turn left on Six Mile Ln.

Contact Information

San Luis State Park
County Ln. 6 N (P.O. Box 175)
Mosca, CO 81146
Phone: 719-378-2020
E-mail: sanluis.park@state.co.us

Spinney Mountain State Park

Spinney offers a large reservoir to visitors, which is mainly used for fishing, as many water sports, such as swimming and waterskiing, are prohibited here. These safety prohibitions are due to the well-known gusts of wind that sometimes bring up to 5-foot waves on the lake.

Although well-known to knowledgeable anglers for its fishing, there are no accessible fishing platforms at Spinney yet. There are docks for unloading and loading boats only, and fishing is prohibited from the docks. Fishing is taken very seriously at Spinney, and there are many restrictions concerning bag limits and allowable fishing times. There is no winter fishing here, no live bait allowed, and no fishing during dark hours. Fishing guides heavily utilize this area. A list of these and maps and regulations can be obtained at the Eleven Mile State Park office.

Roadside wildlife near Spinney Mountain State Park. Courtesy of Jack Lenzo

Picnicking is welcome here, and the park has several tables and fire rings on either side of the reservoir that are accessible from the main road.

As this is a day-use only park, no camping is allowed.

Directions

Spinney Mountain Reservoir lies just west of Eleven Mile Reservoir and State Park, south of U.S. Hwy. 24. If coming from the east and Colorado Springs, Spinney is 4 miles east of Wilerson Pass or 55 miles east of Colorado Springs. Turn south from U.S. Hwy. 24 on CR 23 and go 3 miles to CR 59. From here you can see the reservoir, but you have to continue another mile to the park entrance.

Contact Information

Spinny Mountain State Park
4229 CR 92
Lake George, CO 80827
Phone: 719-748-3401
E-mail: eleven.mile.park@state.co.us

St. Vrain State Park

We found St. Vrain to be a wonderfully accessible park, offering five fully accessible restrooms, the short, accessible **Muskrat Run Nature Trail** (with or without tour guide, although we recommend taking the guided option), four accessible fishing piers with accessible parking areas, and accessible campsites. St. Vrain also offers horseshoe pits, a volleyball court, and a playground for families or groups.

We were thoroughly impressed with the adaptation of this park, and with its close proximity to Denver, it's a great first stop out of the city.

The trail is maintained, the camping is cold but open, and the lake is available for ice fishing during winter months. In our opinion, one of the best sights during the winter is the rare bald eagle, and St. Vrain has been blessed with their nesting habitat for many years now. Winter activities such as skijoring are also allowed.

Directions

Coming from Longmont, which is about 12 miles north of Boulder on CO Hwy. 119, head east on CO Hwy. 119 until just before I-25 exit 24. A mile before the interstate is CR 7, which you will take left (north) for less than 1 mile, where it dead-ends at CR 24.5. Turn right (east) on CR 24.5 and continue until you reach St. Vrain State Park. Some signs still call it Barbour Ponds State Park, so don't be confused, you're in the right spot!

Contact Information

St. Vrain St. Park
4995 Weld CR 24 $^1/_2$
Longmont, CO 80504
Phone: 303-678-9402
E-mail: st.vrain.park@state.co.us

Stagecoach State Park

This beautiful park is a wetland and wildlife preserve for waterfowl and water mammals. There is a full marina here, with rentals, a pelican-observing pontoon tour, the full variety of water sports, and, of course, world-class fishing during all seasons.

Stagecoach is very accessible and offers picnic tables, campgrounds, showers, and even a moderate lake-view trail system, accessible for visitors with disabilities. It's almost better for wheelies than walkers because of the floating (and sometimes wet!) sections of the trail. Two of the fishing areas along the **Wetlands Trail** were built for accessibility, and this is the most accessible of the three trails at Stagecoach, which winds through the wetland with bridges and interpretive signs.

This is definitely one of our favorite parks, but we're not alone, so make your reservations in advance.

Directions

This reservoir is only a 10-minute drive south from Steamboat Springs. From town, head west on U.S. Hwy. 40 for 4 miles and turn right before the Haymaker Golf Course onto CO Hwy. 131. If you get to the pass of Rabbit Ears, you've gone too far. Follow this for 5 miles and look for CR 14, about 1 mile after the big bend in the road. Turn left onto CR 14 and you will find the park entrance about 8 miles up, on your left.

Contact Information

Stagecoach State Park
25500 R CR 14 (P.O. Box 98)
Oak Creek, CO 80467
Phone: 970-736-2436
E-mail: stagecoach.park@state.co.us

Steamboat Lake State Park

Steamboat Lake State Park is open during all seasons and offers the full variety of recreation options. During the summer months, camping and water activities bring thousands of visitors to the area, including many locals, for fishing and other water sports on this 1,050-acre reservoir. During winter, the park still sees die-hard ice fishers and occasional campers, but the area is mostly home to snowmobiling. A nearby outfitter, **Steamboat Lake Outfitters**, provides tours to those with special needs. See the winter activities section on Steamboat for information (page 103).

There are two trails at Steamboat Lake, **Tombstone Nature Trail** and **Willow Creek**, both of which are accessible and well maintained. Tombstone is a 1-mile loop with interpretive plaques and the Willow Creek loop connects the marina, the **Sunrise Campground**, and the **Sage Flat** day-use area. There is an accessible fishing pier at Sage Flat, which is close to the dam on the main, or east, side of lake.

The camper-services building has fully accessible restrooms and showers, and although none of the campsites are labeled for accessibility, they are all flat and very accessible. Because this area is popular, we recommend reserving one of the sites close to the camper-services building.

There are also 10 six-man cabins for rent at Steamboat Lake, two of which are accessible. The cabin rentals include an electric heater, beds without bedding, a small refrigerator, and a coffeepot and should be reserved in advance.

Directions

From downtown Steamboat Springs, follow U.S. Hwy. 40 for 2 miles and turn right at the 7-11 onto Elk River Rd. (CR 129). Follow this road for about 26 miles through the small town of Clark and look for a left-hand turn just past the visitors center. There are several turn-ins to the lake. Follow the signs for marina and fishing access.

Contact Information

Steamboat Lake State Park
P.O. Box 750
Clark, CO 80428
Phone: 970-879-3922
E-mail: steamboat.lake@state.co.us

Sweitzer Lake State Park

Sweitzer is known for its water recreation, power boating, sailboating, and canoeing. Jet Skiers, scuba enthusiasts, and swimmers are all allowed and frequently use Sweitzer Lake. There is a swimming area, which is mostly accessible, with picnic sites and shelter from the sun. There is an accessible concrete pier near the boat ramp for fishing, although the parking lot has a level gravel surface that might not be suitable for some chairs.

The park office offers accessible parking and bathrooms as well as picnic tables with some shade.

Directions

This was one of the easiest of the state parks for us to find. From Delta, take U.S. Hwy. 50/Main St. south through town and continue for about 1.5 miles. The entrance to the park will be on your left, and there are signs marking the turn on CR E.

Contact Information

Sweitzer Lake State Park
P.O. Box 173
Delta, CO 81416
Phone: 970-874-4258
E-mail: sweitzer.park@state.co.us

Sylvan Lake State Park

Surrounded by the **White River National Forest**, Sylvan Lake is a hidden recreation area offering all-season use for camping, hiking, and fishing to enthusiasts in the know. Although blessed with very beautiful scenery, the trails to the lake are narrow and sloping so are quite difficult to navigate in a wheelchair. All fishing is off-shore and there are no platforms. However, the boat ramp pathway is considered accessible.

The camping here is popular and offers 44 tent and RV sites in two campgrounds. There are eight cabins that sleep six each and three yurts that are, unfortunately, located up a switchback trail. There are several options for accessible camping. There are two accessible sites in **Elk Run Campground** (13 and 16). Both of these sites are closest to the camper-services building, which has accessible toilets and showers. All the paths are of level gravel surfaces. **Fisherman's Paradise Campground**, located closest to the lake, has one accessible site (46), which is closest to the restrooms, but they are vault only here. They have three accessible cabins (2, 3, and 8), and we recommend booking these in advance. Cabins 2 and 8 allow pets.

The yurts are located on E. Brush Creed Rd.; number 1 is accessible. There is a ramp, and accessible restrooms are next to the parking area.

Directions

The best way to get to this park is from the town of Eagle, and you won't see signs for it until you get south of town. From I-70, take exit 147 and head immediately south over the river. Take the third right onto U.S. Hwy. 6 (also called Grand Ave.) and go two blocks. Turn left onto Broadway St. (The streets are one-way, so stick with these directions for the easiest route.) Continue for 4 blocks through town and take a left at 5th St. Go 1 block and then turn right on Capitol St. After 2 blocks, Capitol turns into Brush Creek Rd. Follow Brush Creek Rd. (CR 307) for approximately 10 miles until you come to fork in the road. Stay to the left on W. Brush Creek Rd. for another 5 miles, until you see the entrance to the park.

Contact Information

Sylvan Lake State Park
10200 Brush Creek Rd. (P.O. Box 1475)
Eagle, CO 81631
Phone: 970-328-2021
E-mail: sylvan.lake.park@state.co.us

Trinidad Lake State Park

Trinidad Lake is a large recreation area supporting three picnic facilities, trails, excellent fishing, as well as camping.

The picnic facilities are large enough to accommodate up to 60 guests and offer grills, horseshoe pits, shelter, restrooms, and a volleyball net.

The trail system presents half a dozen trails of all terrain and length. The **Carpios Cove** trail is the shortest, but also the most difficult. The **Levsa Self-Guided Nature Trail** is the best option for wheelchairs, as it's a 1-mile loop with informative signs and easy terrain. None of the trails, however, offer paved ground, which, depending on the weather conditions, might make them difficult to use.

Trinidad's **Carpios Ridge Campground** is considered very accessible. It offers 62 campsites with several adapted sites, restrooms, showers, picnic tables, and drinking fountains.

Directions
The town of Trinidad is located approximately 85 miles south of Pueblo on I-25. Drive most of the way through town and head west (a right-hand turn at the Colorado Visitor Center) on CR 12, also known as the Scenic Highway of Legends. The entrance to the park is about 3 miles in.

Contact Information
Trinidad Lake State Park
32610 CR 12
Trinidad, CO 81082
Phone: 719-846-6951
E-mail: trinidad.lake@state.co.us

Vega State Park

As with most of the state parks, Vega is known for its water sports and its beautiful campgrounds, but is uniquely set high into the sub-alpine forest at 8,000 feet, offering beautiful views and distinctive warm temperatures.

There is a fully accessible visitors center at Vega with excellent exhibits on the history and wildlife of the area, as well as a small store for maps, books, and more.

Vega is also known for its accessibility. It offers campsites and cabins, and at the **Early Settlers** and **Pioneer Campgrounds**, there are restrooms with pay showers for guests with special needs. There is also an accessible fishing pier at Oak Point. Unfortunately, the trails here have not yet been adapted and are naturally surfaced with some obstacles.

Directions

Located about 55 miles east of Grand Junction near the small town of Collbran, Vega State Park borders the Grand Mesa National Forest. From I-70, look for the CO Hwy. 65 exit just past Island Acres State Park. Head east on CO Hwy. 65 for 10 miles until you reach the turnoff for CO Hwy. 330. Follow this east along Plateau Creek for 12 miles until you see signs for the park.

Contact Information

Vega State Park
P.O. Box 186
Collbran, CO 81624
Phone: 970-487-3407
E-mail: vega.park@state.co.us

Yampa River State Park

Yampa River State Park is split into two locations not far from each other. The newest portion is the **headquarters**, located just west of Hayden on the Yampa River, and the other is at **Elkhead Reservoir**. Both offer camping; Elkhead also offers fishing.

The visitors center and main campground at the headquarters are located on a midway point on the Yampa River and offer many options for travelers with disabilities. The campground here offers 50 sites total, some with teepees, and two paved adapted sites. All sites offer picnic tables. There is a fully accessible camper-services building separate from the main visitors center that has showers, restrooms, snack machines, picnic tables, and laundry services.

From the main center, there is also an expanding trail system winding through the flat meadows along the river located west of the visitors center. The local youth corps worked very hard on this paved trail, so take advantage of it and view some small wildlife.

There are also more than 20 boat-ramp stations spread out along the length of the river, which can be accessed from U.S. Hwy. 40. A large relief map of these spots is displayed at the main visitors center. There are no fishing piers from these spots, but most are gravel or paved launches for either shore- or canoe-based accessible fishing.

Directions

Yampa River State Park is located 28 miles west of Steamboat Springs, 2 miles west of Hayden, or 10 miles east of Craig on U.S. Hwy. 40.

Contact Information

Yampa River State Park
P.O. Box 759
Hayden, CO 81639
Phone: 970-276-2061
E-mail: yampa.river@state.co.us

Resources

The Internet is an eternally growing wealth of information. Much of our preliminary and follow-up research was done there, and we have included numerous Web sites in this guide for that reason. There are also adaptive magazines and newsletters, both online and in print, in addition to the many travel magazines you can subscribe to. In our experience, you can never have too much travel literature!

Following is a list of magazines and Web sites you can tap into for excellent adaptive travel information and resources.

Magazines directed toward those with disabilities:

Ability
Active Living
Disabled Person
Challenge Magazine by Disabled Sports USA
Emerging Horizons
New Mobility
In Motion

Useful Web sites:

www.abilitycenter.org/webtools/links/accessibletravel.html
www.abilityinfo.com/books/mag.html
www.access-ability.org/travel.html
www.access-able.com
www.accessiblevans.com/
www.armchair.com/tour/hc/handcap.html

www.disabilitytravel.com
www.disabilityworld.org

www.emerginghorizons.com
www.enablelink.org/travel/trav_int_links.html?showtravel=1&page=2

www.gimponthego.com/links.htm

www.mossresourcenet.org/travel.htm

www.newmobility.com/links_view.cfm?link_type=community&link_category=Travel

www.sath.org/

www.travelguides.org/magazines.html
www.travelintalk.net/pages/join.phtml
www.travelworldmagazine.com/contributors/detail.php?ColumnID=198

www.wheelchair-getaways.com/Wheelchair-Vans-Travel.htm
www.wheelchairnet.org/WCN_Living/travel.html
www.wheelchairsonthego.com

Index

A

Action Adventure Rafting and Timberline Tours, 65
Activity Center, Breckenridge, 60
Adaptive activity specialists, 127-32
Adaptive Adventures, 127-29
Adaptive Recreation Opportunities, 27
Adaptive Sports Association (ASA), 35, 88-93
Adaptive Sports Center (ASC), 33-34, 82-87
Adaptive travel: activities, 5-6; asking for help, 5; car/van rentals, 2-4; limitations, 5; packing, 1-4; travel time, 2, 4
Adaptive Water Ski and Wakeboard Festival, 128
Adventure Ridge, 66, 116
Adventures in BBQ, 17
Aggie Theater, 30
Alpenglow Stube, 81
Alpen Rose Bed and Breakfast, 124-25
Alpine Lodging, 112
Alpine Oasis, 36
Alpine Outside Recreational Adventures, 33
Alpiner Lodge, 106
Alpine Taxi, 102
Alpine Visitors Center, 164
American Spirit Shuttle, 98
Americans with Disabilities Act (ADA), 150
Amtrak, 98
Anasazi Heritage Center, 35, 44
Animas Museum, 92
Animas Overlook Trail, 37
Animas River, 35-37, 42
Anticline Pond, 194
Arapahoe Basin, 79
Arkansas Headwaters State Park, 169-70
Arkansas Point Campground, 193
Arkansas Point Trail, 193-94
Arkansas River, 48, 63-64, 169
Arthur B. Schultz Foundation, The, 84
Arvada, 139
Aspen, 54-55, 72-75
Aspenglen Campground, 165
Aspen Highlands, 71, 73
Aspen Ice Garden, 72, 76
Aspen Meadows, 74
Aspen Mountain ("Ajax"), 70-71
Aspen Music Tent, 75
Aspen Ski Area, 70
Aspen Skiing Corporation, 69
Avalanche, The, 86
Avogadro's, 30
Avon, 60, 119
Azteca Tacqueria, 107

B

Bacchanale, 86
Back Country Discovery (BCD), 130
Backstage Theater, 78-79
Badger House Community Overlook, 162
Bagali's Italian Kitchen, 119
Balanced Rock, 152
Balloon America, 65
Barr Lake State Park, 171
Bear Creek Lodge, 112
Bear Lake, 166
Bear River Bar and Grill, 105
Beaver Boardwalk, 166
Beaver Creek, 118-19
Beaver Creek Wilderness Area, 186
Beaver Meadows Resort Ranch, 28
Beaver Meadow Visitors Center, 164
Beaver Run Resort, 80
Benedicts, 73
Bent's Old Fort National Historical Site, 151
Bergenhaus, 79
Berman, Joel, 127
Besant Point Trail, 27
Best Western, Durango, 91
Best Western Nederland, 96
Best Western University, 27-28
Bicycle Tour of Colorado, 128
Big Al Trail, 37
Big Billies, 112
Big Horn Balloon Company, 33
Bighorn Sheep Canyon, 63
Big Rack Horseback Adventures, 103
Big Thompsom Campground, 26
Billy's Island Grill, 119
Bisetti's Italian Restaurant, 29
Bison Visitors Center, 25
Bivans, 118
Black Canyon of the Gunnison National Park, 152-53
Black Hawk, 55, 56-58
Blazing Adventures, 54
Blind Outdoor Leisure Development (BOLD), 70
Blue Mesa Reservoir, 155
Blue River Bistro, 81
Blue Sky Balloon and Airplane Adventures, 51
Boardwalk at Rotary Park, 46
Bob's Steak and Chop House, 23
Bockman Campground, 181
Bonnie's, 73
Bonny Lake State Park, 172
Bonny Marina and Store, 172
Bookcliff Campground, 189
Bootleg Bottom, 187
Bootlegger, 198
Boulder, 7-11
Boulder Marriott, 9
Boulder Outdoor Center, 8
Boulder Reservoir, 127
Bowen-Baker Gulch Trailhead, 166
Boxtel, Amanda, 70
Boyd Lake State Park, 173
Breckenridge, 78-81
Breckenridge Brewery, 80-81
Breckenridge Outdoor Education Center (BOEC), 8, 59-60, 77-81
Breckenridge Resort Chamber, 60
Briar Rose, 9
Bridge Canyon, 174
Bridge Creek, 187
Broadmoor Hotel, 16
Broomfield, 140
Brothers Grille, 75
Brown Bag, The, 113
Brown's Canyon, 64
Browns Park National Wildlife Refuge, 157
Bucking Rainbow, 48

220

Bucks Cabin, 90
Buck's Livery, 89
Bud Events Center, 27
Budweiser Brewery, 27
Buena Vista, 169–70
Buffalo Grill, 86
Buggy Whips and Blue Sky West, 48
Bumps, 73
Burlingame Cabin, 73
Buttermilk, 71, 73

C

Cache La Poudre Canyon, 47
Café de los Pinos, 90
Café Diva, 107
Café Orleans, 57
Café Suzanne, 73
Calypso, 57
Camel's Garden, 113
Cameron Pass, 47, 181
Canine-Assisted Psychotherapy, 139
Cañon City, 169–70
Canyon Point, 174
Canyon View Trail, 174
Capitol Hill Mansion Bed and Breakfast Inn, 22
Carbondale, 140
Carlos and Maria's, 125
Carpios Cove Trail, 215
Carpios Ridge Campground, 215
Carter Knolls Campground, 26
Carter Lake, 25, 26
Carter Lake Marina, 26
Carver's Bakery Café, 125
Cascade Grill, 92
Casinos: Black Hawk, 56–58; Central City, 56; Durango, 92; guide, 56
Castle Peak, 55
Castlewood Canyon State Park, 174
Cathy Fromme Prairie Natural Area, 25
Centennial, 140–41
Central City, 55, 56–58
Central Garden Trail, 13
Central Hotel, 92
Central Reservations: Aspen/Snowmass, 76; Breckenridge, 60, 81;

Crested Butte, 87; Durango, 93; Steamboat Springs, 108; Vail, 120; Winter Park, 126
Central Western Colorado, 54–66
Certified Horsemanship Association (CHA), 139
Cervantes Masterpiece Ballroom, 24
Challege Aspen (CA), 54–55, 70, 71–73, 76
Chapin Mesa, 162
Chaps, 118
Charter at Beaver Creek, The, 118
Chasm, 152
Chatfield State Park, 175–76
Chautauqua Ranger Cottage, 8
Cherry Creek State Park, 177
Cheyenne Mountain State Park, 178
Cheyenne Mountain Zoo, 15
Children's Museum of Durango, 92–93
Chimney View Campground, 200
Christina's Grille and Bar, 92
Cimarron, 153, 155
Cirque Bar and Grill, 73, 75
City Park, 25, 137
City Street Bagels, 10
Clear Creek, 56, 63–64
Clear Fork Campground, 183
Cliffhouse, 73
Clifford, Tim and Jeanie, 140
Cloud Nine Alpine Bistro, 73
Club Car, The, 126
Club Med Crested Butte, 85
Coach U.S.A. and Ace Express, 58
Coalbank Pass, 35
Cog Railway, 15
Cold Shivers Park, 154
Colorado Activity Center (CAC), 136
Colorado Chautauqua Association, 8, 9
Colorado Department of Transportation, 68
Colorado Discovery Ability Intergrated Outdoor Adventures (CDA), 98–100

Colorado Division of Wildlife (DOW), 133, 146, 150
Colorado Historical Society, 63
Colorado Mountain College, 78
Colorado National Monument, 154
Colorado River, 48, 52, 61, 66, 179–80
Colorado River Runs, 48, 51
Colorado River State Park, 179–80
Colorado River Trailhead, 166
Colorado Ski Hall of Fame, 101
Colorado Springs, 12–19, 141
Colorado Springs Transit, 12
Colorado State Forest State Park, 181–82
Colorado State University (CSU), 27, 30
Colorado Therapeutic Riding Center, 142
Colorado Trail, 37
Columbine Station, 90
Comfort Inn: Avon, 119; Durango, 91; Ft. Collins, 27
Connected Lakes, 179
Connections: Horses Healing Arts, 140–41
CooperSmith's Pub and Brewery, 29
Coors Field, 21
Copper Mountain, 60, 79
Cornerstone Mine, 55
Corn Lake, 179, 180
Cottonwood Campground, 205
Cottonwood Cove, 200
Cottonwood Grill, 107
Cowan, Houston, 70
Coyote Valley Trailhead, 167
Crag Crest National Recreation Trail, 36
Crags Campground, The, 181
Crags Mountain, 47
Crawford, 153
Crawford State Park, 183
Crazy Horse Outfitters, 130
Creekside Café, 107
Crested Butte, 32–34, 82–87

Index

Crested Butte Brewery/Idle Spur, 86
Crested Butte International Hostel, 85
Cripple Creek, 186
Crook Campground, 156
Crow Canyon, 44
Crown Pub, The, 29
Crystal Reservoir, 155
Cucina Rustica's, 118
Cuerno Verde Picnic Area, 195
Cuerno Verde Trail, 195
Curecanti National Recreation Area, 152, 155
Cypress Café, 92

D

Dam Trail, 193
Dante's, 90
Dave Spencer Ski Classic, 90
Davis, Michael and Kelly, 17
Day Lodge, The, 98, 99
Days Inn, Durango, 91
Delta, 153
DeMuth, Ruth, 115
Deno's Mountain Bistro, 126
Denver, 20–24, 137
Denver Buffalo Company, 23
Denver International Airport (DIA), 20
Denver Metro Office, 150
Denver Pro Limousine, 20
Denver Zoo, 21–22
Derailer, 126
Desert Edge Therapy, Inc., 143
Devil's Gate Viaduct trestle, 63
Devil's Kitchen, 154
Dial-A-Ride: Ft. Collins, 25; Telluride, 110
Diamond Circle Theater, 93
Dillon, 60, 155
Dinaland Aviation, 157
Dinosaur National Monument, 156–58
Disabled Sports USA, 109–10, 129, 130–31
Disabled Veterans Lifetime Combination Small Game Hunting and Fishing License, 146
Divide, 186
Divide Grill, The, 125

Dominguez and Escalante Ruins, 44
Double Diamond, 75
Double Tree, Durango, 91
Druid Mine, 55
Durango, 35–37, 88–93
Durango and Silverton Narrow Gauge Railroad, 41–42, 89
Durango Area Tourism Office, 37
Durango-Denver Colorado Trail, 197
Durango Dog Ranch, 89
Durango Mountain Resort, 90, 91

E

Eagle and Lowells Campground, 26
Eagle Express, 171
Eagle's Nest Observation platform, 14
Early Settlers Campground, 216
East Inlet Trailhead, 167
East Rifle Creek, 204
Eaton, Earl, 115
Echo Park Campground, 156–57
Econolodge, Durango, 91
Edwards, 119
El Chapultepec, 24
Eldorado Canyon State Park, 184
Eldora Mountain, 94–97
Eldora Nordic Center, 95
Eldora Ski Resort, 94
Eldora Special Recreation Program (ESRP), 94–97
Elephant Bar Restaurant, 17
Eleven Mile General Store, 186
11 Mile Sports, 185
Eleven Mile State Park, 185–86
Elk Creek, 155
Elkhead Reservoir, 217
Elk Pool, 52, 53
Elk River Guest Ranch, 103
Elk Run Campground, 214
El Rancho, 92
Equine Assisted Growth and Learning Association (EAGALA), 139

Equine Assisted Psychotherapy (EAP), 138
Equine Facilitated Mental Health Association (EFMHA), 139
Estes Park, 141, 168
Evergreen Lodge, The, 118
Expand Your Horizons, 111

F

Fall River Visitors Center, 164–65
Farmer's Table, 29
Farraday's, 57
Far View Visitors Center, 162
Fat Alley BBQ, 113
Feeney, Matt, 127
Fetchenhier, Scott, 41
Fetch's Mining and Mercantile Shop, 41
Fillmore Auditorium, 23–24
Firehouse Grill, 85
Fish Creek Falls Recreation Area, 47
Fisherman's Paradise Campground, 214
Fishing, 133–35
Fiske Planetarium, 10–11
Fitzgerald's Casino, 57
Flatiron Reservoir, 25, 26
Flatirons, 8
Florence, 169–70
Florissant, 186
Florissant Fossil Beds National Monument, 159
Fly Me to the Moon Saloon, 114
Fontenot's, 125–26
Foolish Craig's, 10
Forest Canyon Overlook, 166
Forest Discovery Nature Trail, 203
Forest Service, Steamboat Springs, 108
Fossil Bone Quarry, 156, 157–58
Fossil Creek Trail, 25
Four Points, 105
14th St. Bar and Grill, 10
Fowler Trail, 184
Fox Hollow, 137
Fox Theater, 11
Fraser, 51, 52, 121, 126
Fraser River Trail, 51
Freedom Cab, 20

Freewheel Vans, 4
Fremont, John, 82
Freshies, 107
Friends of the Dunes, 161
Frisco, 60, 80
Front Range Exceptional Equestrians, 141
Fruita, Colorado River State Park, 179–80
Ft. Collins, 25–30, 141–42
Ft. Collins Chamber of Commerce, 30
Ft. Lewis College, 92

G

Garden of the Gods, 13, 17
Garfinkle's, 120
Gas Café, 86
Georgetown Loop Railroad, 63
Giovanni's, 107
Glacier Basin Campground, 165
Glassock, Bill, 109
Glenwood Canyon, 66
Glenwood Hot Springs Lodge and Pool, 61–62, 205
Glenwood Springs, 61–62, 66
Glory Hole Mine, 55
Gobi Mongolian Grill, 107
Gold Belt Scenic Byway Tour, 186
Golden Bee, 18
Golden Eagles, 141
Golden Gate Canyon State Park, 187
Golden Gates Casino, 57
Goldenwoods/Valley View Condos, 99–100
Gold Mine Tour, 41
Golf, 136–37
Good Fellows, 75
Good Times Tours, 78
Gorrono, 112
Gothic Theater, 24
Grand Adventures, 123
Grand Junction, 36, 98, 100
Grand Lake, 167, 168
Grand Mesa, 36
Greater Colorado Springs Chamber of Commerce, 19
Great Room, The, 114
Great Sand Dunes National Park and Preserve, 160–61, 208
Green Mountain Trailhead, 167
Green River, 128, 156–58
Green River Campground, 156
Gregory Inn, 22
Grouse Mountain Grill, 118
Guiseppes, 112
Gunnison, 82
Gunnison, John, 82
Gunnison River, 35, 152
Guthries Bar and Grill, 18–19
Gwyn's High Alpine, 73

H

Hahn's Peak Inn, 106–7
Hahn's Peak Lake, 106
Hall, Johanna, 49
Hall of Fame Bar, 84
Hamilton Chop House, 91
Hampton Inn: Durango, 91; Ft. Collins, 27
Hartel, Liz, 138
Harts Towncar Service, 20
Harvey Gap State Park, 188
Hawsapple Campground, 201
Haymaker, 137
Hazie's Restaurant, 105
Healing Touch, 111
Hearts & Horses, 142–43
Heide, Kara, 115
Hell Gate, 15
Hensley, Christopher, 82
Herman's Rest, 155
Hernando's Pizza Pub, 126
Hidden Valley Snowplay and Picnic Area, 166
High Country Stampede and BBQ, 52
Highline Lake State Park, 189
High Point, 152
High Point Academy, 143
Hippotherapy, 139
Historic Argo Gold Mine Hill and Museum Adventure Tours, 63
Historic Charlie Taylor Water Wheel, 63
Hog Lakes, 156
Holden House, 17
Holzwarth Historic Site, 167
Honga's, 113
Hoofs 'n Paws Development Center, 139
Hooper Pool, 207
Hornbek Homestead, 159
Horseback riding, 138–45
Horseshoe Park, 166
Horseshoe Reservoir Picnic Area, 195
Hotel Boulderado, 9
Hotel Columbia, 113
Hotel Telluride, 112–13
Hot Springs Park, 38
Hot Springs Resort, 39
Hot Sulphur Springs Resort, 52–53
Humble Ranch Education and Therapy Center, 144–45
Hunting, 146
Hyatt Regency Beaver Creek, 118

I

Ice House Hotel, 113
Idaho Springs, 55, 56, 63–64
Iguanas Bar and Grill, 73, 75
Independence Monument, 154
Indian Dance Presentations, 14
Indian Peaks Lodge, 96
Information Center, Breckenridge, 60
Inn at Beaver Creek, 118–19
Inn at Crested Butte, 85
Inn at Lost Creek, 113
Inn at Wildewood, The, 99
International Novice Tour, 128
International Ski Federation World Championships, 69
Invesco Field at Mile High Stadium, 20–21
Iron Creek Campground, 183
Island Acres Campground, 179, 180
Isle of Capri, 56–57

J

Jackson Lake State Park, 190
Jake's Deli, 57
Jay's Bistro, 30

Index

Jazz Aspen, 76
Jeeping, 32
John Martin Reservoir State Park, 191–92
John Work Arena, 52
Josie's Cabin, 158
Juniper Breaks Campground, 193
Juniper Rock, 174
Just for the Fun of It, 131
JW Steakhouse, 9

K
Kawuneeche Visitors Center, 165
Kelley, Scott "Grizzly," 88
Ken and Sue's Place, 92
Keystone, 60, 79, 81
Keystone Ranch, 81
Khow Thai Café, 10
Kickapoo Lounge, The, 126
Kochevar's, 86
Kona Grill, 23
Kriley Pond, 187
KT's BBQ Outback, 10

L
La Cochina, 113
Lake Fork, 155
Lake Hasty Campground, 191
Lake Irene, 166
Lake Pueblo State Park, 193–94
Lakeside Campground, 190
Laramie River Ranch, 130
Larimer County Parks and Open Lands, 25
La Sal Mountains, 36
Last Dollar Saloon, 114
Lathrop State Park, 195
Leadville, 169–70
LevelZ, 108
Levsa Self-Guided Nature Trail, 215
Lil's Land and Sea, 85–86
Lily Lake, 165
Limelight Lodge, The, 74
Lincoln Center, 30
Lodge, The, 96
Lodge at Vail, The, 118
Lodge Casino and Hotel, 57
Longmont, 142
Longs Peak Campground, 165

Lookout Inn, 9
Loonees Comedy Corner, 18
Lory State Park, 196
Los Amigos, 120
Lost Pond, 198
Louisville, 142
Loveland, 29, 142–43
Lowry Ruins, 44
Lunch Rock, 124
Lynn Britt Cabin, 73

M
MacKenzie's Chop House, 18
Mack Mesa Lake, 189
Mack Mesa Trail, 189
Mad Adventures, 51
Mahogany Ridge, 107, 108
Mahoney, Bill, Sr., 109
Main St. Station Plaza, 81
Mancos, 143
Mancos State Park, 197
Manion, Mary, 82
Manitou and Pikes Peak Railway, 15
Many Parks Curve Overlook, 166
Maori's, 81
Marble Mountain, 44
Mardi Gras Casino, 57
Maroon Bells, 54, 55
Maroon Lake, 55
Marriott Mountain Resort, 118
Martin Lake, 195
Mary Jane, 122, 124
McCoy's Bar, 118
McPhee Reservoir, 44
Medicine Horse Center: Therapeutic Riding and Equine Rehabilitation, 143
Melodrama, 93
Merry-Go-Round, 73
Mesa Verde National Park, 44, 162–63
Metropolitan areas, 7–30
Metro Taxi, 20
Mild to Wild, 36
Million Dollar Hwy., 35
Milner Pass, 166
Miracle Mount Estes Park Therapeutic Riding Center, 141
Mobility Impaired Big Game Program, 146

Moffat Station Restaurant and Brewery, 126
Molas Divide Pass, 35
Molas Lake, 35
Montrose, 33, 153
Monument, 143
Moose Visitors Center, 181
Moraine Park Campground, 165
Moraine Park Museum, 167
Morefield Campground, 162
Morrow Point Reservoir, 155
Mountain Chalet, 74
Mountain Dragon, 75
Mountain Express Shuttle, 83
Mountain High Inn, 57
Mountain Management at Telluride, 112
Mountain Sun and Oasis Brewery, 10
Mountain Transport, 89
Mountain Village, 43, 112, 113, 114
Mountain Village Trail, 45
Mueller State Park, 198
Mugs Underground Lounge, 30
Mummy Range, 166
Muskrat Run Nature Trail, 210

N
National Alliance for Accessible Golf (NAAG), 136
National Disabled Veterans, 73
National parks, monuments, historic sites, and recreation areas, 147, 150–69
National Ski Hall of Fame, 101
National Sports Center for the Disabled (NSCD), 50–51, 121, 126
Native Americans: Anasazi, 44; Ute, 61, 69, 82, 88, 109, 115
Navajo Loop, 162
Navajo State Park, 199
Nederland, 94–97
Needles Picnic Area, 207
Never Summer Ranch, 167
Never Summer Range, 47
New Belgium Brewing Company, 27

New Sheridan Chop House, 113
New Sheridan Hotel, 113, 114
Noah's Ark Rafting, 8
NORAD, 15
North American Riding for the Handicapped Association (NARHA), 138–39
Northern Plains Campground, 193
North Inlet Trailhead, 167
North Michigan Reservoir Campground, 181
North Rim, Black Canyon, 152
North Shore Amphitheater, 185
North Shore Campground, 185
North Sterling State Park, 200
Northwest Colorado, 46–53
Nova Guides, 65
NXT, 75

O

Olde Schoolhouse Café, 92
Old Glendevey Ranch, 130
Old Hundred Mine, 35
Old Town Inn, 85
O'Leary, Hal, 121
Ole' Barn Knoll, 187
Olympic Hall of Fame, 14–15
Ore House, 119
Orvis Hot Springs, 40
Ouray, 35, 38
Ouray Hot Springs Pool, The, 38, 111
Outlook Ridge, 198

P

Pa-co-chu-puk Campground, 203
Paepcke, Walter, 69
Pagosa Springs, 39
Painted Rock Overlook, 152
Palisade, 143
Palmer Lake Brewing Company, 17
Panorama Point, 187
Paonia State Park, 201
Paradise Bakery, 75
Paradise Warming House, 84
Paratransit, 122
Park Avenue Lofts, 80
Parker, 144
Parsenn Bowl, 122, 124
Paved Bike Trail System, 60
Pazzo's, 119
Peak 7, 80
Peak 9, 79
Peak 8 Fun Park, 59
Pearl Lake State Park, 202
Peninsula day-use area, 183
Penrose, Spencer, 15
Pepsi Center, 21, 23
Performance Tours Rafting, 60
Pfeifer, Friedl, 69
Phoenix Gold Mine, 63
Pike National Forest, 186
Pikes Peak, 12–13, 186
Pikes Peak Center, 19
Pikes Peak International Hill Climb, 12–13
Pine Creek Foundation, 143
Pines Lodge, 118
Pinewood Reservoir, 25, 26–27
Piney River Ranch and Conference Center, 65
Pinnacles, 155
Piñon Campground, 195
Piñon Flats, 160
Pioneer Campground, 216
Plateau Creek Canyon, 36
Point Campground, 191
Poncha Springs, 169–70
Poudre River, 25, 47
Poudre Trail, 25
Powderhorn, 98–100
Powderhorn Adaptive Ski School Office, 100
Powderhouse, 90
Praying Hands Ranch, 144
Preachers Hollow, 198
Princess Wine Bar, 86–87
Professional Ski Instructors of America (PSIA), 129
Project Gain, 136
Pueblo, 144, 169–70
Pufpaff, Christine, 121
Pulpit Rock, 152
Purgy's Pub, 92

Q

Q's, 9
Quandry Grill, 81
Queen Ann Bed and Breakfast Inn, 22

R

Rabbit Ears Motel, 106
Rabbit Ears Pass, 47
Rafters, 86, 87
Raft Masters, 63–64
Railroad Museum, 92
Rail Yard Terrain Park, 124
Rainbow Curve Overlook, 166
Rainbow Limited, 29
Ralston Creek, 187
Ramsay-Shockey Open Space, 25, 26–27
Rancho Vista Equine Therapy Center, 142
Randy's, 92
Ranger Lakes Campground, 181
Red Barn Group Picnic Area, 187
Red Canyon, 154
Red Feather, 28
Red Feather Ranch Bed-and-Breakfast and Horse Hotel, 28
Red Lion, The, 120
Red Mountain Pass, 35
Red Rocks Park and Amphitheater, 21
Regional Transportation District (RTD), 95
Rendezvous, 105
Residence Inn by Marriott, Durango, 91
Reverend's Ridge Campground, 187
Ridgway, 40
Ridgway State Park, 203
Rifle Falls State Park, 188, 204
Rifle Gap State Park, 188, 205
Riggio's, 107
Rio de los Animas Perdidas River Trail, 36–37
Rio Grande Railway, 42
Ritz Grill, 18
Riverwalk Center, 60
Roaring Fork Valley, 69–70
Rock Cut and Tundra Nature Trail, 166
Rocky Mountain Bird Observatory, 171

Index

Rocky Mountain National Park, 51, 164–68
Rocky Mountain Riding Therapy, 142
Rocky Ridge Campground, 185
Roma Bar, 114
Room at the Inn, 16–17
Routt National Forest, 47
Roxborough State Park, 206
Royal Gorge, 63, 186
RTD (Regional Transportation District), 20

S

Sage Flat, 212
Salida, 169–70
Sam's Knob, 73
Samuelson Outfitters, 130
Sancho's Broken Arrow, 24
Sand Canyon, 157
Sand Dunes Pool, 207
San Juan Balloons, 110
San Juan Mountains, 36
San Juan Ski Company, 89
San Luis State Park and Wildlife Area, 207–8
San Miguel River Trail, 45
Sato, 119
Sawmill Canyon Backcountry Campground, 160
Scandia Mine, 55
Scenic suggestions: Anasazi area west of Mesa Verde, 44; Aspen to the Maroon Bells, 55; Cameron Pass to Rabbit Ears Pass, 47; CR 12 to Crested Butte, 32; Grand Mesa Scenic Byway, 36; Oh My Gaud Rd., 55; Ouray to Silverton to Durango—The Million Dollar Hwy., 35; Steamboat to I-70 to Vail—Co Hwy. 131 along the Colorado River, 48; Trail Ridge Rd., 51; Vail to I-70 to Glenwwod Springs—Glenwood Canyon, 66
Season's Buffet, 57
Secret Stash, 86
Seibert, Pete, 115
Serrano's Southwestern Grill, 10
Shamrock Café, 57
Shamrock Shuttle Service, 25
Shed, 126
Sheraton Crested Butte, 85
Sheraton Steamboat Resort Hotel, 106
Sherpa and Yeti's, 81
Shoreline Marina, 190
Silverton, 35, 41–42
Silver Tree Hotel, 74
Sink, The, 10
16th Street Mall, 22
Ski Buddy, 111
Skiers Union, The, 114
Ski Resort Information Booths, 120
Ski Tip Lodge, 81
Sky Hotel, 74
Sky Ute Lodge and Casino, 92
Sloan's Lake, 127
Slopeside Bar and Grill, 107
Slough Pond, 187
Smokin' Moes Ribhouse and Saloon, 126
Smugglers, 114
Snoasis, 124
Snowmass, 55, 69–76
Sommers-Bausch Observatory, 10–11
Sonnalp, 118
Sophio's, 113
Sopris Therapy Services, 140
South Boulder Creek, 184
South Cheyenne Canyon, 14
South Ridge Seafood Bar and Grill, 81
South Rim, Black Canyon, 152
South Rim Camground, 152
South Shore Campground, 26
Southwest Colorado, 32–45
Sow's Ear, The, 91–92
Speakeasy, The, 78
Spencer, Dave, 88
Spinney Mountain State Park, 185, 209
Spitzie, 156
Split Mountain, 158
Sprague Lake Camp, 165–66
Spring Creek Trail, 25
Spring Inn, 39
Springs Mobility, 12
Springs Ranch Golf Club, 137
Spruce Campground, 201
Spur Path, The, 45
St. Regis Hotel, 74, 76
St. Vrain State Park, 210
Stagecoach State Park, 211
Staples, Barb, 130
Star Park, 200
State parks, 148–50, 169–217
Steamboat Adaptive Program, 49
Steamboat Adaptive Ski School, 101, 108
Steamboat Grand Hotel, 106
Steamboat Lake Outfitters, 103, 212
Steamboat Lake State Park, 106, 212
Steamboat Powder Cats at Blue Sky West, 103–4
Steamboat Rock, 157
Steamboat Ski Area, 48–49
Steamboat Snowmobile Tours, 103
Steamboat Springs, 46–49, 101–8, 144–45
Steamboat Springs Transit (SST), 102
Stecklein, Cathy, 141
Steven's Creek, 155
Stew Pot, The, 75
Stoker Bar, 105
Streamside Trail, 184
Summer travel, 127–46
Summit Historical Society, 59
Summit House, 12, 16
Sundance Trail, 26
Sundeck Restaurant, The, 73
Sunrise Campground, 212
Sunset Grill, The, 99, 100
Sunset Overlook, 152
Sunspot, 124
Super 8: Durango, 91; Ft. Collins, 27
Super 8 Boulder, 9
Super 8 Motel, Winter Park, 125
Super Shuttle, 20
Sweet Basil, 119
Sweitzer Lake State Park, 213
Swinging Bridge

Campground, 156
Sylvan Dale Guest Ranch, 28–29
Sylvan Lake State Park, 214

T
Take Four Quad lift, 99
Talk of the Town, 86
Tap Room, The, 120
Tavern, 16
Telluride, 43–45, 109–14, 145
Telluride Adaptive Riding Program (TARP), 145
Telluride Adaptive Sports Program (TASP), 43–44, 109–10, 114
Telluride and Mountain Village Convention and Visitors Bureau, 45
Telluride Outside, 44–45
Telluride Ski & Golf Company, 110
Telluride Snowmobile Adventures, 110–11
Telluride Sports, 111
10-mile, 79
Teocalli Tamale, 86
Terrace, 118
Therapeutic riding, 138
Therapeutic Riding and Education Center (TREC), 144
Therapeutic vaulting, 138–39
Thunderbowl Market Café, 73
Thunderhead, 105
Thunder River Theater Company, 76
Tiger Run Tours, 59, 78
Timber Creek Campground, 165
Timber Lake Trailhead, 166
Tombstone Nature Trail, 212
Tomichi, 152
Trade Winds, 57
Trailblazers, 123
Transfort, 25
Trans Shuttle, 20
Treasury Building, 84
Trinidad Lake State Park, 215
Trousil, Cheri, 144–45
Trout, Colleen, 109

Tugboat, The, 108
Two Creeks Mexican Café, 73
221 S. Oak, 113

U
Ullrhof, 63, 73
United States Golf Association (USGA), 136
United States Hand-Cycling Federation, 129
Up 4 Pizza, 73
U.S. Air Force Academy, 16
U.S. Bureau of Land Management, 169
U.S. Disabled Ski Team, 73
U.S. Olympic Training Center, 14–15
Ute Peak, 44

V
Vail, 60, 65–66, 115–20
Vail Adaptive (VA), 115, 120
Vail Cascade Hotel and Club, 118
Vail Resorts On-Mountain Activities, 65–66
Vail Ski School, 116–17
Vasquez Cirque, 124
Vasquez Ridge, 122, 124
Vega State Park, 216
Vendetta's, 119
Victor, 186
Village of Breckenridge, 78, 80
Virginia Canyon, 55
Vista Haus, 79
Vue, 118

W
Wagon Wheel Campground, 172
Wapiti Nature Trail, 198
Warehouse, The, 17
Waterfalls: Box Canyon Falls, 38; Bridal Veil Falls, 43, 63, 114; Crystal Lake Falls, 41; Deadwood Falls, 41; Eureka Falls, 41; Fish Creek Falls, 47; Highland Mary Mills, 41; Ingram Falls, 43; Niagara, 41; Rifle Falls, 205; Seven Falls, 14
West Vail, 119

Wetherill Mesa, 162
Wetlands Trail, 211
Wheelchair Getaways®, 3
Wheeler Opera House, 76
Wheelers, 3
Whiskey Rocks, 76
Whistlepig Farms, 140
White Buffalo Grill, 57
White River National Forest, 214
Wilderness on Wheels (WOW), 131–32
Wildewood Restaurant, 100
Wildflour, 114
Wildlife Recreation Permits, 146
Wildwood Lodge, 74
Will, Sara, 117
Willow Creek, 73
Willow Creek Trail, 206, 212
Windsurf Beach, 199
Winter Carnival, 101
Winter Moon Sled Dog Adventures, 111
Winter Park, 50–53, 121–26
Winter Park and Fraser Valley Chamber of Commerce, 124
Winter Park Mountain Lodge, 125, 126
Winter Park Resort, 126
Winter travel, 67–126
Woodland Park, 186
Wyndham Lodge, The, 113
Wyndham Peaks Resort, 114
Wynkoop Brewing Company, 23

Y
Yampa River, 46, 48, 106, 217
Yampa River Core Trail, 46
Yampa River State Park, 217
Yellow Cab: Colorado Springs, 12; Denver, 20
Yucca Campground, 195
Yucca House, 44

Z
Zane's, 75
Zephyr Mountain Lodge, 125
Zirkel Mountain Range, 47

About the Authors

Freelance writers and consultants on disability adventure travel, Andrea Jehn and Craig Kennedy live year-round in Steamboat Springs, Colorado, and they travel as often as they can. Both writers moved to Colorado for the weather, the outdoor adventure, and the friends that drew them there. They love returning home to the bright-blue skies, pristine white mountain peaks, and the family that were once just friends. They hope to help spread awareness of adaptability and motivation with this new series of adventure-travel guides.